GODDESS OF THE NORTH

GODDESS
OF THE
NORTH

*A comprehensive exploration of the
Norse goddesses, from antiquity to the
modern age.*

LYNDA C. WELCH

🜨 WEISER BOOKS
York Beach, Maine, USA

First published in 2001 by
Weiser Books, Inc.
P. O. Box 612
York Beach, ME 03910-0612
www.weiserbooks.com

Library of Congress Cataloging-in-Publication Data

Welch, Lynda C.
  Goddess of the north / Lynda C. Welch.
    p. cm.
  Includes bibliographical references and index.
  ISBN 1-57863-170-X (pbk. : alk. paper)
    1. Goddessess, Norse. 2. Mythology, Norse. I. Title.

BL863.W45 2001
293—dc21   00–048228

Typeset in 11 pt. Adobe Caslon

Cover design by Kathryn Sky-Peck
Cover art is "The snake holding deity" from Buffie Johnson's *Lady of the Beasts: The
Goddess and Her Sacred Animals*, Rochester, VT: Inner Traditions, 1994, p. 171.

Illustrations on pages 68, 76, 82, 86, 97, 208 are from Dr. W. Wagner, *Asgard and
the Gods: The Tales and Traditions of Our Northern Ancestors* (New York: E. P. Dutton, 1917); on pages 70, 80, 88, are from Donald MacKenzie, *Teutonic Myth and
Legend* (London: Gresham, n. d.); and on pages 128, 212 are from the author's
personal collection, artist Ingrid Ivic.

Printed in the United States of America

VG

08 07 06 05 04 03 02 01
8 7 6 5 4 3 2 1

The paper used in this publication meets the minimum requirements of the American National Standard for Information Sciences–Permanence of Paper for Printed
Library Materials Z39.48–1992 (R1997).

This book is dedicated to the three driving forces in my life:
the Goddess of the North;
my husband, Daniel;
and our beautiful new son, Asa Garrett.

CONTENTS

Part IV: Past to Present

FIGURES AND TABLES

ACKNOWLEDGMENTS

To Asa, my inspiration, and to Daniel, my support, my deepest gratitude is extended. Mary Anne Rodgers, my mother and an educator, has my sincerest appreciation for her constant encouragement. Betty Wink, my friend and also a professional in the publishing field, has my heartfelt thanks for her humor and comments. Ingrid Ivic has my appreciation for her artwork.

My gratitude extends to the authors in the Norse field, including Edred Thorsson and Kveldulf Gundarsson, my advisors and professors, and Regis University, all who assisted me in my spiritual exploration. Dr. Theresa Smith has my deepest regard for asking questions I had yet to explore. She is the essence of a true educator, and the Goddess was smiling at me the day Dr. Smith and I met.

INTRODUCTION

I have been asked countless times how I came to be a Norse polytheist. My affinity to the Norse Tradition seems to be more of a shock to people than my polytheistic choice in general. As I am a woman, this preference is especially hard for many to understand. My response has always been that the Norse Tradition is a sexually balanced, evolving faith deeply grounded in the past. The deities pulled me incessantly, until I answered. I literally had no choice in the matter, and did not feel at peace within myself until I responded to this call.

Regardless of common misconceptions, I have never acknowledged the Norse Tradition as sexist. I have never felt that either the gods or goddesses are dominant over each other. Unfortunately, many texts do not convey this thought very clearly. While two of the main points of faith are undeniably meditation and inner contemplation, written documentation or oral rendition are necessary to truly understand and examine one's choice of tradition. Because I have a deep inner conviction in regard to the balance in the Norse Tradition, I have never been troubled by the scarcity of information on the goddesses.[1] I knew within myself the truth of my thoughts.

With the birth of my son early last year, I sensed a profound change within myself. I was astounded at the miracle of life. I was entranced with the baby I held in my arms and fed at my breast. I witnessed firsthand the pain and exultation of childbirth, the joy of holding my baby for the first time, and the humbling feeling of looking deep into his brand-new eyes. My husband and I could not stop marveling at the birth of a new life. This experience provoked a deep need in me. I was unconsciously preparing for a new life journey.

I found myself becoming more and more drawn to the goddesses of my faith. Previously, I had been content with my

---

[1] Hilda Ellis Davidson, *Roles of the Northern Goddess* (New York: Routledge, NYP). At the time of writing this manuscript, this text was not published. This book is a must for any Northern Goddess study.

perception of the balance of the gods and goddesses. This led me to ponder why, in most of the available literature, the goddesses were not defined as clearly as the gods. I began to understand the misconceptions many people have about the Norse Tradition. Even though I knew, through my meditations, the strength of the goddesses, I became increasingly annoyed that actual written material was so limited. I resolved to research the feminine aspect of the tradition. This book is the fruit of my efforts.

I remember distinctly the night I decided this. I was relaxing after a long day, pondering why so much literature concerning the spiritual side of the Norse goddesses was so vague, as this question had been posed to me earlier by my professor, Dr. Smith. We had just completed a long discussion concerning the possible sexism in the Nordic Tradition. While I could not deny the truth of her words, considering the majority of material available, I still knew, as she did, that this accusation was false. It was patently obvious to me that my professor was insinuating I should consider new possibilities, but was waiting for me to reach my own conclusions.

I was quite dejected; the pull toward the goddess aspect was so strong, I had even started to question my faith choice, which was absolutely devastating to me. It was no longer enough that I knew within my heart the truth of my choice. I needed to see much more actual documentation. I needed to verify that my faith was not simply my own personal conception, but was indeed grounded in the very antiquity of the Norse Tradition. My baby awoke and while I was tending to his needs, I was reminded of a wonderful dream I had had immediately following his conception. I began to re-examine my thoughts on an article I had recently read about Gaia, the primordial goddess of the Greeks.[2] This led me to think about works I had read about Neolithic goddess worship in Old Europe. This, in turn, prompted me to rehash the many Norse texts I had studied. I rocked my baby to sleep and let my thoughts wander.

---

[2] Carl Olson, ed., *The Book of the Goddess, Past and Present* (New York: Crossroad, 1983), pp. 49–59.

I had just begun to contemplate the possibility and validity of a Norse primordial goddess when, all of a sudden, I felt an overwhelming rush of warmth enveloping me. Overpowering love infused the room, encompassing me in its arms. I was being cradled and rocked, just as I was cradling and rocking my baby. I knew this was the Goddess. She was responding to my need. I am Her baby, and She heard my cry just as I heard my child's. I was overcome with emotion. I was elated and overjoyed. She gave me the answer to my question that night. She gave me the strength and perseverance to begin a long and dedicated research into Her being. This book is the accomplishment of that task. My hopes are that my research and perceptions will benefit all women and men desiring to know of Her and the wonderful faith of the Norse.

Today's Norse polytheistic tradition, called Asatru by some, is involved exclusively with honoring and practicing the pre-Christian faith of the early Nordic and Germanic peoples. While this tradition is wonderfully diverse and rooted in ancient times, it is normally perceived inaccurately as primarily a male-dominated faith. This does not imply that the Norse goddesses are ignored, but oftentimes these female deities are downplayed in relation to their male counterparts. While there are many women attracted to this tradition, many others shy away from it. They tend to explore other traditions, or even choose a more eclectic path, in order to fulfill their need for a complete image of the goddesses, or Goddess.

This fallacy of the Norse Tradition being male-centered stems from many different things, most notably the scarcity of accessible written works. The material available emphasizes the male aspect of the divine, and the majority of texts on the Norse goddesses tend to show them as fractured beings needing a male partner to make them complete. The artifacts found in this area are slim compared with other regions and very few scholars are interested in studying this field. While this fracturing of goddesses can be seen in other mythologies, like the Greek, much more literature and research is available in those areas. This enables the seeker to explore the concept of a primordial goddess more easily in other traditions.

This study will reveal the probability of a primordial goddess—not just a group of figures acknowledged merely as the wives, mothers, lovers, and daughters of the Norse gods. This is not to say that these qualities are not meaningful or are demeaning to women. This would be an untruth and would undermine very important aspects of the feminine divine. They in no way, however, give a complete picture of the goddesses.[3] While the concept of a primordial goddess is an exciting one and can certainly fulfill the need of women and men seeking a fully faceted goddess of the Norse Tradition, this same concept must be explored in other pre-Christian traditions in order to establish a precedent in goddess worship. Otherwise, this study will amount to no more than an esoteric wish for a goddess, rather than a factually based discussion of a primordial goddess.

In the rising tide of heathenism throughout North America, our need to rediscover the Goddess and to link ourselves with our ancient roots is becoming a necessity. We, both women and men, are searching for the equality latent in our past and the beauty and love found displayed throughout nature and within our inner selves. Our environment is again being recognized as both life-giving and divine, rather than as an unintelligent, lifeless mass to be plundered and exploited. The heathen movement is an obvious attempt to reclaim our heritage, while directly refuting the male-dominated faith that has reigned so long in our country. The feminine aspect of life can certainly be suppressed for a short period of time, as is evident in the tragic story of our recent past, but it cannot be caged forever. It is alive and well within us all, ready to lay claim again to its deserved equality: both female and male are needed for true balance. The Nordic peoples suffered under this yoke of oppression for almost a thousand years, but we are again ready to take command of our own

---

[3] Hilda Ellis Davidson, *Roles of the Northern Goddess* (New York: Routledge, 1998), pp. 182–190.

spirituality. This time, instead of adopting or being forced into a new easier faith, many of us are reverting to the beauty, strength, and *duality* of the tradition of our ancestors.

Some will probably question my use of the term heathen, so I will attempt to clarify this usage. Paganism and neopaganism are the popular modern terms for polytheistic faiths. Pagan is a Latin term that does not appear in the early Germanic languages. The correlative term in the Germanic languages is "heathen." Many Norse polytheists feel more comfortable with a term applicable to the tradition itself, and prefer to use one of their own choosing rather than a label used to encompass most non-monotheistic traditions. In essence, therefore, this is a word deeply grounded in the language itself, and, as such, is an actual link to the ancestry of the faith. This term also separates heathenism from many other traditions, since heathenism is based upon an actual ancient religion as it has evolved to the present day. Some faiths are a combination of many traditions. Heathenism strives to retain its ancient appeal and roots, even though it grows and changes with time.

Another misconception about the Norse Tradition should be mentioned here—fatalism. Many people mistakenly believe that this faith lacks a belief in an afterlife of any sort. In this book, we will discuss and explore evidence to the contrary. Reincarnation and rebirth are obvious themes throughout the Nordic myths. They may have been downplayed, however, in an attempt to destroy this wonderful tradition throughout recent history.

Before we begin our exploration of the primordial goddess of the Norse, we must address one other fallacy often associated with the Norse Tradition—the notion that the faith is centered around concepts of nationalism, fascism, and racism. Neither the Norse Tradition nor this book advocate or condone such practices. The early texts of the Nordic myths consistently and clearly portray both the deities and the people as being tolerant of other folk, regardless of race or creed. Hitler, his regime, and modern racial supremacists in general are in total opposition to the true faith of the Norse, nor do any true practitioners of this wonderful faith tolerate such behavior. Proof of these statements will be discussed and explored at length later in this book.

All of these misconceptions will be dispelled through an examination of the myths. This book is dedicated, not only to investigating the feminine aspect of the Norse deities, but to putting an end to these fallacies. It is essential in any research to study both truth and falsehood in order to arrive at an objective view. Now begins the exciting journey of discovering the feminine divine: the Goddess of the North.

PART ONE

HISTORICAL EXPLORATION

So men, longing for knowledge and loving the history of old Germany, sought for the great goddess Saga with untiring diligence, until at length they found her. She dwelt in a house of crystal beneath the cool flowing river. The eager enquirers went to her, and asked her to tell them about the olden times, and about the vanished races which had once ruled, suffered, fought and conquered, in the north of Europe. They found the goddess sunk in dreamy thought, while Odin's ravens fluttered around her, and whispered to her of the past and of the future. She rose from her throne, startled by the numerous questions addressed to her.

—W. WAGNER, *Asgard and the Gods*

ONE

WHY A PRIMORDIAL GODDESS?

The purpose of this book is to present factual, intuitive, and spiritual evidence for the existence of a primordial Norse goddess. Before we begin, however, we must address the motivation behind this task. Why, indeed, is the need for a primordial Norse goddess so important? For many years, the Nordic worldview has been seen as male-dominated by many academics, heathens and pagans alike, so why should we even bother to explore the ostensibly negligible feminine aspect?

The answer to both of these questions is fairly simple. First, the search for the primordial Norse goddess is of utmost importance as She indubitably exists. She has been forced into the dim shadows of our thoughts by ill-used words that have caused many misconceptions and misinterpretations. This situation has gone on far too long, and it is time to join others in re-examining the long-ignored facts. Second, the almost universal *modern* practice of ignoring the feminine divine causes an unnatural imbalance among the human race. It is detrimental to society, as it lessens the inner strength of the people as a whole. It ignores the inherent strength of the female and lowers its value to that of an inferior companion to the male.

Today, Goddess study has again become an avenue for concentrating on many different areas of ancient religions. Unfortunately, the Norse Tradition has been almost completely ignored, until fairly recently. This is due to the dearth of consistent

Nordic literature or to the misunderstanding caused by much of the literature that does exist. Of course, this misinterpretation can only be blamed on the misperception many Americans have of the Norse people in general. Most of us have been taught very little about these magnificent early people, except to hear that their one purpose in life was to "rape, pillage, and plunder." Because of this horrific image, many choose to actively avoid Nordic literature. This negative attitude actually perpetuates the hold that the monotheistic view has over us, as we are not accurately taught, nor do we have the desire to learn, about the wonderful and long history of the Norse. Fortunately, there are a few remarkable scholars and authors determined to keep the interest in Norse literature alive and well.

For many of us, our limited knowledge is focused on the 250-year reign of the Vikings. While the Vikings were indeed fearsome warriors, their goals were not limited to bringing death to other cultures. Unfortunately, this mistaken picture does not include the fact that the Vikings were in need of land, as their homelands were being invaded by waves of monotheistic people willing to do anything to force conversion on the natives. The Norse people were protecting their own—violently, if need be. They were searching for new homes and were willing to do what was needed to preserve their families, friends, faith, and lifestyle. Needless to say, they failed in their ultimate goal. They did manage, however, to retain some of their beloved culture. Fortunately, a few legends have lived on to touch our minds and hearts.

It has been assumed inaccurately by most that the only characteristic worthy of exploration in the Norse worldview is the male pantheon normally associated with battle and death. Because of this, a great deal of emphasis has been placed upon the god Odhinn. He certainly plays a vital role in the Norse myths, but Odhinn must not be viewed as all-encompassing. He has many divine peers, both female and male. Historically, we know Odhinn was not worshipped as frequently as other Norse deities, most likely because, in the mundane sense, he has little to do with fertility, birth, crops, and love, all of which are important areas of everyday life. Odhinn has various attributes, the most

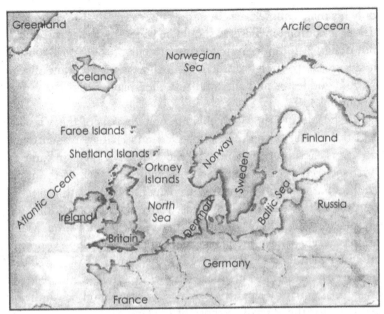

Figure 1. Land of the Norse Goddess. Artifacts have been discovered throughout Northern Europe proving the existence of peaceful native tribes dating back to at least 5900 B.C.E., if not earlier in many areas. Among these artifacts, countless findings are feminine in nature, often exhibiting both divine and unearthly qualities. Many scholars have studied these artifacts in great detail and believe them to point to the religion of these early people. There is no doubt, as many of these scholars will agree, these early people worshipped a primordial goddess encompassing all phases of life—birth, youth, maturity, old age, death, and rebirth. In later years, this primordial goddess came to have numerous aspects with numerous names, many of which are known to us today. This is a map of their land, Northern Europe, where the Norse goddesses were revered, honored, and worshipped.

obvious being magic, death, and war. He is called the All-Father of the Norse deities. This title leads many to unconsciously align his status with that of a monotheistic god. This is an incorrect correlation. We are by no means attempting to undermine Odhinn's importance and placement in the Norse cosmos. He certainly *is* the All-Father, but this title differs greatly from what we are accustomed to believing. To believe that he outweighs not

only his male counterparts in importance but also the Norse goddesses is completely false. It should be stated here that this text is
not designed to undermine the importance of the Norse gods. It
is designed to offer a different and more accurate view of the
Nordic goddesses and the vital role they play within the Norse
Tradition.

Considering the vastly misinterpreted goals of the Vikings,
and the dismal misperception of Odhinn's character and attributes, it is easy to understand how the concept of fatalism came to
be associated with the Norse faith. Fatalism is one of the most
frightening ideas for humanity. To deny life after death is abhorrent. It makes us feel that our present lives are spent working toward goals that simply will not matter in a few years' time. Many
people falsely believe the Norse people had this outlook concerning their own individual demise, and the demise of their beloved
goddesses and gods. This idea is ludicrous. Indeed, the legends
make it abundantly clear that each goddess and god had individual halls for the express purpose of housing souls before rebirth.
These halls will be explored later at greater length. The important thing to remember is that fatalism is not an idea of Norse
origin, but stems rather from later people attempting to twist native concepts to further discourage people from forming an interest in Norse polytheism. These fatal misconceptions can fool us
into overlooking the actual truth and beauty of the Norse Tradition, as portrayed in part by the gods and goddesses, and also by
the very culture of the people.

It is an acknowledged fact that uniform religious choices ordain society's structure, laws, and biases. This is evident in our
personal culture. In recent centuries, women's sole purpose in our
society has been the care of the home and the birthing and rearing of children. Women were normally not given control of the
home, nor were they allowed to make decisions pertaining either
to the home or child. Women were merely considered maids,
convenient daycare providers of future male heirs, and guardians
of often undesired female children. The tasks of home care and
especially child care are obviously important, valued, and skilled
functions within any society, but they certainly do not encompass
all of the wonderful abilities and talents women naturally possess.

Women have been treated as second-class citizens at best, slaves and property at worst. Women have been labeled inferior solely based on their sex. They have suffered the debilitation of twisted superstition and have died horribly as a result. These superstitions led to two of the most heartrending atrocities of our human history, the European and New England witch hunts.

In many cases, women have been considered worthless, dirty, and foul creatures lacking initiative, desire, and intelligence. The physical fact of a woman's menstruation, once believed to be sacred, now was deemed unclean. Women's bodies, once viewed as a beautiful testament to the awesome mystery of creation, were now deemed mere sexual objects. Women's worth in some cultures was considered less than that of livestock and property. Women became cruelly dominated, stripped of dignity, and were forced into oppressive submission, totally against their own inner longings and abilities. The saddest part of this entire affair is that this behavior was not only condoned, but actually approved, by church, government, and the masses.

After many years of persuasion and demonstration, women's voices slowly started to be heard. In our country, women won the right to vote in 1920. In the next decades, it became easier for them to own property. Eventually, it became much easier for them to have their own bank and credit accounts. In the 1960s, women burned their bras as a physical expression of freeing themselves from oppression. They re-acknowledged and lovingly embraced both their bodies and their individual sexuality. Women finally rediscovered the pride their ancestors had in being female.

The Equal Rights Movement continued building momentum. Abortion was legalized, rape and domestic violence were judged punishable acts, and childhood molestation became recognized as a heinous crime. Women came roaring into the workforce, rivaling men in previously male-dominated fields. Educational opportunities expanded. Women finally became respected members of the armed forces, instead of being ridiculed and shamed for choosing to embark upon a military career. Women were slowly proving their indisputable right to be treated as first-class citizens in a country long accustomed to taking every possible freedom away from them. This sexual revolution began to affect other countries as well, and we began to hear almost daily about new advances made by women overseas. We became one of the countries leading the battle for equality of the sexes, and we have yet to accede to the negative influences of derision, discrimination, or hatred.

Women entered politics, and have become respected members of Congress and legislatures. Both their voices and actions continue to support our right to equality. While there has not yet been a female president or vice president, it is only a matter of time. Hillary Clinton is a prime example of our feminine progression. She did not sit back meekly behind her husband, concentrating only on issues he deemed worthy. This First Lady had her own agenda, which she rigorously worked toward achieving. She lent her vibrant voice and all her abilities to enhance the office of the President. Regardless of the scandal and tension that invaded the White House and our country, the former President and Hillary Clinton were symbols of sexual equality in *leadership*. They demonstrated the beauty and power of true balance.

As we can see, women have come a long way in their fight for equality. But this path is long and winding, and a continuous battle must be waged to reach ultimate success. The biggest obstacle to women's equality actually falls into the realm of spiritual faith. Most women and men in this country have been conditioned to believe that the male is the divinely anointed superior, and the female created solely as a companion. The dominant monotheistic spiritual dogma prevalent in this country presently emphasizes women's submissive role and condones previously mentioned negative attitudes and behavior. It must be noted that there has been headway made in this area as well. Many churches and temples are re-examining their former views toward women, and adjusting accordingly to the current overwhelming demand. Unfortunately, as positive as this new trend sounds, it is still a detriment. Regardless of how one wishes for such a change, the dogma attached to these faiths will always remain the same. This monotheistic dogma teaches its practitioners to worship only the male divine, thus this discrimination will continue to perpetuate the suppression of women as the norm.

Many women and men have historically gone against this monotheistic hold on our society. In recent decades, their voices have become increasingly loud and their message increasingly strong. These foremothers and forefathers of ours may have been forced into silence and secrecy in years past, but this isolation is slowly fading. These women and men have unearthed what many Native Americans know and what our ancestors inherently knew. In their spiritual and emotional strength, they are helping us to rediscover the same beauty. The divine is not a singular, untouchable, aloof male being, but a warm, balanced, and interactive presence of both female and male. These men and women have rediscovered the wonderful mystery of the Goddess and God.

Many of these modern-day pioneers are concentrating their spiritual exploration within the perimeters of traditions known only to our ancestors, who were more in tune with both themselves and their surroundings. Many of us have also heard this wonderfully persistent and unavoidable call, and we are slowly beginning to respond to the lovely voice of the Goddess. We are happily leaping into voluminous texts previously scorned as "myths and fairy tales." We are finding out that these "stories" hold glorious gems of spiritual truth and harmony. It is past time to recover the long-hidden feminine side of the divine. This is the only way we as humans can again come into balance, not only with ourselves, but with others and with the natural world.

Of course, the search for the feminine divine has been an ongoing process throughout the centuries. Examples of this can be seen in the reverence shown for the Christian Virgin Mary, the high regard in which female saints of the Catholic Church are held, and the fact that we still use the term "Mother Nature" to describe the elements. This search for the feminine divine is especially apparent in the American Equal Rights Movement. While women and men fighting for this movement may not have been aware of it, the Goddess was certainly calling to them. These people responded loudly and in unison. Women slowly took their place in the mainstream of society. They refused to remain hidden deep within kitchens, wearing aprons and wiping sweat from their prematurely wrinkled brows. Women have fought and won on many levels concerning equality of the sexes.

They have learned again to be proud of their individual sexuality. For each of these battles won, the Goddess smiles quietly and rejoices in watching Her children of both sexes come ever closer to Her loving embrace. These recent advances achieved by women and men are but a few of the subtle signs of the resurgence of the Goddess in our consciousness.

Humanity is slowly coming into closer touch with its natural environment. We are learning and finally acknowledging the appalling destruction we have previously caused the Earth and all Her varied species. We have also accepted the fact that, by continuing this destruction, we will eventually destroy ourselves. We are slowly but surely learning as individuals how to cease such uncaring behavior. We are gradually, but inevitably, learning tolerance for other cultures, religions, and species. This alone is indicative of the Goddess speaking to us, and we are finally beginning to listen. The Goddess does not know the definition of either sexism or racism. She does not acknowledge hatred. She does not condone intolerance of any sort.

Considering these issues, and the fact that polytheism and animism are ancient religious traditions, the question, "Why is a primordial goddess so important?" is not nearly as important as the question, "Why did we neglect the feminine divine?" The second question will be explored at length later in this book. As for the first, the answer is very simple. She is of inarguable importance, for She is a strong elemental part of ourselves, our surroundings, our heredity, and the very ancestry of Earth. Without Her, the gods are incomplete and become, themselves, fractured beings. The Goddess is what nurtures us, sustains us, and shows us the beauty and love inherent in all our surroundings. Through Her very essence, She gives us the gift of a promise of everlasting life. This gift is not one filled with fear, dread, compromise, and conformity, but one filled with beauty, love, challenge, and peace.

PRECEDENTS

To establish a basis for the possibility of a Norse primordial goddess, one must begin with the available material in the Nordic Tradition, and look to other comparable traditions as well. While the focus of this book will certainly be on ancient scholarly works, modern texts will be included for they contain useful information, as their authors most likely started with the same fundamental documentation as we. Some authors of these wonderfully insightful modern works are heathen or pagan, so their spiritual interpretation of the ancient texts is much different from that of authors with a purely academic outlook. By considering both academic and "New Age" works, however, we will arrive at a well-rounded view of the Norse primordial goddess.

In order to assess the multitude of Norse goddesses described in the literature, one should begin with a study of the variety of translations of the *Edda* and the *Prose Edda*, both written by Snorri Sturluson in the 12th century. *Heimskringla: History of the Kings of Norway,* also by Snorri Sturluson, is another wonderful and irreplaceable source. One should note, however, that Snorri was, in all likelihood, a faithful Christian in an era when neither the worship, acknowledgment, nor even discussion of heathen gods and goddesses was tolerated, unless they were talked and written about as mere myths. Icelandic sagas and folk or fairy tales from other related Germanic cultures are also extremely important. They all contain many important, albeit hidden, mythological themes and hints pertaining to the existence of the Goddess of the North.

Hauksbok, Codex Regius, and *Annamagnaean Codex* are all primary texts, but they are, unfortunately, hard to locate in the United States. Luckily, these sources have been used in many of the above-mentioned works, especially in the *Edda* studies. Saxo Grammaticus, author of the text *Gesta Danorum,* is the only other early author to write about the Norse Tradition from Denmark. His writings are usually either similar to Snorri Sturluson's interpretations, or are not given much credit, as Grammaticus was obviously cynical of the Norse Tradition. Saxo's fanatical belief in the Christian faith led him to incorporate a sarcastic outlook toward other faiths. He relegated the polytheistic gods and goddesses to mere mortals involved in petty undertakings. The early travelers, for example, Tacitus, in his *Germania,* or Ibn Fadlan, can be used as sources, as they each visited these Nordic areas and kept thorough journals about their own observations.[1] Jacob Grimm's *Teutonic Mythology* is another text essential to any study of the Norse, as it incorporates both scholarly and folk perspectives.[2] Hilda Ellis Davidson's works are also necessary, as she has done extensive study in the Norse field, including much on the Norse goddesses.[3] Both Grimm and Davidson have done a great deal of comparative work between cultures, dialects, regions, and names. Their knowledge is essential to this study of the feminine divine.

The purpose of tackling such a daunting group of texts is to compare and contrast the many different renditions in order to achieve a sense of balance in this chiefly male-focused academic and spiritual field. Very few texts go into much detail concerning the entire group of known Norse goddesses. The majority emphasize primarily the gods. If one looks closely, however, one will

[1] Kevin Crossley-Holland, *The Norse Myths* (New York: Pantheon Books, 1980), pp. xxxii–xxxvi.

[2] Jacob Grimm, *Teutonic Mythology*, 3 vols., James Steven Stallybrass, trans. (New York: Dover Publications, 1966).

[3] See bibliography for texts by Hilda Ellis Davidson.

find that, in each source, a small spark of the Goddess appears, mirroring a flame found elsewhere. By painstakingly piecing these small bits of information together, one starts to see the rudimentary beginnings of a much larger picture. These texts also have another advantage: many of these authors had access to some of the materials mentioned above that are no longer readily available. We can hope these authors accurately passed on to us the knowledge they gained through their personal studies of the Norse goddesses.

To truly establish a factual precedent for a primordial goddess, a cursory study of other cultures is needed, especially emphasizing those ancient religious cultures in or near the same geographical region as the Norse. In our society, truth is a many-faceted jewel, and the only way to find the ultimate truth is by looking above, underneath, around, and within each facet. In this way, we are able to ascertain not only the probability of the existence of a Norse primordial goddess, but also the factual data needed to determine if, indeed, this search will end at an age-old, universal truth. Since this book concentrates solely on the Norse feminine divine, a few comparisons to other cultures will be made, but the bulk of this preliminary study will be left to the reader. This book would otherwise be overly long and our specific focus would be entirely lost. To assist the reader in this separate task, I have included in the bibliography a list of highly recommended texts concerning goddess research in various cultures.

While we, of course, cannot take a step backward in time to witness the lives of early people firsthand, we can study the comprehensive remains left by these cultures and get a fairly accurate idea of how they lived. By studying early archeological finds in Old Europe, we will find numerous instances of goddess worship, presumably focused on one deity. There has been extensive research done in this area, and the results are astonishing. Until the tribes from the southern area of what we today call Russia invaded, it is obvious that early European peoples did indeed worship a goddess. While there are differences in physical artifacts throughout different regions, most likely due to climatic influences, the similarities pointing to a primordial goddess are certainly observable. Numerous scholars have studied early myths in great detail and many have acknowledged a predominate underlying female theme. Both groups of works point to the existence of a primordial goddess. Robert Graves, in his *Greek Myths*, states:

> Ancient Europe had no gods. The Great Goddess was regarded as immortal, changeless, and omnipotent; and the concept of fatherhood had not been introduced into religious thought. She took lovers, but for pleasure, not to provide her children with a father. Men feared, adored, and obeyed the matriarch; the hearth which she tended in a cave or hut being their earliest social centre, and motherhood their prime mystery. . . . the goddess became identified with seasonal changes in animal and plant life; and thus with Mother Earth who, at the beginning of the vegetative year, produces only leaves and buds, then flowers and fruits, and at last ceases to bear. . . . Her devotees never quite forgot that there were not three goddesses, but one goddess. . . .[4]

Historically, we know early people were primarily hunters and gatherers. As some tribes evolved by adjusting to their surroundings, many learned the art of agriculture. Eventually, through traveling and intermingling, all tribes either had knowledge of or utilized the life-sustaining skill of growing crops. Regardless of whether they were nomadic or agricultural, these people lived off of the resources of the Earth. Their lives depended on fair weather, good crops, accessible roots, berries, and vegetation, and available animal prey. In such a close-knit society, where starvation, injury, or death could happen in an instant due to various unpredictable reasons, there was a deep respect and veneration for the Earth. These people quickly learned to be overjoyed at the advance of abundant spring and saddened at the onset of cold winter. They saw firsthand the cycles of birth, maturity, and death, and understood how each of these deeply affected their

---

[4] Robert Graves, *The Greek Myths*, 2 vols. (London: Penguin, 1960), pp. 13–14.

lives. These ancestors of ours huddled together in their homes during a fierce blizzard, not knowing when the storm would end. They felt a deep sense of thanksgiving for the food they had been able to store, the animal pelts covering their bodies, and the warmth of a raging fire at their feet. As a tribe, they offered thanks for each item protecting them from starvation and death. They were led in this thanksgiving by a respected elder, either female or male, an individual with the gift of experience, who could help the tribe to understand intuitively the subtle signs of the Goddess. This elder, able to interpret and share the messages of the Goddess, eventually was viewed as a person of prophecy and magic.

Led by this holy person, these people learned to notice melting snow and ice, and recognize the warming winds as heralds of spring. They cheered the blossoming of new shoots and the beginning signs of budding flowers washing the valleys and fields in splendid color. They reveled in the sight of newly grown fruits, nuts, and vegetables. The buzzing of bees and the return of migrating birds were signs for the tribe to hold a festival in honor of the Earth and the impatiently anticipated coming of spring. They were overjoyed at the birth of an animal that, upon maturity, would become not only a new food source, but a source of even more animal young. They gave thanks for every infant born to them, for each new child guaranteed the survival of the tribe and represented a direct gift of the Goddess. The tribe mourned the death of anything within their environment, for each death affected them in some way, however minute. They also learned, however, that death did indeed bring forth new life, so the concept of regeneration was respected and honored as well. Every animal, plant, tree, stream, and rock was sacred and acknowledged as having an individual soul. Some were credited as guardian spirits.

To such tribes, the planet Earth was the entire universe— their livelihood and their sustenance. It dictated their very survival and continuation as a species. Earth controlled where they lived, when they would next move, and how long they would stay in each area. They certainly observed that Earth exhibited feminine traits, including, but not limited to, creation, birth, and

nurturing. These tribes understood these characteristics and worshipped them. They named Earth their Mother Goddess.

By researching the many available texts of Nordic and other
comparable religious traditions, studying archeological finds of
early goddess worship, and striving to see Earth through the un-
shadowed eyes of our ancestors, one can certainly begin to see
the blossoming of an ancient truth. The existence of a primordial
goddess is indeed a spiritual fact long accepted by many ancient
cultures. This truth has been established by numerous experts
and scholars. The idea, therefore, that the Norse goddesses are
excluded from this divine status is extremely doubtful. The
Asyniur, the Norse term for goddesses, are actually separate
facets of the Nordic Goddess Herself. Snorri Sturluson's *Edda*
says:

> All Asyniur can be referred to by naming the name of
> another one and referring to them by their possession
> or deeds or descent. . . . Woman is also referred to in
> terms of all Asyniur or valkyries or norns or *disir* [(di-
> vine) ladies].[5]

Since Sturluson was one of the few early scholars to document
the Norse myths and legends, these few words hold a deep
meaning to us in the modern world. He tells us, in no uncertain
terms, that the Nordic goddesses are indeed one, and displays, in
a quiet, understated fashion, the deep reverence the Norse held
for women. Sturluson has essentially given us the most important
piece of evidence needed to prove the possibility of a primordial
Norse goddess. Thanks to his diligence in recording Nordic
myths, we know that the goddess, in fact, exists. This truth is further demonstrated by the discoveries made by experts in both the
Norse and other comparable cultures, all of which point to a primordial goddess of Old Europe.

---

[5] Anthony Faulkes, trans., *Snorri Sturluson Edda* (London: Everyman's Library, 1987), pp.
86, 94.

A chant discovered in England has been preserved and lovingly passed down through the centuries. It has been Christianized, as have most written Nordic works. Even so, this simple prayer still holds a deep beauty and binding truth. H. R. Ellis Davidson, in *Gods and Myths of Northern Europe*, shares this translated chant with us:

> *Erce, Erce, Erce, Earth Mother,*
> *may the Almighty Eternal Lord*
> *grant you fields to increase and flourish,*
> *fields fruitful and healthy,*
> *shining harvest of shafts of millet,*
> *broad harvests of barley . . .*
> *Hail to thee, Earth, Mother of Men!*
> *Bring forth now in God's embrace,*
> *filled with good for the use of men.*[6]

This prayer states unequivocally that the Nordic Goddess was thought of as Mother Earth. This is true throughout early Old European cultures, as has been mentioned previously. The Norse were no different in their veneration of the feminine divine, but they suffered from the misconceptions of others who were not willing to listen and learn about their perceptive religious tradition. It is fortunate, indeed, that some written documentation and artifacts have survived from our Nordic ancestors, otherwise this wonderful and misunderstood culture would remain hidden from us forever in the dim recesses of the past.

There is one last piece of incontestable proof of a primordial Norse goddess—the documented, unarguable oppression and, in many instances, hatred, of women in recent centuries. If women had not been a threat to a patriarchal society and, later, to a male-dominated monotheistic one, there would have been no historical suppression of women. The violence exhibited in the rape, murder, and degradation of women would simply not have played such a large role in recent history. This intimidation and

---

[6] H. R. Ellis Davidson, *The Gods and Myths of Northern Europe* (London: Penguin, 1964), p. 114.

domination would not have been necessary. It is a fact that tribes migrated from the southern part of Russia. They surely must have had some contact with the Far East, and women have been dominated and suppressed in that area for countless centuries. While these migrating tribes certainly cannot be blamed for the suppression of women as we know it today, their more war-like cultures certainly may have led to a *vague* acceptance of an attitude of female inferiority.[7] It is also a fact that the monotheistic movement came from the Middle East. This area has also had a long recorded history of female oppression. It is very simple to see how this second group of migrating people would have been shocked at the lack of control the natives had over their women. The intermingling of cultures and, eventually, horrible conversion techniques ultimately allowed the new faith to override the old.

The reason for this male domination is simple: these patriarchal warring societies, and especially the later male monotheistic cultures, found themselves in direct competition with the deities of the Nordic Tradition, especially with the Goddess and Her loyal practitioners. As they could obviously not war with the Goddess Herself, they chose to overpower Her worshippers and eventually termed them "the weaker sex." By subduing women, these new cultures succeeding in twisting and hiding knowledge of the Goddess, at least for a time. They were not totally successful, however, for nothing can repress the Goddess forever. She is always around and within each of us. The early nomadic tribes planted the seed, whereas the later monotheistic tribes managed to make it grow. The result was a temporary blindness, deafness, and coldness toward Her divine being.

---

[7] Hilda Ellis Davidson, *Roles of the Northern Goddess* (New York: Routledge, 1998), pp. 147, 162.

THREE

DISPLACEMENT AND FRAGMENTATION OF THE GODDESS

Humanity has, in its religious evolution, experienced a severe sexual imbalance rarely found in other species inhabiting Earth. This imbalance has been caused by the domination of the female sex by the masculine. This is a direct result of an involuntary—for the most part—turning from a balanced, polytheistic, and animist faith toward, first, a patriarchal faith, and, in more recent years, a monotheistic faith centered around a single, male god. In this religious development, we not only turned from the feminine divine, but also lost our inherent respect for those beings representing Her sacredness—namely Earth and all Her wondrous species. We have also lost the wonder and curiosity for the unknown exhibited in the concept of an afterlife or in the possibility of life existing elsewhere in the universe or in different dimensions. We have replaced this interest with fear, disrespect, loathing, and hatred.

Some people have an intense desire and a driving need for faith on a spiritual level. We can intuitively sense that a divine presence exists, but because of the way human spirituality has evolved, we have learned, for the most part, *not* to physically sense the divine due to the fear of it, which in turn is caused by unwarranted superstition. This is a devastating blow to humanity, as the divine is all around us. The Goddess is in the air we breathe, the water we drink, the ground we tread, the clothes we wear. She can be observed, not only in the natural, untouched environment, but also in the beauty of the lawns, flowers, and trees throughout our cities. In more rural areas, we occasionally see a lone coyote devoted to the hunt, the magnificence of a soaring raptor, and the beautiful and delicate shadowy forms of a deer herd silhouetted against the far, sunlit horizon. We can hear the voice of the Goddess in the whisper of tree limbs gently caressing each other, the faint roaring of waves hitting a softly carpeted beach, and the quiet melody of pebbles falling lightly from the side of a cliff. We are continually nestled in Her arms, but the majority of us have lost the ability to see, hear, or even feel Her presence.

As we discussed briefly in the previous chapter, this lack of acknowledgment of the feminine divine is obviously not a new occurrence, nor can it be blamed solely on the growth of monotheism. The first act of displacing the Goddess most likely occurred long before monotheism was introduced to the early Norse society. To be accurate, it probably occurred when the migrating tribes from the Russian steppes relocated in northern Europe and slowly melded with the native tribes. As will be discussed in chapter 4, part of the creation myth of the Norse is the long drawn-out war between two separate races of gods. No matter their battle skills or magical strength, neither side could conquer the other. Eventually, the two groups of gods agreed to a truce and learned to live comfortably side by side. They finally became close, intimate comrades and friends.

This mythological war of the gods depicts in precise detail what actually happened when the two different tribes of the native Nordics and the migrating European people met. The nomadic people obviously wished to conquer and subdue, whereas the natives were determined to retain and preserve their long-held domain. They warred against each other for a long period of time. The myth that portrays this on a spiritual level still survives. As with the gods, neither tribe was able to triumph. They finally, probably reluctantly, agreed to a truce. In actuality, however, this compromise most likely led to the initial phase of the displacement of the Goddess worshipped by the natives.

There is no doubt that the migrating tribes were nomadic. They survived by moving, constantly searching for a steady food supply and appropriate shelter. As such, they were more inclined to be warlike, as they always had to be prepared to fight other tribes for their very survival. On the other hand, the native tribes were content to live off the land around them. While they may have had nomadic tendencies, archeological evidence shows that they were an agricultural people. They had a deep respect for the natural world and lived intimately with the earth. They clearly were proficient in war, but their philosophy most likely did not consider war a sacred action, but rather a means of protection. The migrating tribes certainly had a similar reverence for the Earth, but their outlook also included respect and reverence for speed, endurance, weapons, and battle strategies.

This is a fairly easy deduction to make, as many religious myths are based upon actual human experience, as is documented throughout our history. As has been noted, the war of the gods is a divine reenactment of the lengthy war between two different tribes. The race of gods most likely worshipped by the native tribes was called the Vanir. These were gods of love and fertility. Fertility, throughout the ages, has been both a male and female attribute, but it has mainly been associated with the feminine aspect, as it is the female who actually gives birth. The gods of the nomadic tribes were called the Aesir. These gods were revered for their warlike qualities. Indeed, many Norse goddesses are known today for their strong warriorlike characteristics. This lends credence to the combining of faiths. It is unlikely that an agricultural society would have considered war a divine attribute.

Religion, usually due to its interpreters and leaders, plays a much larger role in our society than is generally acknowledged. Religion dictates our ideas of morals and ethics. It is the underlying foundation on which we unconsciously base our decisions concerning law, order, and well-being. Religion sets the trend for our educational and employment expectations and goals. It determines who and what are considered important assets to the community at large. Religion also suggests how we, personally, view Earth, including how we perceive and subsequently treat the numerous other species with which we share this planet. The perception and practice of a culturally chosen religion sets the course for sexual balance or imbalance.

Since women have, throughout the ages, been associated with fertility and earth, the recent emergence of a male-dominated monotheistic faith has been detrimental to both women and the feminine divine. It displaced women from a position in society that they were long accustomed to holding. This was not a position of superiority, but of equality. Because of this newfound faith, opinions and behavior changed drastically, creating an environment in which women were born unwanted, lived their lives under the control of others, and ultimately died, all without ever sharing their innate abilities and talents with society. Not only did women suffer horribly from this displacement, the Goddess did as well. She was relegated to the position of a simple myth, an old wives' tale, even an evil and demonic creature.

As the Goddess came to be viewed so negatively, so, too, did Her aspect as Earth. People began to view Earth as an inanimate object, a tool, an inexhaustible supply of riches to be squandered at will. She was ravished, plundered, scarred, raped, and victimized. The newly created, horrific and terrifying underworld, where "sinners" were said to spend eternity, was located within the very bowels of the once sacred Earth. Cultures that loved and adored Earth were called heathens, barbarians, and savages. Their members were often brutally maimed or slaughtered for their beliefs, or forced to abandon their beloved faith in order to survive. Earth, once so loved, adored, and cherished, became an adult, suffering molestation from its own children.

While the pattern of displacement is easily discernible, the fragmentation of the Goddess is far less observable. Fragmentation probably first came about through different people worshipping different aspects of the Goddess. For example, young maidens were more apt to associate with the youthful, fun-loving Freya than the more mature, stately Frigg. Mothers were drawn to the strong sense of motherhood embodied by Frigg, female warriors to the fierce Skadi or the unconquerable Valkyries. While the Goddess *is* all of these aspects, the human mind is inclined to differentiate, naming each attribute individually.

Naming and associating with separate characteristics of the Goddess actually strengthened the later monotheistic belief that

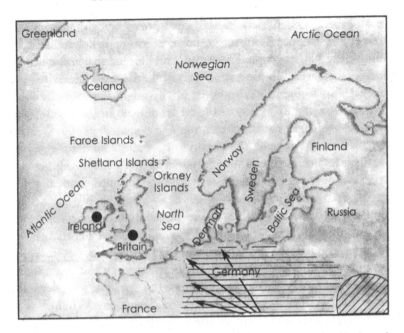

Areas showing the influence of the first nomadic invasion which occurred in eastern and southern Europe in approximately 4300—3500 BCE. These nomadic tribes are often referred to as Kurgans.

● Evidence in England and even the eastern part of Ireland has been linked to the first nomadic invasion.

3500—3000 BCE. Area of Europe inhabited by the nomadic tribes, Kurgans.

Further areas influenced by the nomadics in yet another invasion in 3500—3000 BCE.

Figure 2. Probable origin of the initial displacement and fragmentation of the Goddess of the North. Shows the movement of the nomadic invasions, and the influences felt by them, through Western and Northern Europe. Conflict arose between the peaceful, agricultural native tribes and the warrior tribes of the nomadics. Information shown here from Marija Gimbutas, *The Civilization of the Goddess: The World of Old Europe* (San Francisco: HarperSanFrancisco, 1991), pp. 358, 368, and Ralph Metzner, *The Well of Remembrance* (Boston: Shambhala, 1994), p. 33.

each aspect was, in fact, an individual divine being. The explicit recordings of Snorri Sturluson, however, show that there is little doubt the Norse people knew and never forgot that these separate aspects were simply a small part of the Goddess Herself. The initial displacement, incorporated by the migrating tribes honoring the Aesir gods, was nonetheless reenforced in later years as a result of this original fragmentation.

With the advent of Christianity, championed by zealous leaders of the early Catholic Church, this feminine fragmentation worsened. Each aspect was recognized as an individual goddess, allowing the new religious leaders to view the Norse goddesses with scorn. They could not respect or accept a deity whom they, as humans, viewed as incomplete. The fact that these goddesses were female further incensed these leaders, for the goddesses were seen as being in direct competition with their chosen god. The femininity of the Norse goddesses relegated them to an "evil" class as demons and witches. Witches and witchcraft were abhorrent to the Church leaders. The rituals of witches were not considered holy, nor was the practice of witchcraft, regardless of the benefit it might give others. Herbal knowledge and midwifery became suspect. As exclusively feminine arts, they were also eventually classified in the same negative light as the goddesses. Eventually, all creatures, practices, and rituals pertaining to the worship and observance of the Goddess were reclassified as "of the devil." The punishment for such acts and worship was certain, tortured death.

With the Goddess fragmented and Her worship repressed, Her final displacement was easily accomplished. The Norse people did not have a vernacular written language as the Greeks and Romans did. They recorded their culture in runes, a magical sequence of symbols used primarily for the practice of magic, divination, and meditation. Runes played only a small role in actual communication. Runic knowledge was held by a few select healers, runemasters, leaders, and spae-wives. The Norse depended entirely on an oral tradition to pass on their religious and spiritual stories from generation to generation. They did not commit their myths and legends to paper. As the Norse slowly became converted to the new invading faith, the practice of passing down

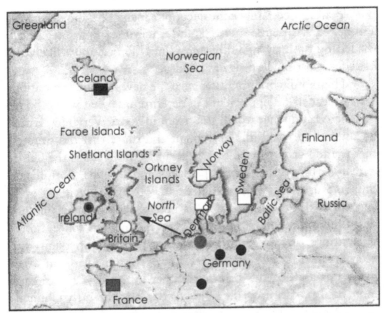

350—500 C.E. Christian conversions began in these and surrounding areas. Often, these conversions amounted to attacks on the pagan people. During this same time, the Bible was translated for the first time into a Germanic language, Gothic.

Approximately 430 C.E. Ireland converts to Christianity.

498 C.E. The tribe known as the Franks, lead by King Clovis, convert to Christianity.

Approximately 500 C.E. Britain converts, under the realm of King Arthur in his attempt to gain unity within the country.

772 C.E. Saxons forced to convert to Christianity by King Charlemagne, leader of the Franks. 30,000 Saxons were murdered.

Approximately 878—965 C.E. These and surrounding areas converted to Christianity.

1000 C.E. Iceland converts.

⟵ Saxons invaded England in the 5th century C.E.

Figure 3. Another stage of competition with the Goddess of the North. The role of Christianity. This map shows how the conversion from polytheism to monotheism often came about through torture, war, and death. This was also the period of time when the Goddess of the North and other Norse gods were considered "demons" by the Christian clergy. Information in map from Kveldulf Gundarsson, *Teutonic Religion: Folk Beliefs and Practices of the Northern Tradition* (St. Paul: Llewellyn, 1993), pp. 378–381; Ralph Metzner, *The Well of Remembrance* (Boston: Shambhala, 1994), pp. 104–106.

the old stories certainly continued, but many of the older myths and legends became twisted and their meanings negatively shaded by the new monotheistic values. This is most likely the basis for most modern-day fairy tales.[1]

The Nordic oral tradition gave the new religious practitioners and leaders an upper hand in determining what would be remembered and what would pass from memory. Very few written documents survived this movement and those that did were either written or translated by Christians. This explains the Christian undertone in many of the sagas and legends. Fortunately, Snorri Sturluson, while a Christian, obviously went to great lengths to record as accurately as possible the myths as he had heard them throughout his life. This is the modern conception of his writings, anyway. Snorri's work began after Christianity had been in effect for a few centuries, however, so many of the original myths and legends had been either lost forever or edited to more easily conform to the rigid standards of the early Church.

This religious direction explains the final displacement and fragmentation of the Goddess. Her documented traditions and practices, and the possibility of future growth were not in the hands of Her beloved worshippers, but in the hands of followers of the new monotheistic faith worshipping a fearful male deity. Nothing could be more abhorrent to such a faith than the concept of the feminine divine. While these monotheistic practitioners were not able to completely eradicate the Goddess, they were able to downplay Her role to that of simple female companions to the gods. Later these companions came to be viewed as demons.

---

[1] Jakob and Wilhelm Grimm, *Grimm's Tales for Young and Old*, Ralph Manheim, trans. (New York: Anchor, 1977), pp. 1–2; and Jacob (Jakob) Grimm, *Teutonic Mythology*, 3 vols., James Steven Stallybrass, trans. (New York: Dover, 1966), pp. 267–268.

PART TWO

THE FRAGMENTS

She pointed to the scrolls which were lying scattered around her, as she said: "Are ye come at last to seek intelligence of the wisdom and deeds of your ancestors? I have written on these scrolls all that the people of that distant land thought and believed, and that which they held to be eternal truth."

—W. WAGNER, *Asgard and the Gods*

CREATION

The Nordic creation story is one of beauty, awe, and wonder. It also has an underlying theme of harshness, which is a shocking reminder of the sometimes disastrous and unavoidable side of nature. It warns us of our own violent behavior, but also applauds our creative talents. To many modern people, it is both surprising and amazing to realize that early cultures had such an intimate understanding of the world. The Norse creation myth exemplifies this discovery. Note how this story and the metaphors it contains closely resemble the scientific knowledge recently attained in the modern era. Interestingly enough, the Nordic people did not believe their gods created the universe, but only seven of the nine worlds the Norse knew intimately.

In the beginning, or what we humans can comprehend as a beginning, there existed a huge void in the heavens. To be more accurate, this void did not exist in any sense we can readily understand. It contained not the faintest glimmer of light, not the smallest spark of fire, not the tiniest drop of moisture, nor any hint of the faintest breath of a breeze. No living soul could be found dwelling within. This space was so filled with darkness that its color can not even be described, for no color exists in our present world that can be called darker than the blackest of black nights. This void, called Ginnungagap, was a huge empty sink of stagnant nothingness settled deep in the vast area we today call the universe.

Eventually, after innumerable eons, two worlds dwelling in the great universe drew closer to this void. Their slow, stately dance finally brought them to the very edges of this vast nothingness. These two worlds are known as Niflheim and Muspellheim. Niflheim, a world of unbearably cold ice and mist, was located to the north. Muspellheim, positioned to the south, was filled with unbelievably scalding hot fire. It is said that, on Muspellheim, a fire giant by the name of Surt dwelt, grimly waiting to be a part of the end of worlds not yet created.

While these two majestic planets did not initially enter the void of Ginnungagap, their innate characteristics eventually gained access to this silent space. After countless millennia, the two elements, water and fire, met deep within this lifeless void. Through this cosmic action, these two primal forces created the very essence needed to generate the seeds of life within the vast, lonely, dark, and empty reaches of the womblike region of Ginnungagap.

Out of the icy moisture of Niflheim, heated by the searing flames of Muspellheim, a being eventually appeared. This creature was huge—bigger than any animal we humans have ever seen. Named Ymir, he was the grandfather and grandmother of all grandfathers and grandmothers of the race we term giants. He dwelt by himself on the layer of clouds formed by Niflheim and Muspellheim. He learned to amuse himself by taking long walks to explore his new environment. On these walks, he never met another soul. We have no idea how long he remained solitary, but surely it became a lonely ordeal.

Ymir became hungry and searched diligently through the clouds of his home, unable to find a morsel of food to satisfy his ever-growing hunger. Dejected, he stopped and rested, viewing his quiet world. All of a sudden, he saw a hint of movement. Miraculously, from a great distance, approached the cow named Audmula. He was overjoyed at seeing another living creature. The huge giant and Audmula bonded quickly, becoming as close as mother and son. Audmula tenderly cared for Ymir, allowing him to nourish himself from her full udders of life-sustaining milk. Ymir's need for food was now satisfied. He grew weary and, under the watchful eyes of his new companion, Audmula, he lay down to sleep on the billowing clouds, ever warmed by the breezes from Muspellheim.

The heat from the world of fire caused Ymir to sweat profusely in his sleep. From this sweat, Ymir's descendants were created. From under one arm, a little girl appeared. The other arm produced a little boy. Yet another little boy was created from Ymir's legs. Ymir awoke and was overjoyed with his new family. He immediately introduced them to his foster mother. Audmula lovingly took these children under her protection and offered them nourishment. The children dwelt, side by side, under the watchful eyes of their great father, Ymir, the ancestor of all giants, and Audmula, the sacred nurturer of all life.

Audmula, either desiring sustenance herself, or feeling a tremendous desire to create yet another wonderful being, began licking a salt block she discovered hidden deep within the billowing clouds. With great effort, patience, and precision, she licked the salt continually for three days. In her diligence, she either uncovered or shaped a full-grown man, whom we call Buri.

Buri, not willing to live a solitary life, met and fell in love with one of the children born by Ymir, now grown to adulthood. Buri and his new wife eventually had a son, whom they named Bor. Bor grew up happily in his new world of clouds. When he reached adulthood, he grew lonely and desired a female companion. He met a young maiden by the name of Bestla, the daughter of the giant Bolthorn, who was another descendent of the great frost giant, Ymir.

This couple fell in love and married. Soon they had three sons, whom they named Odhinn, Vili, and Ve. We believe these are the first gods of the Aesir race. Even though they were gods, they were not immortal. We are not sure why this is, but some may think it is because Bor descended from a divine being while Bestla was of the race of frost giants. This heritage may explain why their three sons were not truly immortal. As we do not know what happened to Buri or his son Bor, their divinity is questionable at best. Why the gods are not truly immortal will always remain a mystery.

Odhinn, Vili, and Ve, for reasons unknown to us, detested the frost giants from birth. As the gods grew to adulthood, they resolved to slaughter them. They warred with Ymir and won the battle. As the huge unforgettable frost giant lay dead at their feet, the blood from his wounds streamed from his body in such large amounts that it flooded the clouds where the frost giants dwelt. The giants panicked and tried to flee, but only two survived—a young giantess and her husband, Bergelmir.

The three brothers, faced with the dilemma of what to do with Ymir, decided to perform their first act of creation. They resolved to use the dead body of their foe to bring into being something new and wondrous. They shaped his body into a round sphere, which they named Midgard. This is the place we now call Earth. Not satisfied with that, they tossed Ymir's brains up into the sky and watched them transform into yet more clouds. Then they directed the giant's blood to flood the empty ravines, craters, and caverns meandering over the surface of Midgard. They caused the blood to transmute magically into water. Thus the rivers and oceans came into being. The brothers decided to form a ring of ocean around Midgard. That is why, today, every continent is surrounded by vast amounts of water.

The gods used Ymir's spine to create mountain ranges. His teeth were made into boulders and rocks. Midgard, previously the body of Ymir, eventually produced maggots, as do most carcasses. When the gods discovered this unsavory fact, they magically changed these unsightly creatures into the race of beings we now call dwarves. They then took Ymir's skull and placed it in the sky. They assigned a dwarf to hold up each of the four corners: east, west, south, and north. These dwarves hold our sky in place.

The gods, never failing to find something new to create, decided to form even more worlds above, adjacent to, and below Midgard. Hel became the part of the realm of Muspellheim and Niflheim that the gods placed at the lowest level. Jotunheim and Svartalfheim were joined along the same level as Midgard, and above them all towered the magnificent worlds of Asgard, Vanaheim, and Ljossalfheim. The brothers then decided to place the giants in the world of Jotunheim and the dwarves in

Svartalfheim. The upper worlds were saved for the deities, and Ljossalfheim became the home of elves. The lower worlds, namely Hel, were reserved as the underworld, housing the dead until they returned to a new life.

All these newly created worlds needed more illumination than Muspellheim was able to provide by itself, so Odhinn searched throughout Midgard for ideas. He finally discovered a beautiful mortal woman, Sol, and placed her in a chariot drawn by two shimmering steeds. He threw them into the heavens, and this is how our Sun came into being. Sol rides through the skies in a neverending pattern, constantly pursued by a wolf, Skoll, the son of a giantess. How this wolf came to chase Sol through the sky is unknown, but the chase is foretold to continue until the beginning of Ragnarok, the end of the worlds as we know it. Sometimes, we are just able to see the wolf's mouth start to close around Sol—during what we now call an eclipse. The brothers also decided to throw sparks of fire into the sky, resulting in what we now call stars.

All species, even gods, need a time for rest. Mani, the god of the Moon, was given his chariot in the skies in the same way that Sol was. He follows her daily, shepherding in the darkness of night, which allows all of us—gods, mortals, and animals—to partake of the peace of slumber. Mani is also pursued relentlessly by a wolf named Hati. The god of the Moon rescued two children, a little girl named Bil and her brother, Hjuki, who now assist Mani in his nighttime flight. These two children represent the waxing and waning times of the Moon. Mani rarely travels at the same time as Sol, for his evening journeys fall within the dark realm of Nott, the goddess of the night. She is "black and dark in accordance with her ancestry."[1] It is said that Nott was married three times, and had two sons, Aud and Day, and a daughter named Earth. Odhinn gave Nott and her son, Day, their own chariots to drive through the skies. They spend every day in a great chase, son following mother, laughing and having great fun all the while.

---

1 Snorri Sturluson, *Edda*, Anthony Faulkes, trans, 2nd ed. (London: Everyman's Library, 1992), p. 13.

The gods were overjoyed with their creation—especially with the new world, Midgard. Odhinn, Vili, and Ve wandered endlessly to explore all of its wonder. In their travels, they came across two logs beached at the side of a stream. These two pieces of wood were so beautiful that the gods were determined to find a use for them. After much contemplation and discussion, they decided to embark on yet another act of creation. The brothers picked up the logs and breathed the essences of life, intelligence, and soul into each one. They joyously watched the logs transform into new shapes, both filled with new life. The gods then named these two new creatures Embla and Ask—our ancestors, the first woman and man of the human race.

To assist the gods in their worldly travels, they created a beautiful colorful bridge, called Bifrost—what we mortals now call the rainbow. When we see this appear, we know the gates are open to either visit or to be visited by the deities of the upper realms. All of these creations of Odhinn, Vili, and Ve are supported by the great tree, Yggdrasill. This tree is a majestic sight, towering over the universe, with three roots delving deep below the nine worlds and cradling them. At the foot of each root lies a well. Animals live in and under this wonderful tree, and a dragon lives below one of the roots. Yggdrasill was here before the beginning of time, and will continue long past the end of time.

One spectacularly fine day, Odhinn and his brothers were lounging in his great hall. All of a sudden, a woman approached from a place unknown. Her name was Gullveig. She was offered hospitality, which is the custom of both gods and mortals, and she happily accepted. Gullveig settled herself quite comfortably on a lounge next to the three brothers and began to converse with Odhinn, Vili, and Ve. They discussed various topics, but eventually began a conversation concerning Gullveig's favorite material possession in all the nine worlds. She told them of her great love for gold, and how she craved this special metal above all else. In due time, Odhinn wearied of this talk and tried to divert the conversation in a new direction. Gullveig would not be that easily dissuaded, and continued to share her love for gold. Odhinn then became furious, and cruelly struck her down with a bolt of fire. Unfazed and unhurt, Gullveig arose. This shocked the brothers, and they were unsure what to do. Odhinn tried to kill Gullveig two more times with fire, and each time Gullveig rose from the floor unscathed. She was furious at the lack of hospitality shown to her by the three gods, and walked to the door. She turned and with an unfathomable look, stared deeply into each of the brother's eyes. She then left the premises to return whence she had come.

Odhinn was unaware, at this time, that Gullveig was actually a goddess of another race of gods called the Vanir. Gullveig is one of the names used by the goddess Freya. The guise of Gullveig is Freya's magical side, whom some call a witch. When Freya returned from her visit with the gods of the Aesir, she immediately called together the Vanir gods. She told them of her experience with the Aesir and how Odhinn had tried to kill her three times with bolts of fire. The Vanir were understandably outraged, and they instantly began to prepare for war. The race of the Vanir were furious at the treatment their beloved goddess had received, and were fired with the need to avenge the unacceptable treatment given to her by the neighboring gods.

We have no idea how long this war of the gods lasted, but we do know it raged constantly for many, many years. Neither side was able to best the other. Both opponents used every resource in their considerable power—battle strategies, weapons, and even magic. Each new attack was countered with a new method of defense. The battle raged on relentlessly, both sides eventually tiring and becoming ever more despondent.

Finally, the Vanir and Aesir sent messengers to each other requesting a truce. The gods soon came to an understanding, mutually agreeing to end the war. Part of the agreement was the exchange of hostages. The Vanir agreed to send a goddess and two gods to dwell with the Aesir. These deities were Freya, her twin brother, Frey, and their father, Njord. The Aesir sent the two gods Honir and Mimir to reside with the Vanir.

Both groups of gods were overjoyed with this new arrangement. The Vanir had the privilege of having two gods notorious for their incredible knowledge living in their midst. The Aesir, especially Odhinn, was ecstatic at the prospect of having Freya as a guest. He looked forward to her tutelage in magical skills. The

Vanir, Freya, and Aesir became fast friends, and the prospects for peace looked good.

The Vanir soon began to experience problems with one of their Aesir hostages. Honir, though known for his vast knowledge, was always silent at the Vanir council meetings. No matter how hard the gods tried, they could not get him to participate. The Vanir started to question whether they had been told the truth about Honir's knowledge. At each meeting, they requested his opinion, but he always declined to answer. His continued silence so infuriated the Vanir, that they finally came to the conclusion that the Aesir had deceived them.

The Vanir held another meeting among themselves to discuss possible solutions. They decided that the Aesir needed a serious warning and punishment. The gods of the Vanir called into the chamber the other hostage god, Mimir, and killed him. They removed his head and sent it to Odhinn as a warning against any further trickery. Apparently, this warning was heeded, for no further problems between the Aesir and the Vanir were ever recorded.

Odhinn received the package containing Mimir's head and was stricken with grief. The two of them had been very close comrades, and Odhinn would miss his friend dearly. He remembered the lessons he had recently been taught by Freya, and decided to implement a particular spell. He discovered that he was able to use his new magical skills to preserve Mimir's head. Odhinn was also able to restore the head's ability to speak. Odhinn then set off on a journey down to the very roots of the World Tree, Yggdrasill. He gently placed the head in a well he found there and took to visiting his old friend whenever he needed counsel. Even though Odhinn performed such a miraculous action for his friend, Mimir required a sacrifice from Odhinn in return for his vast wisdom. Odhinn understood. He plucked out an eye and tossed it into the well. There the head of Mimir still resides, willing to share his knowledge with any willing to sacrifice of themselves.

The Aesir and Vanir finally worked through their mutual suspicions. They implemented a second article of their truce. They all spit into a bowl and, from this, made a god who had all

the wisdom of both the Aesir and the Vanir. They named this
new god Kvasir. The gods finally became close friends and soon
united their kingdoms. They shared in all tasks both divine and
mundane. The Aesir continued to focus primarily on battle,
whereas the Vanir continued to concentrate on fertility and love.

This is the story of the creation, and so things shall be until
the call of the birds announce that the time for Ragnarok has
come.

THE GODDESSES IN THE CREATION

One of the first things a reader will discern in the Norse creation
myth is the common thread of male domination throughout the
story. The first creature, Ymir, is male. He is able to reproduce
himself to begin the race of frost giants. His body is used to create Earth. The first reputedly divine being is male, and he mates
with a "lesser" female and produces the first three gods of the
Aesir. These gods are blemished, apparently due to their heredity; they are not immortal. Odhinn's treatment of his guest,
Gullveig, is shockingly violent. All of these facts help foster the
incorrect belief of male dominance in the Nordic culture, and
strengthen the belief that the female is less than perfect, possibly
even inferior. As with most creation myths, metaphor is heavily
used here. This myth is not meant to have one simple, easily understandable meaning. The reader must be careful to look far beneath the surface of the written word to find the hidden message
of the spiritual tale.

It is fairly easy at first to ignore the presence of Audmula,
because she is described as a cow. Today, cows are not highly respected creatures. They are viewed, inaccurately, as docile animals
bred as an easy food source. Many people have the misconception that cattle are not very intelligent. Of course, the cattle of
today are not what they were in the past. Through domestication,
they have evolved into more complacent, docile creatures,
forcibly stripped of their higher qualities so cherished by earlier
peoples.

The divine cow, Audmula, is, in fact, a representation of an
early breed of wild cattle called aurochs. This particular species of

cattle were highly respected by the Norse. They were aggressive, large, independent, and very similar to the American buffalo. While dangerous to hunt, they were large enough to supply a tribe with food for a long while, along with various other items used from the carcass. The sacred horn used for mead and other drink described throughout Norse myths is, in fact, an aurochs horn. This gives us a useful insight into the ways of the Norse people. They utilized everything from the animals they hunted for food. Nothing went to waste. In this way, the Norse people were very much like the Native Americans in their deep respect and reverence for the sanctity of all life.

The aurochs, as an aggressive species, was especially respected and considered sacred by the Norse people. To have a *female* aurochs in the creation myth holds special significance. As was made abundantly clear in the story, Audmula was the sole provider of nourishment for Ymir and his children. She was actually the creator of Buri, the father of Bor, who, in turn, is the father of Odhinn and his brothers. Without her divine presence, the life of Ymir would have been forfeit long before Audmula shaped Buri.

Audmula is our first glimpse of the Goddess, representing the aspect of female creation we see hinted at in Ginnungagap. In the guise of an aurochs, the Goddess is indisputably in control of the story after Ginnungagap was infused with water and fire. The aurochs seemingly disappears immediately after the man Buri is shaped. This gives us the impression that the Goddess's role in the creation is finished. Instead, She was not overly interested in the everyday lives of the gods, but retreated to Her own unfathomable domain and later emerged as the giantess, Bestla.

The being of Ymir must be explored in a different light, however. The gods did not create Ymir. The great giant was already in existence long before the gods' ancestor, Buri, was shaped. Displacement of the feminine is very common when patriarchal and monotheistic religions gain dominance over polytheistic and animistic faiths. In chapter 8, the reader will discover numerous goddesses likened to the earth element. Furthermore, many goddesses are named Mother Earth, Earth Mother, etc. Because of this, the idea that Ymir is male is entirely contradictory to the Norse worldview. Some readers may argue this by pointing out that the god Loki reputedly bore an eight-legged horse, which he then gave as a gift to Odhinn. The difference between Ymir and Loki is that Ymir's children were born in a fashion *natural* to his mythological bodily functions, whereas Loki was forced to *shape-change* into a female to perform his act of creation. Furthermore, Loki is actually a giant, which lends credence to the Norse concept of giants and giantesses being Earth's creatures.

This leads us to the speculation that Ymir is possibly a more recent addition to the Norse creation myth, or, even more likely, that he was originally of the female sex. The race of Vanir are associated with fertility and love, while the Aesir represent war. In the creation, there are two distinct categories of beings. One is symbolized by Ymir and his offspring, all watched over by Aud-mula. The other is symbolized by the newly born Aesir gods. The logical conclusion is that Ymir is a representation of Earth, or the feminine divine. This association with Earth allows us to liken Ymir to the Vanir, as they are noted for their gift of fertility, which is an obvious trait of Earth. Ymir's only function in the myth is as the foster son of Audmula, and as the ancestor of his race, who will be reborn as the new world, Midgard. The ability to bear children is a distinctly female role, not only in most mythological stories, but in reality as well. Ymir's change of sex and violent death were, most likely, incorporated originally with the blending of the conflicting human tribes. This blending would have been reenforced in later years by the monotheistic wave. The concept of birth, death, and rejuvenation normally falls within the realm of the Norse female divine, which will be discussed at greater length in the following chapters.

The story of Gullveig and her visit with Odhinn and his brothers is certainly abominable, and a prime example of the wretched treatment women have received in the past. It is imperative that we examine this section of the Nordic creation myth closely. We have to question if this treatment of Gullveig would have happened had she been male. Considering the Aesir's hatred of male giants, it can be assumed that Gullveig's sex played little part in the gods' behavior. We can also see that the Aesir had a tendency toward arrogance by examining their past actions. Most likely the gods simply did not consider the consequences of their actions, and acted on the spur of the moment.

It is particularly important to consider the Vanir's response to the attempted burning of Gullveig. Their rage and immediate plans to go to war against the Aesir give us an important clue to the actions of the native and migrating tribes of Europe. Obviously, the Vanir held their goddess in high esteem, whereas the Aesir were more male-oriented, as has been discussed in previous chapters. This further strengthens the idea of the Vanir and the Goddess as deities of the native tribe. While we cannot assume these tribes fought for religious purposes, the innuendoes contained in Odhinn's and Gullveig's dispute give us a strong idea that these tribes waged a spiritual, as well as a territorial, war. We will learn in the next few chapters that Odhinn had a great deal of admiration for Norse goddesses, so his behavior toward Gullveig is certainly perplexing. It is probable that the eventual combination of the tribes helped each side to better understand, accept, respect the other and, in so doing, incorporated the Goddess, the Vanir, and the Aesir into their evolved spiritual beliefs.

Regardless of the original role of Ymir and the story of Gullveig, the facts exhibited throughout the story point us toward a new train of thought. Audmula, as an obvious representation of the Goddess, is, in fact, the pivot around which the other characters of this tale revolve. When Her role as the aurochs ends, She reappears as Bestla. Later, we see Her as Gullveig, and finally as all the various goddesses of the Norse. The essence of the feminine is more than prevalent. It is the dominating force throughout this myth of the Norse creation.

FIVE

THE AESIR, THE VANIR, AND THE GIANTS

This chapter is intended to assist the reader in identifying and understanding Norse mythology. It is impossible to thoroughly investigate the Norse goddesses without acknowledging the active role their male counterparts play. We will not discuss all of the many Norse gods and giants here. Nor will we describe all of their various attributes or the numerous myths surrounding many of these figures. This is meant, rather, to be a brief overview of the male deities and other male figures, many of whom are mentioned throughout this book in relation to the goddesses. A much more detailed discussion devoted entirely to the gods is planned for another book, intended as a companion volume to this one.

Aegir: God of the sea. He shares this particular attribute with the Vanir god, Njord. Aegir is the husband of the sea goddess, Ran, and the father of the nine youthful and fun-loving Wave Maidens. Aegir assists Ran in her constant search for drowned mortal souls, bringing them to live in their hall deep within the sea.

Aesir: The creation myth describes Buri, Bor, and Bestla respectively as the grandfather, father, and mother of the brothers Odhinn, Vili, and Ve. The remainder of the Aesir gods are believed to be the descendants of the goddess, Frigg, and the god,

Odhinn. Prior to the war of the gods, the term Aesir was the exclusive name for all the gods commonly portrayed as either battle or war gods. Even though the early Aesir gods are normally associated with war, they can be called upon for fertility rites as well. This is especially evidenced by Thorr, the god of both thunder and fertility. After the war of the gods ended in truce, both the Vanir and Aesir gods generally became known under the term of Aesir. While it is normally assumed that the goddesses fall under the category of either Aesir or Vanir, this is inaccurate. Although there are a very few goddesses who can claim parentage in either category, the majority of the goddesses do not have known parents, or, if they are known, the parents do not fit into either group.

Balder: God of mercy, beauty, and wisdom. Son of Frigg and Odhinn. Brother of Hod, Thorr, Heimdall, Tyr, Bragi, Vidar, Vali, Hermod, and Skiold. Husband of the goddess Nanna and father to Forseti. Balder was foretold by Heith, another name for the goddess Freya, to die prior to Ragnarok. This did come to pass, as he was killed by his blind brother, Hod. Hod was tricked by Loki into throwing a mistletoe dart at his brother in fun. All creatures except the mistletoe had promised Frigg, prior to this incident, that they would not harm Balder. He will be avenged by the god Vali and reborn at the conclusion of Ragnarok.

Bergelmir: He and his wife were the only giants to survive the great flood caused by Ymir's blood.

Bolthorn: A giant. The father of Bestla, and grandfather of Odhinn, Vili, and Ve.

Bor: Son of the first supposed first divine being, Buri. Husband of the giantess, Bestla, and father of Odhinn, Vili, and Ve.

Bragi: God of poetry. Husband of the goddess Idun and son of the giantess Gunnlod and Odhinn. Brother of Balder, Thorr, Hod, Heimdall, Tyr, Vidar, Vali, Hermod, and Skiold. Bragi loved his wife so much that he spent part of each year with her in the world of Hel, caring for her and guarding her in her sickness.

Buri: The man or god whom Audmula, the sacred aurochs, shaped out of a block of ice. He is the father of Bor, and the grandfather of Odhinn, Vili, and Ve.

Fenris: A monstrous wolf. Son of Loki and the giantess Angrboda. Fenris is the brother of the goddess of death, Hel, and the world serpent, Jormungand. Fenris is foreseen to war on and defeat Odhinn by swallowing him during Ragnarok. Odhinn will be avenged by his son, Vidar, who will, in turn, slay Fenris.

Forseti: God of justice. He is the son of Balder and Nanna. Forseti judges and settles all quarrels of the gods.

Frey: God of fertility. Husband of the goddess Gerd, twin brother to Freya, and son of the goddess Nerthus and the god Njord. Frey was one of the Vanir given as a hostage to the Aesir to strengthen the truce of the gods. He shares many attributes with Nerthus and it is very probable that he actually displaced her in the Norse cosmos. During Ragnarok, Frey is said to battle Surt, the giant who guards Muspellheim, and die.

Hati: One of the numerous wolf giants born from the Giantess of Ironwood. Hati continually chases the three aspects of the Moon throughout the evening sky. He is foretold to actually capture the Moon during Ragnarok, and presumably cause the death of this orb of nighttime light.

Heimdall: The white god. One of Heimdall's main tasks is to guard the rainbow bridge, Bifrost, constantly. He is prophesied to sound a horn warning the Aesir of the onset of Ragnarok. During Ragnarok, he will furiously fight Loki and both will perish. Heimdall's ancestry is a Nordic mystery, but some say he is the son of the nine Wave Maidens. Other tales claim that these young goddesses are the lovers of Odhinn, which makes him a possible candidate for father of Heimdall. If this is indeed the case, Heimdall is the brother of Balder, Bragi, Hod, Thorr, Tyr, Vidar, Vali, Hermod, and Skiold. Heimdall, also thought to be known as Rig, is the forefather of the three social classes of the human race. These are the workers, the warriors and the nobles.

Hermod: Called Hermod the Bold. Son of Odhinn. Brother of Balder, Bragi, Hod, Heimdall, Thorr, Tyr, Vidar, Vali, and Skiold. He bravely rode deep into Hel's realm at the request of the grieving Frigg to attempt to convince Hel to release Balder. Hermod was able to reach an agreement with Hel, although Loki deliberately broke it to insure Balder's continued imprisonment deep within the underworld of death.

Hod: The blind god. Son of Frigg and Odhinn. Brother to Balder, Bragi, Heimdall, Hermod, Thorr, Tyr, Vidar, Vali, and Skiold (see Balder). Hod was tricked into killing his brother, Balder, by a cruel ruse of the giant/god Loki. Even though Hod's part in this act was admittedly unintentional, he was punished with immediate death. He was then sent to the hall of Hel, along with his brother, to await the end of Ragnarok. At this time, Hod's rebirth is foretold.

Honir: The quiet god. Honir is a companion of Odhinn and Loki. Many academics name Honir as one of three gods credited with the creation of the human race. Since this is also known to be the work of Odhinn and his two brothers, Vili and Ve, we can speculate that Honir may be another name for one of Odhinn's brothers. Honir was one of two gods given as hostages to the Vanir in the truce of the gods. As Honir was so silent, he presumably withheld advice, causing the fertility gods to became angry. They thought the Aesir had deliberately tricked them. As punishment, the Vanir killed the other hostage, Mimir, and sent his severed head to the Aesir. After Ragnarok, Honir is prophesied to be Odhinn's heir. He is the only one of the older gods thought to survive "The Twilight of the Gods."

Hraesvelg: A huge giant reputed to have the ability to shape-change into a massive eagle. It is said that the flapping of his huge wings causes the winds to rage across Midgard and the other eight worlds. This wind can be so strong that it is said to shake the very trunk and limbs of the World Tree, Yggdrasill.

Jormungand: The world serpent. Son of Loki and Angrboda. Brother to Hel and Fenris. Jormungand will battle Thorr during Ragnarok and perish. This creature will have his revenge, as Thorr will also die of Jormungand's lethal venom after taking nine steps backward from the slain serpent's body.

Kvasir: Kvasir was created through the spit of the Aesir and Vanir as one of the initial acts of their truce. Kvasir was viciously killed by some dwarves, who managed to use his blood to create vats of magical mead. It was highly prized because it contained universal wisdom, and was finally given to a giant named Suttung. Odhinn went to great lengths to retrieve this mead from Suttung, who had placed it deep within a mountain and charged the giantess Gunnlod to guard it.

Loki: It is unclear whether Loki is actually a god. His giant parentage casts some doubt on this. Most likely, he was given god status when he became Odhinn's blood brother. Loki is the main cause of mischief and wrongdoing among the gods. In punishment for the death of Balder and Loki's refusal to assist in bringing him back from the world of Hel, the gods bound him in a cave to await Ragnarok. Loki is the father of Hel, Fenris, and Jormungand, husband of the goddess Sigyn, and lover of the giantess Angrboda. During Ragnarok, Loki will fight Heimdall and both will die.

Magni: Son of the giantess Iarnaxa and Thorr. Brother of Modi, Thrud, and stepbrother of Uller. Magni will survive Ragnarok along with his brother, Modi. They will become the new tenders of Thorr's hammer, Mjollnir.

Mani: God of the Moon.

Mimir: God of wisdom. According to the legends, a spring at the foot of one of the three roots of Yggdrasill houses Mimir's head.

Mimir was very wise and, even though he was killed by the Vanir, his head was preserved through Odhinn's use of herbs and charms. Odhinn then placed Mimir's head in a spring and, through his use of magic, was able to give it the gift of speech. This enabled Odhinn to increase his own wisdom by requesting Mimir's advice. Mimir did require, in exchange for his wisdom, the sacrifice of one of Odhinn's eyes. This spring also held the runes for which Odhinn sacrificed himself to himself. These runes are the very essence of all universal wisdom and magical ability. We must remember that Freya taught Odhinn all her magical skills, so it is probable that she already knew the universal and magical strength embedded within the runes.[1]

Modi: Son of Iarnaxa and Thorr. Brother of Magni, Thrud, and stepbrother of Uller (see Magni).

Njord: Vanir god of the sea, fire, and wind. He is called upon for sea travel and fishing, and is also able to grant financial and property gain. Husband of Nerthus, and later, the goddess Skadi. Father of the twins, Freya and Frey. Njord was one of the gods given as hostage to the Aesir in the truce of the gods.

Od: Probably a name for Odhinn. Husband of Freya. Od leaves her on yearly journeys. She searches diligently throughout the nine worlds for him, crying tears of gold and amber all the while, until they are reunited again.

Odhinn: The Aesir All-Father. He is the son of the giantess Bestla and Bor, and brother of Vili and Ve. Husband of the queen of all gods, goddesses, and mortals, Frigg. Odhinn is the presumed lover of the goddesses Iord, Rind, and Skadi, the giantesses Grid and Gunnlod, and the nine Wave Maidens. Father of Thorr, Balder, Hod, Heimdall, Tyr, Bragi, Vidar, Vali, Hermod, and Skiold. Odhinn and Frigg are said to be the ancestors

---

[1] Edred Thorsson, *Gildisbok, the Inner Workings of the Rune-Gild*, 1994ce, pp. 15–16. Private text within the Rune Gild. Through meditation on this text, I received my first glimpse into the feminine concept of the runes.

of the Aesir race of gods. Odhinn is sometimes called the one-eyed god, as he was required to sacrifice an eye to Mimir in exchange for wisdom. Odhinn is known as the hanged god as well, because he hanged himself from the World Tree, Yggdrasill, as an act of sacrifice to gain the knowledge of the runes.

Odhinn and his brothers are responsible for the initial creation of Midgard. These brothers killed the first frost giant, Ymir, and used his deceased body for this massive effort. This act drove them to desire greater achievements, so they shaped the worlds of Hel, Jotunheim, Svartalfheim, Ljossalfheim, Vanaheim, and Asgard. Still not satisfied, they went on to bring into being the heavens surrounding the worlds. They filled vast caverns with the blood of Ymir and thus created all the waters of the worlds. The brothers then discovered two logs floating gently in a cool stream of slowly moving water. Finding these dead pieces of wood to be full of beauty and enchantment, they breathed life into each, shaping them into the first mortals, Ask and Embla.

Odhinn, through the attempted burning of the witch, Gullveig, actually was the cause of the war between the Aesir and Vanir gods. As stated previously, this war finally resulted in a truce. Afterwards Freya (also known as Gullveig) taught all her magical skills to Odhinn.

Odhinn oversees three halls: Valaskialf, which is roofed with silver and is the home of the magical chair, Hlidskialf; Val-Halla, where half of those killed in battle will go to await Ragnarok; and Gimle, which will survive Ragnarok and be the hall of the surviving gods. All good and noble people are destined to live in either Gimle or the Asynuir's hall, Vingolf, after death.

Odhinn is the leader of the Wild Hunt and of the Valkyries. He has two ravens, Hugin and Munin (thought and memory), two wolves, Geri and Freki, and an eight-legged horse, Sleipnir, mothered by Loki. He also owns the powerful spear Gungnir and the magical ring Draupnir. After giving this ring to his dead son, Balder, on his funeral bed, Draupnir began to reproduce itself eight times every ninth night.

At the onset of the dreaded "Twilight of the Gods," otherwise known as Ragnarok, Odhinn will resolutely lead all the Aesir and Vanir gods to his last battle on the plains of Vigrid. He already knows he is to die in this raging battle, but will valiantly fight to attempt to change his age-old destiny. This is not prophesied to happen, and he will finally be swallowed by the horrid wolf, Fenris. Odhinn will be avenged immediately by his young son, Vidar.

It has been conjectured by some scholars that Odhinn displaced Tyr as the original All-Father. This is of great interest because it would amount to the displacement of a male god similar to the displacement we have discussed of the goddesses. This could mean that Tyr was the actual ancient male partner of the Goddess of the North. At the present time, however, our interest lies with the Norse feminine.

Ottar: Lover of Freya. She gives him the shape of a boar, which Freya then proceeds to ride.

Skiold: Son of Odhinn. Husband of the goddess Gefjon. Brother of Balder, Bragi, Hod, Heimdall, Hermod, Tyr, Thorr, Vidar, and Vali.

Skoll: Giant wolf who continually chases the goddess of the Sun, Sol, along her daily trail through the sky. It is said he will finally catch up with her during the battle of Ragnarok and swallow her. Skoll is the son of the Giantess of Ironwood.

Surt: Giant who dwells in and defends the world of Muspellheim. Husband of Sinmara. He owns a flaming sword that he will use during Ragnarok to fight and slay Frey. He is prophesied to set fire to all the nine worlds at the conclusion of Ragnarok.

Suttung: Giant. Father of the lovely gaintess Gunnlod. Suttung briefly owned the magical mead of Kvasir.

Thorr: God of thunder and fertility. He drives a chariot pulled by two goats. He is the husband of the goddess Sif and lover of the giantess Iarnaxa. Thorr is the father of Magni, Modi, the goddess Thrud, and is the stepfather of Uller. Thorr is the son of Frigg or Iord, and Odhinn. He is brother to Balder, Bragi,

Heimdall, Hod, Hermod, Tyr, Vali, Vidar, and Skiold. Thorr will battle and kill Jormungand in Ragnarok, but will sacrifice his own life in doing so.

Tyr: God of bravery, wisdom, justice, and war. Some name him the son of Odhinn. If this is indeed true, Tyr would be the brother of Balder, Bragi, Hod, Hermod, Heimdall, Thorr, Vidar, Vali, and Skiold. During the binding of Fenris, Tyr sacrificed his right hand to the wolf in order to display the courage and honor of the Aesir. Tyr will battle the monstrous dog from Hel's kingdom, Garm, in Ragnarok and perish.

As previously mentioned it has been hypothesized that Tyr could be the original All-Father of the native Nordic tribes. Considering his various qualities, this possibility does not seem farfetched.

Uller: God of winter and archery. Son of Sif and stepson of Thorr. Stepbrother of Magni, Modi, and Thrud. Uller's real father is unknown. Because of his attributes, many believe him to be an able mate for the goddess of winter, Skadi. Even though this is a logical theory, no documentation survives to support it. Uller is frequently called upon to assist in both godly and mortal duels.

Vafthrudnir: Giant of incredible wisdom. He was challenged to a contest of knowledge by Odhinn, with the head of the loser as prize. Vafthrudnir was so intelligent that Odhinn finally resorting to trickery to win.

Vali: Bold god. Vali is accurate with weapons. Son of Rind and Odhinn. Avenger of Balder. Vali is one of the gods said to survive Ragnarok. Vali is brother of Vidar, Heimdall, Hermod, Hod, Balder, Skiold, Tyr, Thorr, and Bragi.

Vanir: Early name for gods of fertility. After the war of the gods, the Vanir became known as the Aesir.

Ve: Son of Bestla and Bor, brother of Odhinn and Vili (see Odhinn). Ve and his brother, Vili, were accused of attempting to take over the rule of Odhinn's kingdom when he was away on a lengthy journey. These two brothers were also thought to have had sexual relations with Frigg, Odhinn's wife.

Vidar: Silent god. Son of the giantess Grid and Odhinn. Brother of Vali, Thorr, Tyr, Heimdall, Hod, Balder, Bragi, Skiold, and Hermod. Vidar is very strong and owns a thick shoe made from the scraps of mortals' shoes. Vidar will use this shoe to avenge his father's death by defeating Fenris the wolf in Ragnarok. Vidar is one of the young gods foretold to survive this incomprehensible battle.

Vili: Son of Bestla and Bor, brother of Odhinn and Ve (see Odhinn and Ve).

Ygg: Another name for Odhinn. This name could be the reason why the World Tree is known today by the name of Yggdrasill.

Ymir: The first frost giant. He was created in the void, Ginnungagap, by the elements from the worlds of Niflheim and Muspellheim. During a deep sleep, his sweat formed a boy and a girl under each arm, and his legs created another boy. In this way, Ymir was the forefather of the race of the frost giants. He was nourished from the milk of the sacred cow, Audmula. Ymir was eventually killed by Odhinn and his two brothers. They used his body to shape Midgard, including the sky and sea.

As demonstrated by the creation, the gods' ability to utilize every part of Ymir's deceased body aptly describes the Nordic tribes' behavior. They used every part of an animal they killed for food, wasting nothing. Their reverence for the life of any living creature is a lesson we of the modern era are slowly relearning.

SIX

GIANTESSES

The role of giants and giantesses is an example of the misunderstanding and confusion surrounding the interpretation of Norse mythology, something we previously glimpsed in the discussion of the creation myth. According to the story of the creation, the giants were enemies of the gods prior to the creation of Midgard. Interestingly, there is no justification given for this hatred, nor does there appear to be any easily rationalized reason for this behavior. There are no tales explaining anything that Ymir, the first frost giant, might have done to anger the gods. It is almost implied that the gods' hatred for him stems from their own inability to obtain immortality. The assumption is that their lack of immortality stems from their giantess mother, Bestla. As she is never named a goddess, it allows for the easy misinterpretation that she might not be divine in origin.

Throughout the myths, the gods battle the giants and win each contest, regardless of strength of body, mind, or magic. Occasionally, a few select giantesses are involved in these disputes, and they are beaten as well. In the modern era, this warring has been simplistically likened to the age-old battle of "good versus evil," but this concept does not ring true in the Norse worldview. Evil is not an idea widely accepted by the majority of heathen or pagan traditions. They do not acknowledge demons or a burning underworld. Nor do they use the term "evil." "Evil" in the Norse

Tradition is a lack of responsibility—either personal or communal. These monotheistic concepts—demons, burning underworlds, and especially "evil"—indicate a fear of the unknown, and this fear is indeed far from a polytheistic and animistic outlook. Of course, this unreasonable hatred of the gods toward the race of giants can and has been misconstrued; some people actually believing falsely that it lends credence to racism. This is another concept totally foreign to the Nordic path, as can be seen clearly by the description given in chapter 4 of the goddess Nott. Other facts throughout this chapter and those following also disprove this false justification of Norse racism.

While the concept of the gods participating in racist behavior has been seen in the past as plausible, it simply cannot be accepted as true. Witness the giantesses, some of whom are adored lovers and wives of the gods. Numerous giantesses are elevated to the status of goddesses through their marriages and/or sexual acts with the gods. It should be noted that these giantesses are not *gifted* with divinity; it is a natural progression of their spiritual evolution. This fact alone demonstrates that racism cannot be the reason for the gods' hatred of giants.

It could be construed that the gods favor the giantesses simply to display dominance over another race, therefore viewing male giants as mere unworthy opponents. This idea does not ring true, as the gods never *suppress* the giantesses. The gods show no aggression or ill behavior toward giantesses chosen to be friends and partners, but rather display love and reverence for them. The gods also listen carefully to the giantesses' counsel, and some are even sought after for their healing abilities. These female beings are equal in standing and divinity with the gods themselves.

A more likely scenario is that the myths of battles between the gods and giants are, in reality, caricatures of actual battles between the two human tribes of natives and immigrants. This theory suggests that the gods, representing the warrior tribes, are in competition with the race of giants and giantesses, representing the native tribes. This is a fairly logical deduction, as giants and giantesses are chthonic beings, or beings of the Earth. This being the case, acts of aggression toward the giants on the part of the gods would have originated during the time of the intermingling of the native and nomadic tribes. So what we see here is competition, coupled with love and envy.

This idea lends credence to the previously mentioned theory of Ymir being originally of the female sex and being displaced to fit more easily into a patriarchal and monotheistic worldview. We will never know the true story concerning Ymir, as the intermingling of spiritual outlooks began long before monotheism rose to the top of the religious ladder. It is certainly possible that the original creation myth remained in the minds and hearts of the Norse people, but, due to the negative view of women imposed by the followers of monotheism, the unaltered story has no doubt been lost forever. Regardless of when the myth was modified, we must theorize based upon the documentation we presently possess. What we know is this: the three gods, Odhinn, Vili, and Ve, detested the great giant, Ymir, so much that they killed him and shaped his dead body into Midgard. Somehow, after this shaping, Ymir was reborn as a female entity named Earth. The gods did not create the living form of Earth, but merely the shell. They love and cherish the spirit of Earth, but are always in competition with her as she obviously enhanced their original creation.

Ymir's death and reshaping into Midgard reinforces the fact that all giants and giantesses are representative of Earth. As such, they hold a powerful place within the myths. Without Earth, there would be no other species besides the deities. Even though the gods detest and war against the giants and a few giantesses, they still love, cherish, and marry many of the giantesses. This is an indication that they are in constant competition with Earth herself. Earth, regardless of the truth behind Ymir, is always feminine in the Nordic Tradition. This warring is simply another example of the displacement of the Goddess. She is loved and revered by the gods on one hand, as demonstrated by their desire for the beautiful giantesses. On the other hand, the gods strive to control Her, which is shown through their constant warring against Her very being. Regardless, the giantesses hold a very special place in Norse mythology, and to know and understand them gives us a key to understanding the Goddess. The following list provides a key to understanding their place in the mythology.

Angrboda: Lover of the giant/god Loki and mother of the monstrous children, Hel, Fenris, and Jormungand. Angrboda means "boder-of-sorrow."[1]

Aurboda: Member of the mountain-dwelling giants. She is the mother of the beautiful giantess Gerd, who so overwhelmed the god Frey that he resolved he would do anything to have Gerd as his wife.

Bestla: Daughter of the giant Bolthorn and descendent of the first frost giant, Ymir. She married Bor, son of the first presumably divine male, Buri. Bestla and Bor had three sons, all gifted with divinity and longevity, Odhinn, Vili, and Ve. Many people interpret Bestla's ancestry as the cause of her sons lack of immortality.

Fenia: Two young giantesses named Fenia and Menia were very hearty and had great strength. Somehow, through no fault of their own, they became slaves of a great king named Frodi. This king was ever on the lookout to gain prestige for his kingdom. One day, he overheard a rumor concerning two millstones in Denmark so magical that they could grind whatever the owner desired. These stones were tremendously heavy, however, and no human could move them. Frodi, knowing the strength of his two new slaves, was determined to travel to Denmark to use these stones for his personal benefit.

After they arrived, he immediately tested Fenia's and Menia's strength against the incredibly heavy millstones. King Frodi was correct. The new slaves did have the physical power and stamina to operate the stones. The young giantesses worked laboriously. They were under Frodi's orders to grind him gold,

---

[1]Snorri Sturluson, *Prose Edda, Tales from Norse Mythology*, Jean I. Young, trans. (Berkeley, University of California Press, 1954), p. 56.

peace, and prosperity.[2] Fenia and Menia eventually tired, and requested rest from their owner and king. Frodi, overwhelmed with greed, would only grant them a few minutes of rest at a time before forcing them back to work. This caused the giantesses to become very angry.

Eventually, disgusted with the king's treatment of them, Fenia and Menia started to plot revenge. They continued grinding, but suddenly burst into a powerfully beautiful song of great magical strength. From the grain they were grinding there arose a huge army that immediately assumed battle formation and set upon King Frodi and his men. The new army won the conflict almost immediately, with every man and the old king, Frodi, lying dead at their feet.

The king of the victors, Mysing, soon discovered how he and his men came into being and was astounded at the magical properties of the millstones. Foolishly, he did not heed the power of the young giantesses to control this magic. He, like King Frodi, was overcome with greed and arrogantly took ownership of the two young slaves, forcing them to resume grinding. This time, he ordered them to grind for a totally different commodity, salt. When Fenia and Menia requested rest, Mysing denied them outright.

The two giantesses again grew frustrated, tired, and angry with the treatment they were receiving. But this time, they were even more furious, as they had given King Mysing life and he, in exchange, was treating them atrociously. Fenia and Menia began a new magical song, this one even more powerful than before. In seconds, the sea rose up in a vast, tumultuous, angry flood. Huge waves engulfed the men of Mysing's magical battalion and dragged them under the frothing, swirling waters. Soldiers and king alike met their death deep beneath the ocean. The sea finally calmed to a mirror surface, except for one area. The power behind this new spell of the young giantesses had created a vast whirlpool located in the very same spot where the two giantesses had been tediously grinding with the millstones.

---

[2]Snorri Sturluson, *Edda*, Anthony Faulkes, trans., 2nd ed. (London: Everyman's Library, 1992), p. 107.

Because of this powerful and magical action, sea water today is salty.

Frid: One of the handmaidens of the healer, Mengloth.[3] Her name means "peace" (see Eir in chapter 8).

Gefjon: Gefjon's heredity can be a bit confusing, as her name can be used to describe a giantess.[4] She is actually a goddess, but the confusion of her heredity may have come about because she bore four sons, all sired by a giant (see chapter 8).

Gerd: Daughter of the giantess, Aurboda. Gerd was so beautiful that she enchanted the Vanir god Frey. He would not settle for anything except her hand in marriage. She declined this offer numerous times, until she was threatened with the magical power of the runes. She finally agreed to wed Frey, but only under her conditions. This marriage resulted in Gerd becoming a goddess (see chapter 8).

Gialp: A young giantess who attempted to deter the god Thorr from a mission he was on to visit her father, a giant named Geirrod. As Thorr was crossing a river, Gialp stood over it and, through magic, caused it to rise up in a fury of rushing water. Thorr saved himself from being carried down river by plunging a staff deep into the river bed and hanging on tightly. Seeing the threat to his life, he looked up and down the river to see who or what was causing this catastrophe. He spotted Gialp standing some distance upriver, smiling at the trouble she was causing the great god. Thorr, seeing the young giantess and guessing she was the cause of his trouble, took a rock and viciously threw it at her. It hit Gialp hard enough to knock her from her stance over the river. This broke her magical hold over the raging waters and allowed the river to revert to its normally calm, gently flowing

---

[3]Jacob Grimm, *Teutonic Mythology*, 3 vols., James Steven Stallybrass, trans., 4th ed. (New York: Dover Publications, 1966), p. 1149.
[4]Snorri Sturluson, *Edda*, p. 81.

demeanor. Thorr then finished his crossing without further mishap.

Continuing on his journey, Thorr finally reached the home of Geirrod. Thorr and his companion, Loki, were offered shelter in an outlying shed. This was unusual treatment for the gods, but they were exhausted and hungry, so readily accepted the offering in good faith. Once settled in the shed, Thorr sat on the only bench available. It immediately started to rise rapidly toward the ceiling. Thorr, knowing he would soon be crushed, grabbed the same staff that had saved him in the river. This staff was very special and possessed magical qualities. It had been lent to him by another giantess, Grid. He pushed this staff against the ceiling and, using his incredible strength, caused the bench to crash to the floor.

The god immediately heard loud, piercing wails resonating throughout the shed. Thorr finally looked underneath the broken bench and discovered two young giantesses, Gialp and her sister, Greip. They were the ones who had lifted the bench and tried to crush Thorr against the ceiling. When the bench fell with Thorr still seated on it, Gialp and Greip were unable to move in time to avoid being injured. The two young giantesses were both mortally wounded, with broken backs.

Giantess of Ironwood: This giantess lives deeply hidden in a fabled forest named Ironwood. Her sons are all said to be giants with the gift of shape-changing into wolves. Two of the descendants of these shape-changers are the wolves Skoll and Hati, who chase Sol and Mani, goddess of the Sun and god of the Moon, throughout the heavens. Supposedly, another of these shape-changers will be born who will bear the name of Moongarm. It is said that he will feed off the dead and will eventually eat the Moon.[5] As a result of this catastrophic event, blood will course through the skies, causing the sunlight to become dim and the winds to thrash the nine worlds with unheard of force.

---

[5]Snorri Sturluson, *Prose Edda*, p. 39.

Greip: See Gialp.

Grid: Lover of Odhinn and mother of Vidar. According to one legend, Grid prepared special shoes of protection for her son at his birth in response to a prophecy which claimed that her son would avenge his father, Odhinn, in Ragnarok.[6] Vidar would need protective shoes, as he would kill Odhinn's slayer, Fenris the wolf, by prying his mouth apart with his feet.

Grid was very protective of the god Thorr. On one occasion, she sheltered and counseled him on a journey he was making. She advised him of possible treachery and lent him three objects: her belt of strength, her iron gloves, and her staff, called Grid's Stick.[7] This was the staff Thorr used to save himself from drowning and to stop himself from being crushed against the ceiling (see Gialp). The story of Grid shows us a new side of the giantesses—their gift of prophecy.

Groa: This giantess is known for her healing abilities. She was once requested to remove a piece of stone from the forehead of Thorr. As she was working and reciting magical spells, Thorr felt the stone begin to loosen. He wanted to express his thanks to Groa, so proceeded to tell her that he had found her husband and that it would not be long before he returned home. Groa was so overjoyed at this news that she stopped in the middle of one of her spells, leaving the stone embedded in Thorr's forehead.

Gunnlod: As an act of faith between the Aesir and the Vanir, both groups of gods spit into a bowl. From this spit, the gods together created the god Kvasir. Kvasir was very knowledgeable, as he was gifted with the attributes of both the Aesir and the Vanir. He enjoyed wandering the worlds, observing and learning everywhere he went.

On one such journey, Kvasir was tricked and killed by two dwarves. They used his blood to make a magical batch of mead. The dwarves continued to cause distress and dissension wherever

[6]H. A. Guerber, *The Norsemen* (London: Senate, 1994), p. 159.
[7]Snorri Sturluson, *Prose Edda*, p. 107.

they went, and were eventually tracked down and captured by a giant named Suttung. They were terrified and, in exchange for their lives, gave this specially brewed mead to the giant. Suttung, not being a fool, knew the value of the mead. He resolved to protect it at all costs. He decided to hide it deep within a mountain and gave guardianship of the mead to his daughter, Gunnlod.

One day, a beautiful man miraculously showed up in Gunnlod's chamber. Unknown to her, this man had just used an armory of magical stunts and tricks to enter her abode. Gunnlod was so beguiled by the beauty of this man that she immediately fell deeply in love with him. They ended up spending three days and three nights together. The man was actually the god Odhinn, shape-changed into this breathtakingly handsome man. At the end of this three-day tryst, he stole the mead from the trusting and adoring young giantess and took it back to his godly realm of Asgard.

Hel: Hel is indisputably a giantess, as she is the child of Angrboda, a giantess, and Loki, a giant-turned-god. It is most likely she came to be termed a goddess when Odhinn, in defense against a prophecy that named Hel as a key figure leading to the eventual demise of the gods, gave her dominion over the underworld and the dead criminals within. Through this action, Odhinn undoubtedly thought he could better control the coming of Ragnarok through the constant supervision of the giantess Hel.

Hyrrokkin: This giantess possesses unheard-of strength. When the Aesir god, Balder, was murdered, the gods gathered to mourn his untimely passing. Balder was placed in his ship, Ringhorn, and funeral ceremonies were held. When all preparations were made and it was finally time to launch the ship with its sad cargo, none of the gods, no matter how hard they tried, could budge Ringhorn. It was firmly stuck in the sands of the beach. They finally sent for the giantess Hyrrokkin and requested her assistance. She came immediately, riding a wolf and using snakes for reins. She gave the ship one nudge, and off it went into the sea.

Iarnaxa: Lover of Thorr and mother of Magni. Her name means "Iron Cutlass."[8]

Laufey: Also called Nal. Laufey is the wife of the giant, Farbauti, and the mother of Loki, Byleist, and Helblindi.

Menia: See Fenia.

Rind: No one seems to know if Rind is a mortal or a giantess by birth, although the latter is most likely due to the gods' attraction to giantesses. Through her association as a lover of Odhinn, she is acknowledged as a goddess (see chapter 8).

Sinmara: The giantess who guards a sword named Laevateinn. This sword is apparently meant to kill one of the birds who will forewarn of Ragnarok. She is the wife of the giant Surt, who guards the world of Muspellheim.[9]

Skadi: A giantess by heritage, who became a goddess through her marriage to the Vanir god Njord (see chapter 8).

---

[8]Snorri Sturluson, *Prose Edda*, p. 105.

[9]Kevin Crossley-Holland, *The Norse Myths* (New York: Pantheon Books, 1980), p. 123–4.

SEVEN

DIVINE SEERESSES
AND GUARDIANS

T he following groups of goddesses and guardian spirits are all directly involved with the unfolding of each individual life—human and god, female and male. Most of these feminine beings are present at every birth, marriage, and death. They all have the gift of prophecy and most help to shape our destiny. Many visit battles, and some take it upon themselves to become guardians and protectors of chosen warriors. This aspect of the feminine divine is with each of us constantly, intermingling in our lives, usually for good, although sometimes we who are shortsighted may perceive these helping hands as actively working toward negative results.

Disir: These supernatural women may also be called Idises. The Disir are the spirits of deceased women who oversee and protect members of their ancestral family line. They view all individuals in their kindred group as "children," guarding and watching over each person from birth until death. While the thought of such guardians may be comforting, not all Disir appear to work in a positive way. Some actually seem to devote themselves to bringing challenge and adversity into our lives. Pure negative workings, however, are not very common. We may perceive such an action as "bad luck," but we have no idea what our guardian Dis is actually attempting to accomplish.

For example, "Jane" wakes in the morning and prepares for the upcoming workday. For some reason, the car won't start, so she calls in to inform her supervisor of the situation. The supervisor, furious, terminates her. She is completely taken aback by this "stroke of bad luck," but then hears on the radio that she had just missed being involved in a terrible auto wreck that just occurred on the direct route to her old place of employment. Granted, the loss of the job may seem extreme, but the Dis only protects and guides her family members, not those of another kindred group. Therefore, her concern in this instance would be for her "child's" safety, not for her continued employment, over which she may not necessarily have active control.

Disir are often likened to Norns, as both groups of divine females have the ability to shape our destiny and are present at every birth, marriage, and death. Unlike the Norns, however, Disir are said to ride on horseback in their comings and goings. This is an important distinction, as the Norns are never known to ride horses, with the exception of one Norn, Skuld. The goddess Freya is also associated with the Disir, as she is also known by the name of Vanadis. This implies that one of her roles is as a Dis. The yearly festival of Winternights is celebrated to acknowledge and give thanks to each family's guardian Dis.

Fylgje: A female guardian spirit who attaches herself to every infant's soul at birth. She will stay connected to this person throughout life and sometimes, in rare instances, will exhibit protective or guiding qualities. While most people are not able to see their personal Fylgje, legend has it that, at death, she may make herself visible as she is leaving the body. Sometimes, she will take on the shape of the animal that most exemplifies the dying person's character and personality. Another part of a person's soul, the Hamingjes, is a feminine spirit whose sole purpose is to assist the individual in attracting good luck throughout his or her mortal time on Earth.

Norns: In the Nordic legends, myths, and sagas, Norns are sometimes referred to as prophetesses, seeresses, or Valas. The Norns are goddesses who weave and spin the strands of destiny for all creatures residing throughout the nine worlds, including the gods. This action is not performed according to the Norn's motives, but is controlled by a higher power called Orlog. Put simply, Orlog is the destiny of all that has ever been and all that will ever be. It is not limited to mortals, but includes all the beings dwelling on all the worlds, and even the worlds and universe themselves. The Norns are answerable to no one, nor are they controlled in any fashion by the gods of the Aesir.

The Norns take responsibility for watering the World Tree, Yggdrasill, and packing clay around its trunk for added preservation. This prevents the great tree from perishing, and protects it from the destruction caused by worldly doings. The Aesir visit these goddesses daily to request their astonishing insight and to hold council meetings by the Norns' well, the spring of Urd, located at the foot of one of the roots of Yggdrasill.

Interestingly enough, although the Norns are perceived to spin and weave fate, legends also state that they foresee destiny by cutting and reading runes. This is a fascinating insight into the very nature of the runes themselves. Normally, this magical and divinatory tool is associated with the god Odhinn. Legend has it that he sacrificed himself by hanging himself on the tree, Yggdrasill, for nine days and nights. At the end of this life-threatening ordeal, Odhinn grabbed the runes from where they resided deep within the spring of Mimir, which is located below one of the roots of the tree.

We know that the Norns control destiny, have the gift of prophecy, live near Yggdrasill, care for the great tree, and have one of the magical springs of Yggdrasill at their disposal. We also know that a Norn is present at every birth, including those of the gods. We do not know much about the Norns' origin, except that they simply appeared, in a way similar to the sacred aurochs, Audmula. All of these facts, further supported by the fact that Freya taught Odhinn all of her considerable magical skills, leads us to the conclusion that the runes are of feminine, not masculine origin, as is commonly believed.

While it is normally assumed there are only three Norns, who have been compared to the Greek Fates, this belief is inaccurate. Not only are there more than three Norns, but these divine women are present at every transition phase of an individual's life. We actually have no idea how many there truly are. For these reasons, they are sometimes confused with the other female divine guardians, the Disir and Valkyries. The three most notorious of all the Norns are the sisters Urd, Verdandi, and Skuld.

It is certainly easy to assign only the simple concepts of past, present, and future to these three Norns, however, this is obviously not an idea widely accepted in the Norse worldview. The past is always intermingled with the present, as the past is what has brought us to the present. Hence, past and present can be seen as one driving force bringing us ever closer to the future. The future is an intangible idea, for none of us knows for certain what tomorrow may bring, regardless of preparation or planning. The best we can hope for is what should happen as a result of what has happened and what is presently happening.[1]

Urd: Possibly the oldest of the Norns, she symbolizes fate, or the past. She can also be called Wyrd, which is the precursor of our present-day English word, weird. As the Norse did not believe in the concept of predestination, to use the word "fate" as understood in the modern day, can be confusing. Basically, in this context, the term means that every action or nonaction we take will result in a reaction somewhere along the pathway of our lives. Because of this, we should be able to ordain our fate in certain matters by the choices we make as individuals. This does not always hold true, of course, hence the disposing of the notion of predestination. It is a fact, however, that our past does, to a certain extent, shape our present circumstances.

Verdandi: Represents the concepts of being, present, or becoming. Verdandi is the natural ongoing force that shows us the direct results of our past. She is the reactive force portraying our

---

[1] Kveldulf Gundarsson, *Teutonic Magic: The Magical and Spiritual Practices of the Germanic Peoples* (St. Paul: Llewellyn, 1994), pp. 7–8. Mr. Gundarsson has a superb explanation of the idea of time in this text. His works are highly recommended for all persons interested in the Norse Tradition.

previous choices, actions, and nonactions—the past becoming the present. She characterizes everything we have done with our individual lives and gives it physical, emotional, mental, and spiritual shape in our present. The present is a slim, fleeting moment, slipping rapidly through our hands and turning toward the unknown and unpredictable future even as we speak.

Skuld: The youngest of all the Norns, Skuld symbolizes an unusual range of concepts: necessity, future, guilt, and debt. Because we are controlled by the physical element of linear time, by necessity our present always continues on into Skuld's domain of the future. She represents what may happen in the future as a result of our past and present choices. The future, however, is changeable at best, and even the best or worst choices in the past do not always accurately determine its outcome. The choices we make in the present can always outweigh those made previously. Because of this ever-present possibility of chance, Skuld is always seen veiled, with a scroll in her hands.

The idea of Skuld representing guilt and debt is a little more difficult to comprehend. To the Norse, it is obvious that we owe a debt from the moment we are born. Our very lives depend on the deaths of other creatures, animals and plants, to nourish us. Because of this, guilt comes into play, for we literally have to kill to survive. Even vegetarians are at fault, for the death of one species always occurs to feed, shelter, clothe, or warm another.

Each of us owes a tremendous debt to other species and the Earth for the very fact that we are alive. The only way we will repay this debt is through our own eventual physical death. At this time, we will, in turn, nourish another species, and so the cycles of life continue their spiral dance. Through death, our guilt and debt is alleviated, allowing us a new beginning in another realm of existence.[2]

---

[2]Ralph Metzner, *The Well of Remembrance* (Boston: Shambhala, 1994), pp. 217–218.

This youngest Norn, Skuld, is oftentimes linked to the battle goddesses called Valkyries. She is known to lead the other Valkyries to battle. Skuld is also connected with the elves.

Valkyries: A group of young, beautiful, fierce battle-oriented goddesses normally viewed as the maidens of Odhinn. They are reputed to serve food and drink to the god and his guests, special warriors who have been killed in battle and selected to become elite members of Odhinn's personal army of mortal soldiers. When the Valkyries are not waiting on these blessed men, they are overseeing all battles waging on the world, Midgard. The Valkyries purpose is to bring about the death of any warrior chosen by Odhinn to become a new member of his force. The battle goddesses then escort the soul of the man back to Odhinn's hall, Val-Halla, in preparation for the coming of Ragnarok.

Although this is the common, modern theme behind the purpose and duties of the Valkyries, it is inaccurate and requires further exploration. These lovely goddesses are also known as wish maidens and battle maidens. They are indeed fierce warrioresses who tend to thrive on war and conflict. They not only visit every battle, but *they* choose who will win the conflict and who will perish. The Valkyries accompany the souls of those soldiers who have met death over the rainbow bridge, Bifrost, to a new, higher level of renewed life. It is doubtful, however, that every warrior, female or male, chosen by the Valkyries goes to Val-Halla. There are many different halls in the heavens, and various goddesses and gods head each hall. It is more likely that the Valkyries escort the souls to the hall these goddesses feel is most fitting to each individual soul.

The very name, Valkyrie, means "choosers of the slain." Although Odhinn may request the Valkyries to accompany a particular hero back to his hall, these goddesses do not always heed his wishes. They are known to protect their chosen warriors vehemently, and, in some cases, will go deliberately against Odhinn's wishes. He may decide to attempt to punish the Valkyries for their disobedience, and he may even succeed in the short term, but these goddesses always prevail.

When a Valkyrie chooses a favorite mortal, she is apt to teach this person special skills of magic. She will protect her chosen and warn the person of upcoming danger or conflict. She will remain her prodigy's guardian spirit throughout his or her lifetime. The Valkyrie has the gift of prophecy, which she can and will use to determine her favorite's most probable destiny. She will sometimes even take the form of a mortal woman in order to marry the hero of her heart. She has been known to give some warriors visions of battle, as a warning of the probable outcome. If one knows their particular Valkyrie-guardian's name, they may call out to her at any time and she will immediately appear. In such an instance, she will protect or assist the individual, whatever the circumstance.

Snorri Sturluson says, in "The Deluding of Gylfi" from the *Prose Edda,* that the names of the Valkyries are as follows: Hrist, Mist, Skeggjold, Skogul, Hild, Thrud, Hlokk, Herfjotur, Goll, Geirahod, Randgrid, Radgrid, and Reginleif.[3] Many of these names have meanings describing war and weaponry. The Valkyries always have female leaders, whom Sturluson lists as Gud, Rota, and the Norn Skuld.

Another leader of the Valkyries is the goddess of love and fertility, Freya. As Freya is also said to take half of the dead from battle to her halls, it can be assumed that the Valkyries may accompany these souls to their destination at Freya's request as well as at Odhinn's. The Valkyries are always seen dressed in battle gear and a helmet, and carrying a shield and spear. We are not sure how many Valkyries there actually are, for different authors and legends list different names and numbers. One possibility, as just mentioned above, is that there are thirteen Valkyries, as Snorri Sturluson does mention thirteen names with three additional leaders in his list of goddesses. He also mentions different names and numbers in other areas of his work, however, that correspond with other authors' literature. Presumably, the confusion of different names and numbers can be explained by some Valkyries having more than one name

---

[3]Snorri Sturluson, *Prose Edda: Tales from Norse Mythology,* Jean I. Young, trans. (Berkeley: University of California Press, 1954), p. 61.

Figure 4. Hilde, one of the Valkyries (from Dr. W. Wagner, *Asgard and the Gods: The Tales and Traditions of Our Northern Ancestors*, New York: E. P. Dutton, 1917, p. 105).

as well as the fact that different groups of them are occasionally involved in separate activities at the same time. It may also be that they are similar to the Disir and Norns, thereby having countless members in their divine ranks. Their ancestry is confusing as well, as some Valkyries are certainly of divine heritage, while others are said to be deceased mortal maidens evolved to a higher level of consciousness.

The sight of a troop of Valkyries is both awe-inspiring and heartrending. Clouds billow furiously throughout the skies, thunder has the sound of a thousand galloping hoofs, and lightning flashes in huge stabs of searing light. The Valkyries and their lather-flecked mounts burst from under cover of the dark, dangerous-looking clouds and the winds whip to a frenzy. Shrieking and wailing reverberate in the skies, causing a frightful array of overwhelming sound. The steeds are huge, fierce, and armed for battle with tooth and hoof. These magnificent creatures are covered in a coat of gorgeous color, tossing their proud heads and flinging drops of sweat from their beautiful silky manes and tails. The sound of their travel is louder than the worst thunderstorm, their gnashing teeth shooting lightning bolts toward the Earth. The lovely goddesses of war are firmly seated upon their mounts, proudly surveying the view around them. They are dressed in full battle gear and carrying their weapons in one hand, their shields in the other. Their hair whips around their faces, and it is their voices we hear on the blowing winds. All of a sudden, the troop turns as one, and bounds off into another group of clouds, with the sounds of wailing and the pounding of hoofs, and flashes of lightning following the Valkyries' trail.

The Valkyries ride these majestic and powerful horses on all their travels through the skies and over vast bodies of water. For this reason, they are often associated with the elements of air and water. These goddesses also symbolize fertility because, when they ride through the skies, their horses perspire and the sweat falls to Earth. This turns into the dew that helps crops and vegetation grow green and lush. As the Valkyries ride their horses through the different realms by way of Bifrost, this emphasizes their connection with death and regeneration.

Valkyries are often associated with the Norns and Disir. One reason for this is that Skuld is both a Norn and a Valkyrie. Other reasons include their skill at prophecy and magic, and their roles as guardian spirits and protectors of mortals. Valkyries also know the art of weaving and spinning, which is always associated with the Norns. One myth relates a vivid image of these goddesses of war spinning a horribly grim vision using the intestines of men with weapons intermingled. Men's heads are brutally impaled upon spindles and various other bloody and

Figure 5. A Valkyrie (from Donald MacKenzie, *Teutonic Myth and Legend*, London: Gresham, n. d., p. 49).

gore-covered implements. As the goddesses continue to spin and weave, they sing an eerily frightening song of prophecy concerning a battle to come. When they finish this morbid work, six Valkyries take half of the terrifyingly vivid battle cloth to the south, and another six take the other half to the north. This is certainly a grisly tale that emphasizes the fact the Valkyries are indeed representatives of death.

Valkyries are associated with a variety of animals: namely the horse, raven, eagle, and wolf. The first has already been mentioned. The others are often seen at battles eagerly awaiting the resulting carnage. After the conflict is completed, these animals can be seen avidly feeding on the dead. Valkyries are occasionally known to ride wolves rather than their preferred steeds. These divine women represent water and, in this aspect, are known to shape-change into swans. In this form, they are called Swan Maidens. It is very probable that the Valkyries are also connected to the Wave Maidens, the nine young sister-goddesses of the sea. This connection can clearly be seen, as the Valkyries are notorious for their swift travels over water and are ever present at battles taking place at sea.

Swan Maidens: Swan Maidens are normally seen in groups of three. As soon as they land on Earth, they shed their feathery skins to reveal breathtakingly beautiful young women. Sometimes, these lovely goddesses can be observed quietly weaving and spinning near secluded lakes, rivers, or streams. They also love to swim in these peaceful places, reveling in the cool water that sensually caresses their womanly bodies. At other times, they can be observed skyclad, happily dancing to a tune known only to themselves.

If the Swan Maidens are caught unaware, a person can steal their swan skins, thereby preventing the lovely young women from shape-changing and flying away to their home far away in the heavens. They have even been known to marry mortals in the hopes of retrieving their swan skins. If the young woman ever touches her swan skin again, she will immediately shape-change and speedily fly away to her divine abode, regardless of the love she may share with her mortal husband. Some of these Swan Maidens wear delicate golden chains. Like their swan skins, if these necklaces are removed, it stops them from shape-changing and escaping Midgard.[4]

---

[4]Jacob (Jakob) Grimm, *Teutonic Mythology*, 3 vols., James Steven Stallybrass, trans., 4th ed. (New York: Dover, 1966), p. 429.

EIGHT

ASYNIUR

This chapter is devoted entirely to the goddesses named and described by Snorri Sturluson. I have made additions to this initial list, such as Erce, Fjorgyn, Hel, and Nerthus, and various dialectal names, in accordance with numerous texts written by other knowledgeable scholars. We will explore each goddess as thoroughly and accurately as possible. This will include discussing the different names by which these goddesses were known or called upon. Some of these goddesses have few or no attributes. It can be assumed myths about these particular goddesses have either been irretrievably lost, or that they were simply different named aspects for more popular goddesses.

This discussion will be the culmination of our initial exploration of the divine women of the Norse Tradition. At the conclusion of this chapter, we will be able to pursue the actual goal of this book—the discovery of the primordial Goddess of the North. For us to know Her, we must know all of the various goddesses of the Norse cosmos in minute detail. This will enable us to piece together ancient knowledge hidden or suppressed for centuries.

Bil: Goddess of the waxing Moon. Bil is a kenning for woman.[1] Mani, god of the Moon, witnessed a father forcing his little girl

---

[1] Snorri Sturluson, *Edda*, Anthony Faulkes, trans., 2nd ed. (London: Everyman's Library, 1992), p. 115.

Figure 6. *Sol, Bil, and the Wave Maidens*. The goddess of the Sun, Sol; goddess of the Waxing Moon, Bil; and the Wave Maidens in their daily and nightly earthly travels. (From the author's personal collection; artist Ingrid Ivic.)

and boy to carry pails of water throughout the night. He immediately snatched the children away from their undeserving father and gave them a secure home with him on the Moon. The Nordic people thought they could see these children with their water buckets on the surface of the Moon. The fairy tale, Jack and Jill, most likely originated with this early legend of Bil and her brother.

Bil travels through the sky driving a chariot that is chased continuously by the wolf Hati. This is the reason we can see her steadily moving across the nighttime heavens. It is said her life will end at the onset of Ragnarok, when the wolf will finally catch up to her chariot and swallow her. Bil is one of three goddesses prophesied to die in Ragnarok. This is certainly due to the fact that, even though Bil is called a goddess, she is, in actuality, mortal woman. Gifted by Odhinn with the status of a goddess, she is given longevity through the nourishment of Idun's apples.

The Nordic view of the Moon and Sun is unlike most other early religious traditions. (See figure 6, p. 73.) In comparable cultures, one normally finds the Sun represented as masculine and the Moon as feminine. To the Norse, both the Sun and Moon were feminine, although the Moon also has two countering masculine personalities.

Eir: Goddess of healing. In the early Nordic tribes, the art of healing was practiced by both sexes. However, it is evident in the writings of Nordic lore that women dominated in this honored and revered field. In the realm of the deities, goddesses exclusively held the skill and power of healing. The only exception to this would be Odhinn's knowledge of healing magic learned from Freya.

In addition to being the name of a goddess, Eir is the name of one of the nine mortal handmaidens of Mengloth, a human princess who is thought to be a representation of the goddess Freya. Mengloth and her nine attendants lived on the very summit of a rock called Hyfjaberg. Any woman who climbed this rock was said to be healed of any illness, regardless how severe. Eir is also a name of one of the Valkyries.

Erce: An ancient, almost forgotten Earth goddess. There is very little knowledge preserved about her. We have written evidence demonstrating that Erce was called upon in fertility rituals during the yearly planting season (see chapter 2). This alludes to her being a very early goddess symbolizing the earth and fertility. According to Jacob Grimm, Erce could mean "the mother of Earth."[2]

Fjorgyn: Mother of Frigg and possibly the god Thorr. Fjorgyn is another name for Earth, as are Iord, Sif, and Hlodyn. Fjorgyn is

---

[2] Jacob Grimm, *Teutonic Mythology*, vol. 1, James Steven Stallybrass, trans., 4th ed. (New York: Dover, 1966), p. 253.

not listed by Snorri Sturluson as a goddess, even though she is mentioned as the mother of a goddess and perhaps a god. As with Erce, Fjorgyn is an ancient goddess barely remembered in the myths. What little documentation remains couples her with another name, Fjorgvin, who may be either her mate or her brother. This is strikingly similar to the divine siblings Nerthus and Njord (see Nerthus in this chapter). While it is not certain Fjorgyn and Fjorgvin are indeed brother and sister, it is true that incestuous relations are not, and never have been, tolerated by the Aesir, but they were accepted by the Vanir in ancient times.

Freya: Goddess of love, fruitfulness, fertility, prosperity, destiny, magic, seidhr, shape-changing, shamanism, and war. Her name means "mistress" and "lady." She is a youthful goddess, ever ready to experiment with love or jump into the midst of war. Freya is normally considered to be of the Vanir race, as she is the daughter of Nerthus and Njord, and is the twin of the god Frey. Freya, Frey, and Njord were the first members of the Vanir race to live with the Aesir, as agreed to in the truce of the gods.

Freya is symbolic of the earth, which is seen clearly through her marriage and yearly separation from her dearly beloved husband, Od. Each year, she searches diligently throughout the nine worlds for him, bitterly crying tears of gold and amber until they are reunited. On this yearly search, she is called Mardel, Mardoll, Skialf, Syr, Gefn, and Horn. Gefn is thought to be another name for Gefjon. Horn, even though another name for Freya, is connected to flax.[3] This plant is normally associated with the divine females whose attributes include spinning and weaving, such as the Norns, the Valkyries, and the goddess Frigg.

In Germany, Freya was considered the same goddess as Frigg, but in Denmark, Norway, Sweden, and Iceland, she is considered a separate deity.[4] Other names for Freya are Vanadis and Vanabride. Freya is also associated with the human healer Mengloth (who is mentioned under Eir).

---

[3] H. R. Ellis Davidson, *The Gods and Myths of Northern Europe* (London: Penguin, 1964), p. 116.

[4] H. A. Guerber, *The Norsemen* (London: Senate, 1994), p. 131.

Figure 7. Freya in her chariot (from Dr. W. Wagner, *Asgard and the Gods: The Tales and Traditions of Our Northern Ancestors*, New York: E. P. Dutton, 1917, p. 303).

Animals sacred to Freya include the cat, swallow, cuckoo, sow, and weasel.[5] She is the owner of a falcon skin and is associated with all birds of prey through her role as leader of the Valkyries. While traveling, she either drives a chariot drawn by two cats (see figure 7, above), or she rides a boar. This boar is actually her lover, Ottar, whom she has shape-changed. Obviously, Freya's love for these creatures and her skill at magic is still

[5] Jacob Grimm, *Teutonic Mythology*, pp. 305–306.

acknowledged today. These same attributes and animals, revered and cherished by the Norse, were the same animals and attributes for which women were slaughtered during the European and New England witch hunts. Even today, many people view these creatures and traits—especially the ability to perform magic—with terror and label them as "evil."

Two tales about Freya revolve around her beautiful golden necklace, called the Brisingamen. One of the tales discusses Freya's purchase of this necklace by exchanging sexual favors with four dwarves, the designers and crafters of the Brisingamen. The other relates her anger at being asked by Thorr to leave her husband, Od, in order to marry a giant. This giant had in his possession Thorr's hammer, and would only return it if Freya agreed to be his bride. She became so angry that her neck enlarged and broke her necklace. Needless to say, she refused this ludicrous request. Brisingr means fire, which, in this case, is obviously associated with the shining gold from which the necklace is fashioned.

Freya is the goddess of all witchcraft, seidhr, and magical abilities. In this aspect, she is sometimes referred to as Gullveig, Heith, or Heid. As discussed in chapter 4, Gullveig is a witch who visited the Aesir before the war between the gods. Her love of gold was so intense it disturbed the Aesir greatly, and Odhinn decided to destroy her. He tried three times to burn her, but each time she came out of the fire miraculously unscathed. This treatment of Gullveig so infuriated the Vanir that it caused the war between the gods of the two tribes.

After this war ended in a truce, Freya voluntarily educated Odhinn in all of her considerable magical skills. He then used this ability to summon a seeress from her lonely grave. He requested information about the destiny of the gods. This seeress, thought to be Heith, told Odhinn about the creation of Midgard and the other eight worlds to prove her psychic skill. She then went on to advise him about the coming of the inescapable, tragic death of his beloved young son, Balder. She also warned Odhinn about the unavoidable coming of Ragnarok, commonly called The Twilight of the Gods.

Freya is often asked to assist in human love affairs. Under the guise of Heith, she enabled a god-favored warrior of peasant

Figure 8. Freya and the necklace (from Donald MacKenzie, *Teutonic Myth and Legend*, London: Gresham, n. d., p. 85).

blood, Frithiof, to marry the woman of his heart. Heith and another witch, Ham, were requested by King Helge to produce a furious storm in order to sink a ship carrying Frithiof. This ship, named Ellida, was given by the gods to Frithiof. King Helge wanted this warrior to die, as he did not approve of Frithiof wedding his sister, Ingeborg. The king did not care that she was very much in love with Frithiof and desired this marriage above all else. Heith and Ham heard the prayers of both the ill-fated couple and the king. The two witches produced a furious storm at the king's request. It was devastating enough to convince King Helge that Frithiof did indeed perish, but not strong enough to actually kill him. Frithiof not only survived, but went on to become a famed warrior and, eventually, through many trials and tribulations, did indeed win the hand of Ingeborg.[6]

As Valfreya, Freya is the leader of the Valkyries and leads them to all the battles on Midgard. In this role, she chooses half of the slain warriors from these battles to stay within her hall, Folkvang.

Frigg: Queen of the Aesir and of the Asyniur. Her name means "beloved." She is a lovely goddess, confident and proud of her maturity. Goddess of societies, marriage, maternity, sky, prophecy, magic skills, destiny, shape-changing, childbirth, children, housewives, women, hearth, home, protection, Earth, fertility, weaving, and spinning. Frigg is married to Odhinn and is queen of two halls: her own, Fensalir, and the Asyniur's, Vingolf. Half of the warriors killed in battle go to Vingolf. This is confusing, as it has previously been stated that half of the slain soldiers reside in Val-Halla, and the other half in Folkvang. Obviously, one of these halls possesses more than one name. All righteous people will ascend to either Vingolf or Odhinn's hall, Gimle, after death. It can be assumed that, as Odhinn's wife, Frigg also oversees his three halls: Valaskialf, Val-Halla, and Gimle.

Legend states that Frigg is in competition with Odhinn's lovers: the goddesses Iord, Rind, and Skadi; the giantesses Gunnlod and Grid; and the nine Wave Maidens. Frigg is the

6 H. A. Guerber, *The Norsemen*, pp. 312–327.

Figure 9. Freya (from Donald MacKenzie, *Teutonic Myth and Legend*, London: Gresham, n. d., p. 55).

mother of Balder and Hod, and is either mother or sister of
Thorr. Frigg is the stepmother of the gods Bragi, Hermod,
Heimdall, Tyr, Vidar, Vali, and Skiold. She is the daughter of
Fjorgyn. Another name for Frigg is Friia, the origin of the mod-
ern word, Friday. This day is holy to both Frigg and Freya. The
star constellation Orion's Girdle was also called Frigg's Spinning
Wheel by the Norse people. The spindle is sacred to Frigg as are
keys, which are always seen on Frigg's girdle.

Frigg, along with Odhinn, sits in the magical chair called
Hlidskialf, which allows her to survey all activities and beings
within the nine worlds. While she is known for her prophetic
ability (she knows all that is to come), she never shares her immense knowledge with anyone—gods, goddesses, or humans.
She, along with the Disir, Norns, and Freya, shapes children's
destiny. She is also called upon by women in labor. Frigg is
known to protect young children in need and bring them to her
hall. These children assist her in watering the earth.

One of the more popular stories about Frigg concerns the
untimely death of her adored son, Balder. She knew that this was
prophesied to happen, but attempted to change destiny to save
him. Needless to say, she failed. At Loki's hands, Balder was viciously killed. Frigg offered a servant all of her considerable love
and gratitude if he would consent to visit the hall of Hel to request Balder's release. Hel was sympathetic and would allow
Balder to leave, on one condition: all things within all the nine
worlds, animate and inanimate, must weep for his death. Frigg
visited everyone and everything within the worlds and received
all of their promises to weep, except from one giantess, who glee-
fully refused. This giantess was actually Loki, shape-changed.
The furious gods of the Aesir captured and imprisoned Loki for
this action and for the crime of causing Balder's death. It is said
that Frigg weeps for the loss of her dear son. During Ragnarok,
she will also weep for Odhinn, who is killed by Fenris the wolf,
another of Loki's offspring. In this aspect of mourning, Frigg is
called Hlin.

Frigg is extremely intelligent and crafty. She portrays these
attributes in several other noteworthy tales. In one instance, she
persuades Odhinn to test his wisdom against Vafthrudnir, the

Figure 10. Frigg engaged in hunting (from Dr. W. Wagner, *Asgard and the Gods: The Tales and Traditions of Our Northern Ancestors*, New York: E. P. Dutton, 1917, p. 7).

most knowledgeable giant in existence. The outrageous prize in this debate is the head of the loser. Odhinn eventually wins not through the use of his wisdom, but through trickery. He finally asks Vafthrudnir a question to which he cannot possibly know the answer. Frigg, through her prophetic ability, certainly knew what the outcome of this debate would be, but Odhinn did not.

In another story, Frigg and Odhinn, disguised as mortal peasants, became foster parents for two boys of noble birth. Odhinn assisted his charge in supplanting his sibling, the rightful heir, as king. Frigg, to punish Odhinn for his actions, told him how poor a king his foster son was, which, unknown to Odhinn,

was a falsehood. Odhinn, disguised as a traveler, left immediately
to visit his grown foster son. In the meantime, Frigg sent one of
her attendants to warn the king of a treacherous visitor, dressed
as a traveler. The king had Odhinn captured, tied up, and placed
between two fires for days. Eventually, through the kindness of
the king's son (or possibly sibling), named after the charge of
Frigg, Odhinn was released. Through the use of magic, Odhinn
forced the present king to commit suicide. Odhinn then crowned
the young prince as the new heir and king.

In yet another story, Frigg and Odhinn were of opposite
opinions concerning two warring tribes, the Winnilers and the
Vandals. Odhinn had decided to grant the Vandals victory the
next day, while Frigg disputed his choice. Eventually, they agreed
that whichever tribe Odhinn saw when he first woke in the
morning would be the victors. As Odhinn knew the Vandals
were camped on his side of the bed, he was quite confident his
promise would result in his favored tribe winning. After he fell
asleep, Frigg sent an attendant to the Winnilers. She told them
to cover their faces with their long hair and move their camp to
right outside Odhinn's window, which they immediately did.
Odhinn, upon awaking, was shocked and asked who the
long-bearded men were. In order to keep his promise, however,
he was forced to award them the victory. Ultimately, he approved
of Frigg's choice and watched over the band of Winnilers, re-
naming them the Longbeards.

Frigg shares the love of gold with Freya, and also has in her
possession a lovely, golden necklace. Frigg is separated from
Odhinn for a few months out of every year, as is Freya from Od.
She is accused of having sexual relations during this lonely period
with his two brothers, Vili and Ve. Again like Freya, Frigg also
owns a falcon skin, which she uses to shape-change.

Frigg has many similarities to other Germanic goddesses—
so many, in fact, that it is probable they are other names for
Frigg. These names of regional goddesses are Wode, Eastre, Frau
Venus, Frau Holle or Mother Holle, Holda or Huda, Huldra,
Vrou-Elde, Frau Gode, Brechta, Bertha, and Ostara. As Mother
Holle, she shakes her bed linens in the air until feathers fly. This
is what creates snow on Earth. Nerthus is also most likely

another name for Frigg. Tacitus said, in his observations, that the Norse people called Nerthus by the name of Terra Mater, or Mother Earth.

Frigg has goddesses as attendants—some sources say at least ten. I have found definite proof of only three. Even though they are said to be goddesses in their own right, it is most likely they are aspects of Frigg, herself. These three goddesses are Fulla, Gna, and Hlin.

Fulla: Frigg's chief attendant and possibly her sister. Fulla is the goddess of fertility and knower of all secrets. She is responsible for guarding Frigg's jewelry and assisting in the Queen's dress. She also accompanies and advises Frigg in worldly matters. Fulla is the goddess who received the gift of a golden ring from Nanna. She is known for her long, golden hair and wears a golden circlet on her forehead. As her name means fullness, Fulla represents the Earth. She may be symbolic of the Full Moon, as well as of fertility.[7]

Gefjon: Goddess of agriculture and associated with the skill of ploughing. All young virgin women go to her hall after death. While visiting a king, Gefjon, disguised as a beggar woman, was given all the land she could plough in a day and night in exchange for sexual favors. She enlisted the help of her four sons, whom she shape-changed into oxen, and ploughed a huge area of land near the sea. The furrows were so massive that they quickly filled with sea water, thereby creating the island called Leire. Gefjon is reputed to live there to this day with Skiold, a son of Odhinn. Leire, modern-day Copenhagen, is also associated with the goddess Nerthus.

Loki accused Gefjon of being free with her sexuality with Heimdall and other gods. Gefjon, like Frigg and Freya, owns a golden necklace that she also gained by trading sexual favors. Gefjon is a name used to indicate both Frigg and Freya. Gefjon and Gefn are most likely the same goddess, as discussed under Freya.

---

[7] Jacob Grimm, *Teutonic Mythology*, pp. 308, 889.

Gerd: Goddess of the frozen field. Wife of Frey. Frey took the opportunity one day to sit upon Frigg's and Odhinn's magical chair, Hlidskialf. As he was viewing the nine worlds, he noticed a beautiful giantess going into a house. When she raised her lovely arms to open the door, the entire sky and sea shone with her brightness. Frey fell instantly in love and desired, above all else, her undying love. Frey gave his horse and magical sword to his servant in return for Gerd's hand in marriage. The servant immediately went to win Gerd for his master, even though he had to ride through a fierce curtain of flames surrounding her home to do so. This servant offered Gerd many wonderful gifts, including eleven magical apples and the golden arm-ring Draupnir, which is able to duplicate itself eight times every nine nights. Even with these beautiful gifts, Gerd refused this union, as she had no desire to marry a god. Eventually, under the threat of a terrible runic spell, she relented. Gerd promised to meet Frey in nine nights in the forest called Buri and become his bride. This mythical story exemplifies the ongoing yearly cycle of the cold, frozen fields thawing and being reborn with the coming of each spring.

Gersemi: One of two daughters of Freya (see Hnoss, p. 87).

Gna: Frigg's attendant. Gna is Frigg's messenger and advisor of all that is happening throughout the nine worlds. Like the Valkyries, Gna travels through the skies on a stately horse. In one story, Gna discovered a king named Rerir in a deep depression over his inability to produce a heir. Gna immediately went to Frigg and told her about the poor king's troubles. Frigg, touched by the story, produced a magic apple and requested that Gna deliver it to the king. Gna left at once and, as she flew over the king, dropped the apple in his lap. As he knew this was a gift from the goddesses in answer to his prayer, he went home and shared the special fruit with his wife. They had a child by the name of Volsung, ancestor of the famous Volsung family.[8]

---

[8] H. A. Guerber, *The Norsemen*, p. 48.

Figure 11. Holda, the kind protectress (from Dr. W. Wagner, *Asgard and the Gods: The Tales and Traditions of Our Northern Ancestors*, New York: E. P. Dutton, 1917, p. 7).

It can easily be assumed from reading the saga that the Volsung tribe is descended from Odhinn, for this saga does portray this family as worshipping him exclusively. This same saga also states that Odhinn is, in fact, the actual ancestor of this particular tribe. This popular belief of the Volsung ancestry is obviously false, but it is a good example of the patriarchal god supplanting the goddess in more recent times.

Hel: Goddess of death and of the underworld. Hel is actually a giantess. She is the daughter of Loki and Angrboda, both of whom are of giant heritage. Even so, Hel is considered a goddess by most scholars. She is sister to the monsters Jormungand and Fenris. It should be noted, however, that Snorri Sturluson, in his list of the Asyniur, does not include Hel with the goddesses.

Hel is described as a terribly hideous being with half of her body alive and vibrant, and the other cold and dead. Her fate was ordained before birth as an enemy of the gods. She is foretold to side with her father in Ragnarok and assist in destroying the Aesir. Upon discovery, Odhinn forced her into the very depths of the underworld. There, he gave her leadership of the world of her name, Hel. This role also included her supervision of the dead. Her hall is called Elvidner, meaning misery. Hel has a dark, reddish colored bird within her hall who will sing at the onset of Ragnarok. When Hel visits Midgard on her three-legged horse, she brings hunger and illness with her. The plague of medieval Europe was attributed to her. Hel, along with Bil, is another of the three goddesses to die in Ragnarok. Her name is the origin of the Christian place of punishment, Hell.

Hlin: Frigg's attendant. Goddess of protection. Hlin listens to all prayers and relays them to Frigg. She protects Frigg's favorite mortals from harm. Hlin is also another name for Frigg.

Hlodyn: Goddess of the Earth. Hlodyn means protectress of the fireplace. As her name is symbolic of the Earth, along with Fjorgyn, it is probable that they are the same goddess. Hlodyn, along with Sif and Iord, is also a namesake for the Earth. Hlodyn is also considered to be another name for Nerthus.

Hnoss: One of two daughters of Freya. Goddess of beauty. The Norse people named lovely things after Hnoss and her sister, Gersemi.

Idun: Goddess of youth and apples. She lives in a hall called Brunnaker. Idun's apples have the gift of longevity, which she willingly shares with the Aesir. A myth tells of her being the brunt of a trick by Loki. She is said to have been led by him to the hall of a giant, Skadi's father, who then imprisoned her. The Aesir,

Figure 12. Idun and the apples (from Donald MacKenzie, *Teutonic Myth and Legend*, London: Gresham, n. d., p. 49).

weakened and aging from lack of her apples, ordered Loki to return her. Loki had to borrow the falcon skin from Freya, and was forced to turn Idun into a nut in order to carry her safely home.

Another Norse myth describes her as sitting in the World Tree, Yggdrasill, and falling off her branch into the realms of Hel. She is unable to get back up, as she is taken with a violent illness. She is snugly wrapped in a wolf skin by her husband, Bragi, who stays with her throughout the months until she is well enough to leave. Both of these tales are obvious metaphors for the death of winter and the rebirth of spring. Idun was also accused by Loki of sleeping with other gods besides Bragi.

Ilm: Mentioned as a goddess although no other information is available.

Iord: Although a goddess, Iord is similar to Fjorgyn, Hlodyn, and Sif, as all are names for Earth, as mentioned under Fjorgyn. Iord is the daughter of Nott, mother of Thorr, lover of Odhinn, mother-in-law of Sif, and sister of Aud and Day.

Lofn: Goddess of permission. She listens to prayers from mortals and helps couples in matters of love and marriage.

Nanna: Married to Balder and the mother of Forseti. When Balder was killed through the terrible workings of Loki, Nanna was so overwhelmed with grief that her heart broke and she died. She and Balder were then trapped together in Hel's domain. Nanna, knowing she would be unable to leave until the end of Ragnarok, gave to Frigg's messenger a beautiful headdress for Frigg and a golden ring for Fulla.

Nerthus: Earth Mother. Nerthus is most likely another name for Frigg and Hlodyn, as has been mentioned previously. She is the mother of the twins Freya and Frey, and wife and possibly sister of Njord. While not much Nordic literature has been preserved about Nerthus, it is known that she was drawn in a wagon on a yearly visit to the people. This visitation brought harmony to the folk. They all stopped warring and put down their weapons in her presence to show their respect and reverence. The people held lively festivals in her honor, as her visits always resulted in peace and fertility. After her visit to the people, she was bathed by her attendants in a secret lake known only by her priests. Today, this lake is thought to be the Schwartze See, located on the island of Rugen.

Nott: Also named Niorun.[9] Goddess of the night who drives a chariot through the sky. As discussed in the chapter on the creation, we know Nott has dark skin and hair, and that this is a result of her heritage. This is of great significance, as many people, both Asatru and others, believe the Norse Tradition emphasizes white supremacy. Historically, no group of people will worship a deity of a different race or ethnic group if they practice racism. Nott, as a goddess of the Norse, obviously refutes that false belief. Nott is the mother of Aud, Day, and Iord.

Ran: Ran is the goddess of the sea and of death at sea. She uses a net to catch people who are drowning. If they have gold, they are treated well within her deep sea hall. Families know if their drowned kin are accepted within Ran's hall if they appear as ghosts at their own funeral. In one myth, Ran lends Loki her net to help save Odhinn and Honir from a horrible situation in which they found themselves due to yet another of Loki's pranks. Ran is the wife of Aegir and mother of nine divine daughters, called the Wave Maidens.

Rind: Goddess of the frozen earth. Rind, the daughter of Billing, refused to marry anyone, including the great god Odhinn. As Odhinn knew he had to marry her to fulfill his destiny as prophesied by Heith, he tried everything in his power to convince her to wed him. Finally, he resorted to placing a spell on Rind to gain her love. Rind did then marry Odhinn and the couple soon had a son named Vali, who grew up anticipating avenging his dead stepbrother, Balder, at the onset of Ragnarok.

---

[9] Snorri Sturluson, *Edda*, pp. 144, 157.

Saga: Saga, meaning seeress, is the goddess of prophecy.[10] Saga is said to drink with Odhinn every day in her hall, Sokkvabekk. As Frigg is known to do the same, it is most likely that Saga is another name for Frigg.

Sif: Goddess of fertility. Sif is often called the fair-haired goddess for her beautiful, long golden hair. She is considered a representation of vegetation, especially of mature crops. She is the daughter-in-law of Iord, wife of Thorr, and mother of Uller and Thrud. Sif is the stepmother of Magni and Modi. She supposedly had a husband prior to Thorr, but he is not named. She is accused by both Loki and Odhinn on different occasions of being wanton with her sexual favors. The only myth surviving about Sif involves a prank of Loki's. While she was sleeping, Loki cut off all her hair. When she awoke and discovered her hair gone, Sif was devastated. Thorr, ever the protector of his loved ones, proceeded to threaten Loki with his life unless *weregild* (amends) was paid. Loki, through the help of the dark dwarves, had new hair fashioned from gold thread. This lacy web of gold miraculously became real and more beautiful than Sif's old hair when it was placed on her head. Sif is another name for Earth, as has been previously mentioned under Fjorgyn, Hlodyn, and Iord.

Sigyn: Very little is known about Sigyn. She is married to Loki and is the stepmother of Hel, Fenris, and Jormungand. During Loki's imprisonment, while awaiting Ragnarok, Sigyn holds a bowl above his head to prevent the venom of a serpent from falling on Loki's face. Sigyn is obviously a symbol of loyalty, even in adverse conditions.

Sjofn: Goddess of love. She assists couples in affairs of the heart.

Skadi: Goddess of winter, skis, snowshoes, and hunting. She is symbolic of death and harm.[11] She is known for her courage, strength, honor, and her warrioress capabilities. Her hall, which

---

10 Edred Thorsson, *Northern Magic* (St. Paul: Llewellyn, 1993), p. 35.
11 Kevin Crossley-Holland, *The Norse Myths* (New York: Pantheon, 1980), p. 195.

she inherited from her father, is called Thrymheim. Skadi is actually a breathtakingly beautiful giantess, who becomes a goddess through her association with the Aesir. She is called the "bright bride of the gods."[12] Upon a trip to the Aesir to avenge her father's death, she is given Njord as a husband, although she really desired Balder. She is also given the gift of having her deceased father's eyes thrown into the sky as stars. As Njord was god of the sea and Skadi goddess of winter, they were totally incompatible and eventually separated. While this marriage can lead to the conclusion that she is the mother of Freya and Frey, she is, in fact, their stepmother. Both Freya and Frey were a part of the initial truce of the gods, whereas the marriage of Skadi and Njord happened much later in the mythology. Skadi is also thought to be a lover of Odhinn. She was accused, as were other goddesses, by Loki of being free with her sexual favors. Skadi is the goddess who hung the poisonous serpent above Loki's head when he was bound in a cave to await Ragnarok.

Snotra: Goddess of wisdom and courtesy.

Sol: The bright goddess of the Sun. She travels the sky in a chariot chased by the wolf Skoll. Sol is one of three goddesses foretold to die in Ragnarok, but not before she gives birth to a daughter who outshines her in beauty. It is possible that her prophesied death was because she was born a mortal woman. She was chosen by Odhinn because of her beauty. He magically elevated her to the rank of goddess, and placed her in the sky to become the Sun. This is similar to what happened with the goddess of the Moon, Bil.

Syn: Goddess of denial. She guards the door to a hall, presumably Frigg's. Her help is requested by defendants on trial. Syn is also a kenning for woman.[13]

Thrud: Daughter of Sif and Thorr. Sister of Magni and Modi, and stepsister of Uller. Thrud is both a goddess and a Valkyrie. She is

---

12 Snorri Sturluson, *Edda*, p. 24.
13 Snorri Sturluson, *Edda*, p. 115.

incredibly beautiful and is desired as a wife by many males, divine and mortal. In one instance, a dwarf by the name of Alvis thought he could win her hand. In the cool dark of night, he confidently made his way to the gates of Asgard where the gorgeous maiden resided. Thorr met Alvis at the gate and was appalled that such a creature would attempt to claim his daughter's hand. Thorr challenged the dwarf and refused to grant him permission to marry his lovely daughter. The dwarf continued to taunt the god and finally they agreed to a riddle game, with Thrud as the prize. They played all through the night and, as soon as Alvis thought he had finally come up with an unanswerable riddle, the Sun arose. He shrank back, but it was too late. Alvis was immediately turned to stone, as is the fate of all dwarves who see the light of day.

Vara: Goddess of promises. She listens to all oaths by gods and mortals, and either rewards when they are kept or punishes when they are broken.

Vor: Goddess of omniscience. Gifted with wisdom and prophetic abilities, she knows all that has occurred and all that will occur on Midgard and the other worlds.

Wave Maidens: Nine young daughters of the goddess and god of the sea, Ran and Aegir. Sailors strive for good rapport with these stunningly beautiful maidens of the oceans. If they succeed, they are assured safe and uneventful voyages with these powerful goddesses protecting and guiding them. If human voyagers do not gain the approval of the Wave Maidens, they can expect gale winds, creating a frothing, raging tempest, that will most likely cause death at sea. While these lovely goddesses prefer fun and positive workings, they will not hesitate to set upon their enemies with all the fury the seas can possess. The Wave Maidens are the mothers of the god Heimdall and lovers of Odhinn.

According to Snorri Sturluson, these goddesses' names are as follows: Himinglaeva, Dufa, Blodughadda, Hefring, Unn, Hronn, Bylgia, Bara, and Kolga.[14]

---

14 Snorri Sturluson, *Edda*, p. 91.

NINE

RAGNAROK

Ragnarok, commonly called "The Twilight of the Gods," is, without a doubt, the most misinterpreted of all Nordic myths. Many scholars and readers mistakenly believe this story illustrates the fatalism of the Norse people concerning the spiritual views of an afterlife. Nothing could be further from the truth, as a deep exploration and understanding of this legend will show. This myth is deeply moving and portrays a warm sense of comfort with its overt hint of rebirth. There is a suggestion of a definite Christian theme, although it does not mask the actual secret beauty of the legend of Ragnarok.

Before we begin, one point must be made abundantly clear. Neither the legend of Ragnarok, nor the Norse people who believed in this metaphor, nor the Norse polytheists of today acknowledge the arrogant and ridiculous concept of "the end of the world." None of us have the ability to destroy Earth, but we do have the means to destroy all creatures living on her, including ourselves. If such a tragic event ever did take place, which some seem determined to accomplish, Earth and her surrounding planets would continue to survive. Eventually, she would again produce new life.

Prophecy warns that the coming of Ragnarok will be heralded by three winters of bloody and devastating war on an unprecedented scale. Son will fight father, brother will turn against brother, blood-brother against blood-brother. They all will fight until death, nothing and no one will be able to bring them to reason. Humans will be filled with a horrible blood rage that only constant death will soothe. Fidelity in marriage will become a humorous myth, and children will turn against parents. Incest, always a punishable crime, will become common. Bloodshed will be continual, staining the ground red. Death will be all around, the scent of it provoking further savagery. The fighting will worsen, until it has lasted for three unbearably long years. Then true winter will descend, and it will be named Fimbulvetr.

It is said this will be such a fierce and bitterly cold winter that even grandmothers and grandfathers will not have experienced such a thing in their lifetimes. Nor will they be able to remember that their grandmothers and grandfathers, nor theirs, and so on until the beginning of what we call time, ever saw such a bitterly cold and cruelly harsh winter. People will die from cold, exhaustion, and starvation, but there will be no relief in sight. The storm will not weaken. Instead, it will rapidly worsen. The winds carrying the freezing snow will be so strong that the light from Sol will not reach Midgard. One will not be able to see one's hand in front of one's face, the snow will be so blinding. The bitter winds will bite through the thickest of clothing, the heaviest of blankets, and the most solid of homes. Frostbite and freezing to death will become the norm. People, frustrated and scared, will be quick to anger over the smallest of things. As is common among the human race, they will begin to turn rabidly on each other. The unbelievably tall drifts of snow will become stained with the red of blood. Flecks of pinkish snow will lash against unprotected faces, angering people into even greater acts of violence. The cursed winds will howl. This vicious winter will rage on for three interminably long years.

This will be the beginning of the end of life as we know it, and as it has been prophesied. It has been dreaded and feared for eons, but now humans will be so enmeshed in their personal hatred and ongoing fighting that they will fail to see all of the horrid signs. All of a sudden, the barely perceptible dim light of day will cease, and total darkness will descend, cloaking Midgard in a mantle of utter blackness. People will stop, swords dropping to their sides, shields falling to the ground, chests heaving, and they will begin to look around with clearing eyes, finally realizing that the truth is near. They will huddle close together for warmth and comfort, turning their eyes upward. They will wait, hoping against hope that their utmost fears are unjustified.

In depictions of Ragnarok, Sol is viciously killed by her pursuer of countless centuries, the terrible wolf Skoll. Mani, the Moon, is also caught and killed by Skoll's brother wolf, Hati. The ravaging of the heavens affects the Earth deeply. She is enraged, mortified, and saddened. She begins to tremble, then to shake with grief, inadvertently starting the worst earthquakes ever known to humankind.

At the same time, the three sacred birds of prophecy begin their horribly frightening call to battle. Their gruesomely ugly songs are heard through all nine worlds, so piercing that they deafen people, causing them to fall to the ground in severe agony. A red bird sings to the giants. Another, the color of blood, calls to Hel and her companions of the dead. Yet another, the golden brilliant bird of Val-Halla, screeches to warn the gods and the dead warriors of Val-Halla. It is time to go to the final war. Heimdall runs to the beautiful bridge, Bifrost, and lifts his great horn toward the blackened sky. He plays his final song, warning the gods to hurry.

The waters of Midgard rise in huge, tremendously destructive waves. Massive flooding becomes just another fear of the mortals. All of a sudden, the monstrous world serpent, Jormungand, emerges from the ocean. It is because of him that the waters have wrought such deadly havoc. The terrible ship, Naglfar, breaks free of its mooring. It is constructed of all the shavings of mortals' nails from the beginning of time. This ship is loaded with the giants of Jotunheim and begins to sail toward the huge area of land named Vigrid.

Loki, the god of mischief and trouble, has finally been released from his imprisonment by these unheard-of, terribly devastating earthquakes. He frolics around like a child, overjoyed to be free at last. He is already planning his next exciting adventure. This is to be his grand finale, to commence yet another act of devious mischief. Only this time, he is assured through prophecy of his victory over the gods. Loki, joined by his daughter, Hel, and all of her dead wards, begins to sail in yet another ship toward Vigrid.

Figure 13. Valkyries conducting fallen heroes to Valhalla (from Dr. W. Wagner, *Asgard and the Gods: The Tales and Traditions of Our Northern Ancestors*, New York: E. P. Dutton, 1917, p. 216).

Loki and his fearsome host arrive in good time at Vigrid. They are met by Loki's two other children, the world serpent, Jormungand, and the wolf Fenris. The two brothers have just arrived from a long trek, the serpent happily spitting venom over the entire surface of Midgard. This force is soon joined by numerous giants from Jotunheim. There, the tremendous army assembles, anxiously awaiting the upcoming battle, craving the scent of blood and gore, relishing the thought of miserable death. Giants gnash their teeth, the dead clang their shields, Loki screams with laughter, Fenris roars his delight. Hel, quiet as always, turns toward her massive brother, Jormungand, and smiles with deadly glee. The noise is deafening, frightening—worse than the worst thunderstorm known to humankind, caused by the most gruesome foes ever known. The mortals of Midgard bow their heads, waiting and listening, shuddering and terrified, and remain cowering on their knees.

In the distant south, a glimmering hellish light is moving ever closer. Loki and his army turn as one to watch, all with a smile of unsurpassed joy. As the light approaches, faint shapes can vaguely be made out. It is Surt, the giant from Muspellheim, leading his host of fire giants to battle. A reverberating crack is heard throughout the universe; Surt and his host have just crossed Bifrost. The bridge cannot withstand the heat or weight and falls down to places unseen, shattered beyond repair. In Surt's hand, he carries a sword flickering with flames. He joins Loki at the forefront, and smiles with a grim, condescending grimace. Loki, as usual not paying attention to innuendoes, is absolutely ecstatic at his good fortune. His army has joined together as foreseen long ago, and they are ready.

The gods, hearing the proud, yet wretchedly sorrowful call of Heimdall, assemble hastily. They are joined by all the dead warriors brought to Val-Halla for countless centuries by the Valkyries. Odhinn hurriedly rushes to talk with his old friend, Mimir, but there is little advice to give. The gods reassemble and, with strategies planned and weapons checked, they begin to march. Ever closer to Vigrid they approach, all the while hearing the overwhelmingly noxious noise from the foe. They see the unearthly light of Surt's sword, and know without doubt that the prophecy of Ragnarok is about to be fulfilled.

Both armies now stand poised on opposite sides of the vast plain of Vigrid. Each is shocked at the size of the other, but individual fear is no longer an option. Each side stands to lose much more than a simple life; the universe as it is known is at stake. Loki and his host have the confidence of prophecy; the gods and their army have the confidence of divinity. Horns are blown, battle cries are heard, the armies crash and blend together with a force comparable to the previous quakes of the Earth.

The scene is worse than the most vivid nightmare ever experienced. Men and giants are lying dead or dying everywhere, trampled by both friend and foe. Swords clash, shields shatter, axes smash spears, and spears impale enemies. The blood runs in huge torrents, causing entire battalions to stumble and fall, becoming easy prey for the unfeeling predator. Men lie gasping for breath, maimed and bleeding, wondering, at their final moment of life, if this battle could possibly have been avoided. Much too late for such thoughts, they sigh with deep regret, and pass on to the next plane of existence.

The gods are also caught in the midst of savage battle, fighting not only for their own personal lives, but for the continuance of all the worlds as they know them. Heimdall, the shining guardian of the rainbow bridge, Bifrost, is locked in a vicious battle with Loki, the once-beloved friend of the gods, now the most treacherous enemy of all. Heimdall is doomed from the onset, however. The prophecy holds true and he dies bitterly, but not before he seeks vengeance in the death of Loki.

Garm, the dreadful dog of Hel, furiously attacks the valiant, one-handed god of battle, Tyr. Tyr defends himself quite well, and the fight continues for a long time. Eventually, Garm and Tyr simultaneously deal each other a brutal blow, each mortally wounding the other. They fall at each other's side. There they lie, mortal enemies even in death.

Thorr, always the powerful protector of the gods, is enmeshed in the most hideous battle of his life. He is unable to lend a hand to save anyone other than himself. He is locked in combat with Jormungand, the world serpent. This battle continues, neither able to outdo the other. Thorr finally gets the upper hand, and kills the monstrous serpent. In relief, Thorr begins to back away, looking to each side to determine where his help is needed most. At his ninth step, he falls heavily to the ground, astounded to feel his life-force rapidly dwindling. Just before death, Jormungand had managed to spit venom on Thorr. This is how the great god and protector of life finally meets his death.

Frey, the beautiful fertility god of the Vanir, is also engaged in battle. He is fighting Surt, the terrible fire giant from Muspellheim. Frey is without sword or horse, for he gave all he owned in return for his marriage to the breathtakingly lovely Gerd. Even though he is virtually naked without weapons in this grisly battle, he does not regret his choice, for his love of Gerd still remains as strong as when he first saw her lovely face. Regardless of his lack of weaponry, he is magnificent to watch. He holds off Surt and the flaming sword for a long time. Surt finally sees an opening, and attacks viciously with his sword. Frey falls heavily, bleeding from a mortal wound, and dies at Surt's feet. Surt's attention is already elsewhere. He is overseeing the rest of the battle, his concentration on Frey no longer needed.

Odhinn, the All-Father of the gods, is in the death grip of the monstrously huge wolf, Fenris. This individual battle has been raging since the onset of the conflict. Neither are tiring, both are determined to conquer. Odhinn, possibly due to a slip on the bloody ground or some other mishap, loses control for less than a second. This is all Fenris needs to take Odhinn deep within his huge mouth and swallow him. Fenris prances around. He is delighted to know he is the only being in all the worlds to bring death to the fearsome one-eyed god. Fenris is so busy being proud of himself that he fails to see Vidar approaching from behind. Vidar snatches Fenris's jaw and plants one foot firmly on the lower jaw. Vidar brutally rips the wolf's jaws apart, thus killing his father's murderer.

At this time, Surt takes his sword of fire and starts swinging it maniacally in ever-growing arcs. He hurls it toward the east, then west; south, then north. He sets all the nine worlds on fire as easily as one lights a match. All the beings on the battlefield are instantly burned to ashes. All creatures dwelling in the nine worlds immediately perish. Midgard, a huge flaming ball of fire, brighter than the Sun ever was, is slowly drawn downward into the sea's embrace. The skies are again completely black. Silence descends.

All of a sudden, the sky brightens and there is a new Sun dancing the old path of the previous Sun through the sky. She is the daughter of Sol, born just before Sol perished. She is just as beautiful as her arrestingly lovely mother, if not more so. Through her gift of light, Midgard can be seen majestically rising from the vast ocean. The Earth is also even more beautiful than before. Lush with plant life, filled with scampering animals, the skies buffering the calls of birds, and fish splashing in the waters, Midgard is truly a magnificent sight to behold.

A woman and man, named Lif and Lifthrasir, appear. They have been hiding deep within the vast reaches of Yggdrasill throughout the entire battle and its fiery aftermath. They look around them, awed at the renewed beauty and magnificence of Midgard. They will have children eventually, and these children will have children, and so on and on throughout the ages to come. Lif and Lifthrasir will become the new ancestors of the human race.

Yggdrasill is, as always, the center of the universe. Although the great tree has been shaken by the massive earthquakes, flooded with raging sea waters, and subjected to the threat of fire from Surt's sword, it remains, as always, unbreakable. Yggdrasill will continue throughout all the ages and beyond.

The other eight worlds have also been renewed. On Asgard, young gods begin to appear. Vidar, Vali, Balder, and Hod—all sons of Odhinn—arrive at Idavoll. This is the area where the Aesir's halls previously stood. Magni and Modi, both sons of Thorr, show up as well. There they are given their father's hammer, Mjollnir, and are named the new keepers of this powerful talisman. Honir is among the new gods, and he will now predict the new future. These gods will eventually be joined by the sons of Odhinn's brothers, Vili and Ve. Together, they will take up the rule of the new and reborn Asgard.

As they all sit and reminisce, bitterly mourning the deaths of their fathers and uncles, they see some small objects shining in the lush grass. They explore this with much interest and discover golden chess pieces scattered about. These pieces are from the old halls of Asgard. Tears fill their eyes at the memories these pieces dredge up, but the gods tenderly cradle these little tokens; a new connection with the past, still in their hands to help them face the future.

THE GODDESSES IN RAGNAROK

The most common rendition of Ragnarok is fairly simple: the majority of mortals and gods die, to be replaced by a select few of their kin. This is represented by the continued existence of the mortals Lif and Lifthrasir, and the gods Vidar, Vali, Balder, Hod, Magni, Modi, Honir, and the unnamed sons of Vili and Ve. While this interpretation does, indeed, seem extraordinarily harsh and cruel, it is obviously just a simple surface explanation. It has no depth and ignores all apparent symbolism.

Because the myth of Ragnarok is normally taken so literally, it allows for continued ignorance of the role of the goddesses. The blame for this cannot all be laid on the interpreter and/or author, however. As with most spiritual writings, the myth of Ragnarok is metaphoric. This means that it is necessary to decipher all meanings of each simple word. This is not an easy task, but it is essential to the search for the primordial Norse goddess.

As is evident, only two goddesses, Sol and Hel, are mentioned throughout the entire story. Sol is killed by the wolf that has chased her throughout the ages. Before Sol's death, however, she gives birth to a daughter. This daughter almost immediately takes up the pattern Sol had established. There is no mention of Hel's demise, but her death is assumed, as Surt wipes the worlds clean with fire, killing most creatures, divine and mortal, in the process. Hel is, in actuality, a giantess, and her goddesshood is certainly questionable, as has been discussed previously. Her brothers, Fenris and Jormungand, die in battle, as does her father, Loki. Because Hel's role in Ragnarok was foreseen before her birth, it is apparent that her entire function was to build up troops for this battle and die at its conclusion.

What is interesting is that none of the other goddesses are mentioned even briefly in this story. The lack of these goddesses in Ragnarok is surprising. One would think these divine females would play an important role, as some have the gift of prophecy, many have strong magical abilities, and many are endowed with impressive battle skills. Even the Valkyries, some of the fiercest of all warriors, are surprisingly absent. Frigg, the Queen of the Asyniur and Aesir, is also disturbingly missing, as is Freya, sometime leader of the Valkyries and undisputed goddess of magic.

These absences lead to only two possible conclusions: that the goddesses hold so little worth in the Norse cosmos that their deaths were deemed unworthy of note, or that the goddesses were not a part of Ragnarok because this horribly gruesome battle did not pertain to them. They lived through this great war without sustaining any personal harm. The second alternative is the more feasible one.

After the death of Sol and Mani, the skies fall to utter darkness, devoid of all signs of life. Nevertheless, the goddess of night, Nott, is in obvious attendance. She is the blackness surrounding the worlds, symbolizing a womb waiting for the spark of life. In this instance, she represents the void, Ginnungagap, from the story of the creation.

The most obvious proof of the continued existence of the goddesses is the fact that Midgard, even though cleansed with fire and water, remains not only intact, but refreshed and renewed. As we have already explored, many of the goddesses bear the name Mother Earth, Earth Mother, or Earth. This is because they, along with various giantesses, are representations of the beautiful and sacred Earth, and cannot be destroyed by the harmful acts of either gods or humans. Another indication of the goddesses' continued existence is the seemingly insignificant appearance of the chess pieces. The fact that they are golden is a direct symbol of the goddesses Frigg, Freya, and Gefjon. As the gold pieces were still resting in the grasses, so too are the goddesses resting in the wings of this powerful myth.

It is most likely that Lif and Lifthrasir, the female and male humans who survive Ragnarok, are representations of many different women and men. They somehow, most likely with feminine divine assistance, found the World Tree, Yggdrasill, and took shelter deep within to avoid the coming battle. The only way a human could find the tree would be with great mental and spiritual strength. These people were obviously worshippers of the goddesses and were divinely blessed by being saved from the devastation of Ragnarok. The goddesses granted them a new life upon a cleansed and reborn Midgard.

While Ragnarok may be a grand story foretelling the end of the races of gods and humans, it is most likely a simple metaphor for the yearly cycles of death and rebirth as evidenced by the Earth herself. The three winters of inner conflict could be a simple adage describing "spring fever," and the tempers that fly when long winters prevail and spring fails to approach in what we deem a timely fashion. The gods dying and being replaced by their sons would be consistent with Frigg's and Freya's yearly search for their lost husbands. After a long separation, the reunion with one's mate would certainly have the fluttery feeling of meeting a loved one anew.

Regardless of how this myth is interpreted, the fact remains that the goddesses do not play a part in this story of war and death, as they are beyond such antics. They survive, and will continue to do so throughout all time.

PART THREE

UNVEILING THE HIDDEN TRUTH

The men sought out and collected as many of the scrolls as they were able. They arranged them in order, but found, as Saga had told them, that very many were lost, and others only existed as fragments. . . . Nevertheless, they allowed no difficulties to terrify them, but courageously pursued their work of investigation. Soon they discovered other records, or fragments of records, which they had supposed to have been lost. What the storms of time had scattered in different directions, what ignorance had cast aside as worthless, they brought to the light of day . . .

—W. WAGNER, *Asgard and the Gods*

TEN

PIECING TOGETHER
THE FRAGMENTS

In this chapter, we will begin to fit together all the fragments of the divine women and goddesses explored in the previous sections. While much of this section may indeed be called speculation, this speculation is based upon careful research of the Norse Tradition and of other comparable spiritual traditions. The facts we have discovered will demonstrate a truth neglected and ignored for centuries.

Table 1 on pages 108–111 lists the various Norse goddesses, their attributes, and associations. While all these goddesses have already been discussed in previous chapters, this table gives a visual reference to assist us in our study and makes the fragmented aspects of the Goddess of the North easier to understand.

Certain divine feminine beings—giantesses, Disir, Norns, and Valkyries not named as specific goddesses—have not been included in the following tables. They and their varying aspects will be introduced in later chapters.

The reader will note the inclusion of animals in this and following tables. This is important to gain a thorough knowledge of the goddesses, for a creature may incorporate characteristics we would not necessarily connect with the specific goddess with which this animal is associated. These tables do not include all the sacred animals, only those that we know, through common mythological sources, are aligned with the feminine divine.

Table 1. The Goddesses, Their Attributes and Associations.

Attribute	Bil	Eir	Erce	Fjorgyn	Freya	Frigg	Fulla	Gefjon	Gerd
Air	X	X				X			
Apples						X			X
Beauty		X			X	X	X		X
Butterfly					X				
Cat					X				
Childbirth/ Maternity					X	X			
Cuckoo/Swallow					X	X			
Day									
Death		X			X	X		X	
Destiny/Prophecy		X			X	X	X		
Eagle/Falcon/ Hawk/Raven		X			X	X			
Earth/Fertility			X	X	X	X	X	X	X
Fire					X	X	X	X	
Gold					X	X	X	X	X
Healing		X			X	X			
Home/Marriage					X	X			
Horse		X			X				
Judgment		X			X	X			
Love/Sensuality		X			X	X		X	X
Magic		X			X	X			
Moon	X						X		
Night	X						X		
Peace/Prosperity					X	X			
Pig					X				
Protection		X				X			
Shape-Changing/ Shamanism		X			X	X		X	
Spring					X	X			
Sun									
Swan		X							
Water		X							
War		X			X	X			
Weave/Spinning		X			X	X			
Weasel					X				
Winter									X
Wolf		X			X				
World						X			
Youth	X	X			X				X

Table 1. The Goddesses, Their Attributes and Associations (cont.).

Attribute	Gersemi	Gna	Hel	Hlin	Hloydn	Hnoss	Idun	Ilm	Iord
Air		X							
Apples		X					X		
Beauty	X					X	X		
Butterfly									
Cat									
Childbirth/ Maternity		X							
Cuckoo/Swallow									
Day									
Death			X						
Destiny/Prophecy									
Eagle/Falcon/ Hawk/Raven									
Earth/Fertility					X				X
Fire									
Gold									
Healing									
Home/Marriage		X							
Horse		X	X						
Judgment									
Love/Sensuality		X					X		X
Magic									
Moon									
Night									
Peace/Prosperity									
Pig									
Protection				X	X				
Shape-Changing/ Shamanism									
Spring							X		
Sun									
Swan									
Water									
War			X						
Weave/Spinning									
Weasel									
Winter									
Wolf							X		
World									
Youth	X					X	X		

Table 1. The Goddesses, Their Attributes and Associations (cont.).

Attribute	Lofn	Nanna	Nerthus	Nott	Ran	Rind	Saga	Sif	Sigyn
Air				X					
Apples									
Beauty				X		X		X	
Butterfly									
Cat									
Childbirth/ Maternity									
Cuckoo/Swallow									
Day									
Death		X			X				
Destiny/Prophecy							X		
Eagle/Falcon/ Hawk/Raven									
Earth/Fertility			X			X		X	
Fire									
Gold		X			X			X	
Healing									
Home/Marriage	X								
Horse									
Judgment									
Love/Sensuality	X	X				X		X	X
Magic									
Moon									
Night				X					
Peace/Prosperity			X					X	
Pig									
Protection									X
Shape-Changing/ Shamanism									
Spring			X						
Sun									
Swan									
Water			X		X				
War									
Weave/Spinning									
Weasel									
Winter						X			
Wolf									
World									
Youth						X			

Table 1. The Goddesses, Their Attributes and Associations (cont.).

Attribute	Sjofn	Skadi	Snotra	Sol	Syn	Thrud	Vara	Vor	Wave Maidens
Air				X		X			
Apples									
Beauty		X		X		X			X
Butterfly									
Cat									
Childbirth/ Maternity				X					
Cuckoo/Swallow									
Day				X					
Death		X				X			
Destiny/Prophecy			X			X		X	
Eagle/Falcon/ Hawk/Raven						X			
Earth/Fertility									
Fire				X					
Gold				X					
Healing									
Home/Marriage	X								
Horse						X			
Judgment						X	X		
Love/Sensuality	X	X				X			X
Magic						X			
Moon									
Night									
Peace/Prosperity									
Pig									
Protection		X			X	X			X
Shape-Changing/ Shamanism						X			
Spring									
Sun				X					
Swan						X			
Water						X			X
War		X				X			
Weave/Spinning						X			
Weasel									
Winter		X							
Wolf						X			
World									
Youth						X			X

Chapter 19 is devoted to the study of animals and other spiritual symbols affiliated with the Goddess of the North.

The table shows that most of the Norse goddesses do not have a wide range of attributes. This is because they are themselves aspects of other, more fully developed goddesses. The Nordic people would not have worshipped a deity that was hampered by having very few attributes. As humans, we expect our deities to have many different talents and abilities, as we do ourselves. Those with a strong spiritual sense know the divine, feminine and masculine, is all-encompassing, comprised of so many different traits that we are unable to truly comprehend it in its entirety. It is likely that the names shown in this table were used to acknowledge one precise aspect of a goddess, an aspect the Norse people wished to recognize for a particular reason.

For example, the sister goddesses Gersemi and Hnoss are known to have only two attributes—youth and beauty. All early people, including the Norse, had a deep respect for beauty. Their concept of beauty, however, differed greatly from the modern-day definition of the term. The ancients saw beauty in all life, birth, creation, plants, trees, water, etc. Beauty, in many cases, also included the aspect of youth. To the Norse, beauty appeared in almost every animate and inanimate object. Consequently, calling upon the goddess of beauty, Freya, in each instance may not have served the purpose these people desired, for Freya encompasses many other attributes. They may have wanted to name an object after their beloved goddess, but did not wish this item to take on Freya's other attributes. If they simply wanted to acknowledge the beauty of an object, they called the item by a special name reserved for that particular aspect of Freya, such as Gersemi and Hnoss.

This is a very common occurrence throughout Norse mythology and other comparable mythologies. Odhinn himself has various names, fortunately well documented and clearly describing his numerous aspects. This lends further credence to the practice of assigning different names to different aspects of a goddess. This custom is especially apparent in modern monotheistic practices as well, as can be seen by the various names for the prophet Jesus Christ that appear in the Bible. There is also evidence of this practice in the doctrines of Judaism and Islam. The tendency to attach several names to a deity occurs often in later religious traditions, a fact that validates the early Norse practice of performing the very same action. We know that polytheism and animism predate monotheism. This naming of deities to emphasize their individual attributes is, thus, an old and universal tradition.

The following tables enumerate the group of goddesses given by Snorri Sturluson as names of the Asyniur in his *Edda*.[1] His work remains the foundation of any Nordic study, with other authors and texts serving as valuable supplements. Sturluson, to the best of our knowledge, retold the myths and legends as he had heard them throughout his life. Unlike us, he lived in an era in which monotheism was fairly new, and in which the old tradition still retained a strong hold on his culture. This explains his considerable knowledge of the individual Norse goddesses and gods. Other texts, such as works by Jacob Grimm and Hilda Ellis Davidson, combine this knowledge with known folklore from several Germanic countries.[2] These two scholars also provide numerous linguistic, dialectic, and cultural comparisons. The difference in language dialects further demonstrates the practice of assigning multiple names to various goddesses. Table 2 on pages 114–116 combines the names of goddesses that Sturluson mentions with those he does not, and lists the same attributes and associations shown in Table 1.

In Sturluson's list of names, nine goddesses which are listed in Table 1 (pages 108–111) are missing. This implies that those missing are not actually goddesses, but rather duplicate names describing specific aspects of the named goddesses. As we discussed earlier, Hnoss and Gersemi are, without a doubt, prime examples of this.

Eir is allegedly both a goddess and a Valkyrie, so her absence from this list is interesting and insightful, as well as confusing. As a dual being, it is possible that her strength lies more in

---

1 Snorri Sturluson, *Edda*, Anthony Faulkes, trans., 2nd ed. (London: Everyman's Library, 1992), p. 157.
2 See Bibliography for these authors' texts.

Table 2. Sturluson's List of Names.

Attribute	Bil	Freya [Eir, Wave Maidens]	Frigg [Nerthus]	Fulla	Gefjon	Gerd	Gna	Hlin	Hnoss [Gersemi]
Air	X	X	X				X		
Apples			X			X	X		
Beauty		X	X	X		X			X
Butterfly		X							
Cat		X							
Childbirth/ Maternity		X	X				X		
Cuckoo/Swallow		X	X						
Day									
Death		X	X		X				
Destiny/Prophecy		X	X	X					
Eagle/Falcon/ Hawk/Raven		X	X						
Earth/Fertility		X	X	X	X	X			
Fire		X	X	X	X				
Gold		X	X	X	X	X			
Healing		X	X						
Home/Marriage		X	X				X		
Horse		X					X		
Judgment		X	X						
Love/Sensuality		X	X		X	X	X		
Magic		X	X						
Moon	X			X					
Night	X			X					
Peace/Prosperity		X	X						
Pig		X							
Protection		X	X					X	
Shape-Changing/ Shamanism		X	X		X				
Spring		X	X						
Sun									
Swan		X							
Water		X	X						
War		X	X						
Weave/Spinning		X	X						
Weasel		X							
Winter						X			
Wolf		X							
World			X						
Youth	X	X				X			X

Table 2. Sturluson's List of Names (cont.).

Attribute	Idun	Ilm [Erce, Fjorgyn, Hlodyn, Sif]	Iord	Lofn	Nanna	Nott [Niorun]*	Ran [Hel]	Rind	Saga
Air						X			
Apples	X								
Beauty	X	X				X		X	
Butterfly									
Cat									
Childbirth/ Maternity									
Cuckoo/Swallow									
Day									
Death					X		X		
Destiny/Prophecy									X
Eagle/Falcon/ Hawk/Raven									
Earth/Fertility		X	X					X	
Fire									
Gold		X			X		X		
Healing									
Home/Marriage				X					
Horse							X		
Judgment									
Love/Sensuality	X	X	X	X	X			X	
Magic									
Moon									
Night						X			
Peace/Prosperity		X							
Pig									
Protection		X							
Shape-Changing/ Shamanism									
Spring	X								
Sun									
Swan									
Water							X		
War							X		
Weave/Spinning									
Weasel									
Winter								X	
Wolf	X								
World									
Youth	X							X	

*Niorun is used in this text for Nott, as both names are used in other translations to describe the same goddess, the goddess of the night.

Table 2. Sturluson's List of Names (cont.).

Attribute	Sigyn	Sjofn	Skadi	Snotra	Sol	Syn	Thrud	Vara	Vor
Air					X		X		
Apples									
Beauty			X		X		X		
Butterfly									
Cat									
Childbirth/ Maternity					X				
Cuckoo/Swallow									
Day					X				
Death			X				X		
Destiny/Prophecy				X			X		X
Eagle/Falcon/ Hawk/Raven							X		
Earth/Fertility									
Fire					X				
Gold					X				
Healing									
Home/Marriage		X							
Horse							X		
Judgment							X	X	
Love/Sensuality	X	X	X				X		
Magic							X		
Moon									
Night									
Peace/Prosperity									
Pig									
Protection	X		X			X	X		
Shape-Changing/ Shamanism							X		
Spring									
Sun					X				
Swan							X		
Water							X		
War			X				X		
Weave/Spinning							X		
Weasel									
Winter			X						
Wolf							X		
World									
Youth							X		

her identity as a fearsome Valkyrie than as a goddess. This aligns her closely with the goddess Freya. Freya is a leader of the Valkyries—those divine female warriors. In fact, she is the only goddess openly connected with them. Freya has strong tendencies for magic, fertility, beauty, youth, and sensuality, but she also has a natural aptitude for war.

For many of these same reasons, the Wave Maidens are often considered to be an aspect of Freya. These goddesses of the sea perfectly portray both Freya's inescapable charm and her bouts of fury. These nine young sisters love, play, and dance in the calm waters. When enraged, however, they are able to demonstrate their mighty anger in raging tempests and life-threatening waves.

The most interesting combination of attributes appears under the name of Ilm. As seen in Table 1, Ilm has no known attributes. In Table 2, however, she is still listed as a goddess. She has been combined with Sif, Erce, Fjorgyn, and Hlodyn. Even though Sif does play a small role in a myth concerning her lustrous hair and is the wife of the god Thorr, she is not listed by Sturluson as an actual goddess. This tells us her true form lies with the earth, emphasized by the fact that Sturluson goes on to tell us that Fjorgyn, Hlodyn, and Sif are all names used to describe the Earth.[3] We do know that Fjorgyn, Hlodyn, and Erce are all names of Mother Earth in her most ancient Nordic form. Nonetheless, little else is known about these three. Because of the emphasis on the lack of knowledge concerning the Earth Mother, this fact alone pulls these three aspects, plus Sif, into Ilm's realm. This is likely where the original displacement of the primordial goddess actually began.

Ran and Hel are obvious counterparts, as they are both goddesses of death. The only difference is that Ran nets her victims, whereas Hel simply waits for them to appear. They are both perceived to live beneath the realm of Midgard: Hel in her underworld, and Ran deep beneath the sea. As such, they both have a deep connection with the Earth herself. Hel is a giantess. We already know that all giantesses are considered to be of the earth.

---

[3] Snorri Sturluson, *Edda*, p. 163.

This fact is underscored by the fact that they are all descendants of Ymir, whose body is the shell of the earth.

Ran's connection to Earth is a little more vague. Her oceans surround the continents of Midgard. Her glorious hall, lined with gold, is not on the highest level of Asgard, but here in the vast oceans of the Earth. As she represents water, she controls the life-force not only of sea creatures, but of land-bound species as well. She can also prompt their devastation. In the myth of Ragnarok, the Earth sinks into Ran's realm of cool dark waters to be cleansed and reborn as an even more beautiful Earth.

Table 3, pages 120–121, shows the Norse goddesses named by Snorri Sturluson as Asyniur in both his *Edda* and his *Prose Edda*.[4] Unlike the list of names in Table 2, this list gives considerable detail about each of these goddesses, allowing them to be viewed and honored as actual deities. We must realize that, considering the political climate in which Snorri lived, he would not have been able to demonstrate his knowledge of the Norse Goddess in great detail. Therefore, he left future generations these many hints. Table 3 again adds the names of those goddesses not listed by Sturluson, in an attempt to arrive at a more complete catalog.

In this more detailed list, Sturluson names Eir as the goddess of healing, but does not include Thrud. This switching of the two Valkyries as goddesses is telling. It is obvious that neither is actually a "true" goddess, and this interchanging lends credence to the fact that they are both aspects of another goddess, who, as mentioned before, must be the goddess Freya. Eir and Thrud are not only symbolic of Freya's Valkyrie-like nature, they also enhance that specific aspect of Freya by giving this fierceness both visual and physical substance. Valkyries are normally seen as cruel-hearted warriors, attending every battle and either protecting their favorites or escorting departed souls to the next realm of life.

This swapping back and forth between Eir and Thrud tells us the Valkyrie aspect of Freya has the powerful gift of healing as

---

[4] Snorri Sturluson, *Edda*, pp. 29–31; Snorri Sturluson, *Prose Edda: Tales from Norse Mythology*, Jean I. Young, trans. (Berkeley, University of California Press, 1954), pp. 59–61.

well. These divine female warriors seek not only war and death, but also to heal the wounds of the body and of the soul. Therefore, even though they are normally associated with the cause of death, they also are able to sustain life.

Idun, the supposed goddess who, with her magical golden apples, gracefully granted longevity to all the gods of the Aesir and Vanir, is also surprisingly missing from Sturluson's list. It is very difficult to determine exactly to which goddess this aspect of Idun belongs. We know she represents apples, beauty, spring, and youth. The key to this riddle, however, is that Idun does not represent youth by being young herself. Rather, she *gives* the gift of youth to others through her apples. This is metaphorically similar to a mother giving birth to a baby, as the woman gives the miraculous gift of life and youth to the newborn. As Frigg is the only fully developed matron figure among the Norse goddesses, logic tells us that Idun is one of her many aspects.

We have already seen the role played by the Earth Mother in Tables 1 and 2. As we know, Iord is, literally, another name for the Earth.[5] She therefore incorporates all the other names having the same meaning and replaces the name of the goddess, Ilm, in this chart.

Of all the giantesses elevated to goddess status, according to the various myths, Rind is the only one Sturluson names as a goddess. It remains a mystery whether Rind is, in actuality, a giantess or a mortal, but considering the role she plays in the legends, the most likely scenario is that she is a giantess, since the gods of the Aesir and Vanir only marry or entertain lovers that are either goddesses or giantesses. There is no Nordic legend that shows one of the gods wedding a mortal woman, although sexual acts between gods and mortal women are mentioned. Taking this into consideration, and the fact that Sturluson has eliminated all the other giantesses supposedly elevated to goddesses from this list, we must assume that Rind is the only actual giantess-turned-goddess. As such, she would be the giantess from whom all other myths of giantesses-turned-divine actually derived.

---

5 Snorri Sturluson, *Edda*, p. 237.

Table 3. Sturluson's List of Asyniur.

Attribute	Bil	Eir	Freya [Hnoss Gersemi, Thrud, Wave Maidens]	Frigg [Idun, Nerthus]	Fulla	Gefjon	Gna	Hlin
Air	X	X	X	X			X	
Apples				X			X	
Beauty		X	X	X	X			
Butterfly			X					
Cat		.	X					
Childbirth/ Maternity			X	X			X	
Cuckoo/Swallow			X	X				
Day								
Death		X	X	X		X		
Destiny/Prophecy		X	X	X	X			
Eagle/Falcon/ Hawk/Raven		X	X	X				
Earth/Fertility			X	X	X	X		
Fire			X	X	X	X		
Gold			X	X	X	X		
Healing		X	X	X				
Home/Marriage			X	X			X	
Horse		X	X				X	
Judgment		X	X	X				
Love/Sensuality		X	X	X		X	X	
Magic		X	X	X				
Moon	X				X			
Night	X				X			
Peace/Prosperity			X	X				
Pig			X					
Protection		X	X	X				X
Shape-Changing/ Shamanism		X	X	X		X		
Spring			X	X				
Sun								
Swan		X	X					
Water		X	X	X				
War		X	X	X				
Weave/Spinning		X	X	X				
Weasel			X					
Winter								
Wolf		X	X	X				
World				X				
Youth	X	X	X	X				

Table 3. Sturluson's List of Asyniur (cont.).

Attribute	Iord [Erce, Fjorgyn, Hloydn, Ilm, Sif]	Lofn	Rind [Gerd, Hel, Nanna, Nott, Ran, Sigyn, Skadi]	Saga	Sjofn	Snotra	Sol	Syn	Vara	Vor
Air			X				X			
Apples			X							
Beauty	X		X				X			
Butterfly										
Cat										
Childbirth/ Maternity						X				
Cuckoo/Swallow										
Day							X			
Death			X							
Destiny/Prophecy				X		X				X
Eagle/Falcon/ Hawk/Raven										
Earth/Fertility	X		X							
Fire							X			
Gold	X		X				X			
Healing										
Home/Marriage		X			X					
Horse			X							
Judgment									X	
Love/Sensuality	X	X	X		X					
Magic										
Moon										
Night			X							
Peace/Prosperity	X									
Pig										
Protection	X		X					X		
Shape-Changing/ Shamanism										
Spring										
Sun							X			
Swan										
Water			X							
War			X							
Weave/Spinning										
Weasel										
Winter			X							
Wolf										
World										
Youth			X							

We know Gerd and Skadi are lovely giantesses who married gods of the Vanir. Hel is also a giantess. Sigyn is, most likely, a giantess, as she is married to the giant, Loki, and protects him deep within a cave until Ragnarok. Seldom, in all the myths, do we find an example of a goddess wedded to a giant. Nanna remains hidden in the underworld in Hel's domain until the end of Ragnarok. That she is unable to leave hints at her not being of divine ancestry. We have already discussed Ran and her watery connection with the earth. All these aspects are associated with earth in the form of either winter or death. Metaphorically, these two terms mean the same thing, for earth is considered dead in the harshness of winter, and is reborn with the warmth of spring. Nott has been included in this group, as night is another popular metaphor for death. Hence, the only obvious connection these names and attributes have is to the goddess Rind, for she, being a giantess, is of the earth. Furthermore, she represents death through her strong association with winter.

Table 4, page 123, summarizes the results of our detective work. Under the column of Freya, we have already explored at length the connections between the Wave Maidens and the two Valkyries, Eir and Thrud. In chapter 8, we discussed the distinct possibility that Gefjon is another name for Gefn, who we know is Freya. Sjofn is an obvious addition to this list, for she is a goddess of love, as is Freya. They are both called upon to help amorous couples find a way of uniting in love. Bil, the goddess of the waxing Moon, symbolizes the rebirth and youth of the Moon each month. Hence, it is a foregone conclusion that she is also one with Freya, for Freya symbolizes youth.

Iord has been combined not only with all the giantesses from chapter 6, but with the giantesses whom we previously thought might be goddesses that we had already aligned with Rind. We explored these connections thoroughly, so we know the giantesses and goddesses symbolizing winter and death are of the earth. These female beings are also representatives of the two underworlds of sea and darkness.

In Table 4, Frigg is the goddess who has assumed the most numerous aspects. Fulla, Gna, and Hlin are Frigg's handmaidens. This unusual occurrence appears to be more of a human notion

Table 4. Aligning the Aspects.

Attribute	Freya Bil, Eir, Gefjon, Gersemi, Hnoss, Sjofn, Thrud, Wave Maidens	Frigg Fulla, Gna, Hlin, Idun, Lofn, Nerthus, Saga, Snotra, Sol, Syn, Vara, Vor	Iord Fjorgyn, Erce, Gerd, Giantesses, Hel, Hloydn, Ilm, Nanna, Nott, Ran, Rind, Sif, Sigyn, Skadi
Air	X	X	X
Apples		X	X
Beauty	X	X	X
Butterfly	X		
Cat	X		
Childbirth/Maternity	X	X	
Cuckoo/Swallow	X	X	
Day		X	
Death	X	X	X
Destiny/Prophecy	X	X	
Eagle/Falcon/Hawk/Raven	X	X	
Earth/Fertility	X	X	X
Fire	X		X
Gold	X	X	X
Healing	X	X	
Home/Marriage	X	X	
Horse	X	X	X
Judgment	X	X	
Love/Sensuality	X	X	X
Magic	X	X	
Moon	X	X	
Night	X	X	X
Peace/Prosperity	X	X	X
Pig	X		
Protection	X	X	X
Shape-Changing/Shamanism	X	X	
Spring	X	X	
Sun		X	
Swan	X		
Water	X	X	X
War	X	X	X
Weave/Spinning	X	X	
Weasel	X		
Winter			X
Wolf	X	X	
World		X	
Youth	X	X	X

than a divine one. The desire for attendants is what we, as humans, consider necessary or acceptable for royalty and for the very wealthy. There is no doubt that early Nordic noblewomen also had servants to assist with daily chores, to oversee crops, and to care for livestock while their men were away. As such, they would expect their matron goddess to have the same need for attendants.

Lofn assists couples in marriage, as does Frigg. Saga is simply another name for Frigg, and Snotra has the qualities of wisdom and courtesy, already known as Frigg's attributes. Syn is the guardian of Frigg's hall, and is called upon to help in trials. Frigg, in previously mentioned myths, is also seen to uphold the laws of justice. Vara appears under similar guise, for this aspect of Frigg listens carefully to all oaths, and either rewards for completion or punishes for failure. This is exhibited in the myth of Frigg holding Odhinn to his word concerning the warring tribes of mortals. Even though he was tricked, he was required to keep his promise to Frigg or reap the consequences. Vor is simply another name for Frigg when she is cloaked in her prophetic aspect.

Sol, the goddess of the Sun, is also an important aspect of Frigg. In her shining bright glory, Sol gives us the gift of light. She is said to die in Ragnarok, but she will first give birth to a daughter, and this daughter will be even more beautiful than Sol. Three pertinent facts show us the definite connection between Sol and Frigg. First, we know she is a mature goddess, fully comfortable and stately in her matronly elegance. Second, Sol is a mother. Third, as the Sun, she represents the maturity of day, versus the youthfulness of dawn or the aging of dusk. Today, we know many Suns in our universe die while others, newly formed, come into being. Frigg, encompassing this particular aspect, is teaching us that there is no death, simply a rebirth into a more beautiful being surrounded by a more beautiful place.

We do not need another chart to show us which aspect will encompass the other two. Snorri Sturluson was kind enough to give us two other clues. He told us that all Asyniur can be called by another's name and he told us that Frigg is the Queen of the Asyniur.[6] These two comments allow us to narrow the names of

---

[6] Snorri Sturluson, *Edda*, p. 86.

the goddesses down to one, who is obviously Frigg. This is by no means the end of our search, however. We are merely standing on the threshold of an ultimate truth. Our first assumption would be that Frigg is the name our ancestors initially gave to the Goddess of the North in an attempt to comprehend Her with their limited human understanding. Such an assumption, however, is incomplete. Encompassing all the goddesses and their attributes under Frigg should not imply a reduction of the aspects of the Goddess, but rather an expansion of them. We know that Frigg is the daughter of the Earth, Fjorgyn. Freya is the daughter of the Queen, Frigg. Hnoss and Gersemi are the daughters of Love, Freya. This is the only unbroken ancestral line we will find among the goddesses in all Nordic lore. This divine heritage is of crucial importance, as it is a most important hint as to the character of the Goddess of the North.

We have already decided that Hnoss and Gersemi are aspects of Freya, as they are only mentioned in light of Freya's beauty. In fact, what they also represent is the continuance of life on all levels of existence. They show us that the beauty of the Goddess is always around, regardless of the age of the being. Hnoss and Gersemi represent that small spark of the Goddess that we can find deep within ourselves if we look hard enough. This spark of beauty and divine essence, characterized by Hnoss and Gersemi, is the Fylgie who resides within each of us.

This ancestral line demonstrates that Fjorgyn, Frigg, and Freya are the three true aspects of the Goddess of the North. They represent Her beings as Grandmother, Mother, and Daughter.[7] This is of tremendous importance, for the Norse would not have worshipped and honored a stagnant, aloof Goddess. They would only have revered a Goddess whom they could see in every possible situation involving Earth and their very lives.

The Disir, our feminine ancestors who guard over children are, in actuality, the aspect of Fjorgyn, the Grandmother. The Norns, who shape all of destiny for the worlds and all species within, are aligned with Frigg, the Mother. The Valkyries, those

---

7 Hilda Ellis Davidson, *Roles of the Northern Goddess* (New York: Routledge, 1998), p. 89.

wild, loving, and protective warriors, are the aspect of the
Daughter, Freya. We have already discussed the Valkyrie connection at length. We will explore the other two groups in the chapters that follow.

We have almost reached the climax of our search for the
primordial Norse Goddess. She is with us continually in Her
beautiful forms of Grandmother, Mother, and Daughter, and
each aspect deeply affects us throughout our lives. We have a few
more details to explore in order to truly understand the depth—
as much as we as humans are able to comprehend—of the Goddess of the North.

ELEVEN

UNDERSTANDING YGGDRASILL

I t would be easy to stop our exploration here and be satisfied with the aspects of the Grandmother, Mother, and Daughter of the Goddess of the North, but one crucial element of the Norse cosmos has yet to be explored—Yggdrasill, also known as the Laerath, World Tree, or Guardian Tree. (See figure 14 on p. 128) The name Yggdrasill may reflect Odhinn as Ygg is one of his many names, however, this is probably a later addition to the mythology. According to all mythological stories about Yggdrasill, this tree is infinite. On the other hand, Odhinn was born of a presumed god and a giantess. This being the case, it is very possible that the World Tree became known as Yggdrasill after Odhinn's self-sacrifice and discovery of the runes. This is an important detail, as the reason Odhinn is associated with Yggdrasill has nothing to do with the essence of the tree itself. Yggdrasill's state of being is the very issue we intend to investigate. To uncover the truth of the primordial goddess, we must explore Yggdrasill in minute detail.

When reading of the Norse cosmos, some people tend to view the legend of Yggdrasill in a humorous light. They imagine a giant tree filled with scampering animals. They envision three huge tree roots extending downward to literally cradle Earth, the other eight worlds, and the three springs, as described in the mythology. While this playful visualization is helpful in beginning to understand the regions of Yggdrasill, it is inaccurate and

Figure 14. Yggdrasill, the World Tree of the Norse Tradition. (From the author's personal collection; artist Ingrid Ivic.)

naive to assume that this is the entire meaning of the myth. Metaphor is commonly used in spiritual narratives and writings and the legend of the Guardian Tree is no exception. It is unfortunate that the myths of the Nordic ancestors have been reduced in the recent past to mere fables of a primitive, unintelligent, and barbaric people. These stories hold much truth, if we are willing to examine them carefully, with open eyes and minds. The Norse should be commended for their wonderful way of describing that which they did not understand and for explaining in a beautiful, narrative fashion that which they did.

We will begin to explore Yggdrasill by considering the significance of the vivid physical visualization of the World Tree as described in the myths. We will then break the myth down into small, easily manageable parts: the springs, the worlds, the creatures, and, of course, the tree itself. We must begin with the physical aspects and then slowly peel back all the layers to reveal the true significance hidden in each of these symbols. For us to truly comprehend the realms of the World Tree, we must begin with a literal, simplistic description.

The great tree, Yggdrasill, is described as an incomprehensibly enormous ash. It has three roots that cradle three sets of three worlds each: Asgard, Vanaheim, and Ljossalfheim; Midgard, Jotunheim, and Svartalfheim; and Niflheim, Hel, and Muspellheim. Under each group of worlds lie the three springs of water, Hvergelmir, Mimir, and Urd. A horrid dragon gnaws constantly at the lowest root and he is helped by many different smaller serpents of various names. In the spring of Hvergelmir, two swans continually swim. Above all of these creatures, springs, worlds, and roots is a carpet of grass from which the upper reaches of Yggdrasill arise. Countless bees are found drinking dew from the grasses. They will eventually make honey from this moisture. Stags and goats can be seen feeding on the young shoots and leaves of the great tree. Above, in the very summit of the tree, an eagle sits, with a hawk perched between his eyes. A squirrel runs busily up and down the trunk, taking messages back and forth between the eagle and the dragon. It is said that Yggdrasill is infinite, and will always remain so.

To truly discover the mysteries hidden beneath the surface, we must investigate both the actual and metaphorical aspects of the Guardian Tree. While we will uncover much of the mystery in this section, the study of Yggdrasill is the work of a lifetime. Each leaf is a new page of life, each drop of dew is a new future awaiting birth, and each blade of grass is a new thought awaiting fruition. This book is merely a stepping-stone along the way. Hopefully, it will lead to the discovery of the wondrous beauty and spiritual enlightenment of the World Tree.

SPRINGS

At the very bottom of Yggdrasill's three-root system lie three springs, one at the very foot of each root. They are named, respectively, the springs of Hvergelmir, Mimir, and Urd. The obvious reason for the springs is that water is needed for any plant or animal species to grow and flourish. These springs, however, are not merely for nourishment. They hold various other symbolic meanings.

Hvergelmir: The spring of Hvergelmir is at the foot of the lowest root. In this spring, two swans gracefully swim. These swans are the ancestors of their species and are beautiful representations of the birth of all species. There are twelve rivers that flow from this spring into the world of Midgard. These rivers give sustenance to the Earth. This spring is the lifeblood of Yggdrasill and of all the worlds, the universe, and all creatures dwelling therein. Hvergelmir symbolizes nourishment and life. It is the primal source of all beginnings. It is responsible not only for the nurturing of the universe itself, but most notably for the nurturing of all newly created worlds and beings. The spring of Hvergelmir is the metaphoric breast of a loving mother offered to her cherished infant, and the arms of a proud father tenderly cradling his newborn child.

Mimir: The spring of Mimir is at the foot of the second root of Yggdrasill. According to all of the legends, this spring holds Mimir's head. As discussed in chapter 5, Mimir had great wisdom due, in no small part, to an incredible memory of past events. Even though he was brutally killed by the gods of the Vanir, his head was preserved through the use of herbs and charms by Odhinn. Odhinn then placed Mimir's head in this spring. Through the use of magic, he was able to give Mimir's head the gift of speech. This enabled Odhinn to increase his own wisdom by requesting Mimir's council. It must be remembered that Freya gave Odhinn the gift of magic. This spring also holds the runes for which Odhinn sacrificed himself to himself to gain. These runes are the very essence of all universal wisdom. The spring of Mimir represents wisdom, knowledge, memory, and magic, throughout all ages and dimensions. This is not merely a humanistic or godly attribute. The spring holds the wisdom, knowledge, memory, and magic of the universe and beyond.

Urd: The spring of Urd sits at the foot of the highest root. This is the spring of destiny and the home of the Norns. It is the water source from which the Norns water Yggdrasill's roots and limbs daily. The Norns also make clay from this water, which they pack onto the trunk of the Guardian Tree. This clay eventually falls from the limbs and trunk, the moisture in it creating dew on the grass below. The spring of Urd is where the Aesir gather to hold daily councils to gain the Norns' insight into the future. This spring obviously signifies destiny, as it is decided here what will be done concerning divine and mortal events. Also, it shows the reactions to previous actions throughout all lifetimes. This is seen through the constant supply of nourishment to the tree by the Norns. This is a circular concept that is often difficult for modern minds to comprehend. Basically, it is the idea of death causing life, thoughts causing action, and wisdom resulting in strength. Every action results in a reaction, no matter how great or small.

These springs together represent the lifeline not only of humans, but also of the Aesir, the Earth, the planets and stars, the entire universe, and the unknowable beyond. creation must happen for life to begin; nourishment is needed for life to prosper. Knowledge and instinct are necessary for survival, whereas wisdom and magic are necessary for personal evolution and spiritual growth. Death is the catalyst that continually restarts the process. Destiny enables us to see these cycles repeat themselves constantly and, in some cases, can be used to shape the process into a more positive outcome.

WORLDS

Connected to each of the three roots of Yggdrasill is a group of three worlds, making for a total of nine. These worlds have significant meaning in a metaphoric sense and should be explored thoroughly, as they will greatly impact our study of the Goddess of the North.

Niflheim: Above the first spring, Hvergelmir, the third root of Yggdrasill plunges through the world called Niflheim. This is the world of cold, mist, and snow. In the legend of the creation of Midgard, this world helped mold Ginnungagap, where Midgard, Earth, was formed. Niflheim is the complete opposite of warmth and fire, but is still necessary for the creation of life. Niflheim symbolizes the barren womb of the mind and body before the seeds of thought and life are gently stirred into being. It is the resting stage of physical and mental beginnings.

Hel: Niflheim is connected to the world of the dead, Hel. As discussed earlier, it is ruled by a giantess of the same name. All those mortals not immediately chosen to occupy the goddesses' or gods' halls travel here and are sometimes reincarnated. This is shown through the legend of Balder discussed in chapter 5. Hel also represents unconscious thought, as it emerges through deep sleep. Interestingly enough, the world of Hel holds within it nine other worlds. This is a wonderful attempt by early people to explain the concept of infinity. On this level, the further one travels in Hel, the more dimensions one uncovers. Hel symbolizes the concept of life created through death: regeneration. Hel could very well be a representation of Ginnungagap, as it is connected to both Niflheim and Muspellheim. Because of this, Hel may be symbolic of the void in which the roots of creation are conceived.

Muspellheim: This is the world of fire, located on the same level as Hel and Niflheim. This is the world that, combined with Niflheim, created life in the nothingness of Ginnungagap, the space in which Midgard was formed. It is the sunlight that helps crops to grow, species to be created, and evolution to take place. It is the fire of Muspellheim that brings the gift of warming and thought to the womb of Niflheim. It creates the atmosphere for fertilization. This is the realm of awakening mental and physical awareness.

Jotunheim: Above the spring of Mimir lies the world of Jotunheim. This is the world of the giants, who are constantly at war with the Aesir. The giants are so busy trying to battle and steal, they have no time for developing their own world or lives. Very few have the desire of expanding intellectual consciousness. They show little desire for spiritual growth. They do exhibit desire for material possessions, but usually only those that belong to others. This world symbolizes the stagnation that can come from a lack of mental and spiritual growth. It is the opposite of Midgard, as it lacks the ability and the desire to evolve. As the giants are immensely strong, this world also warns us how powerful the state of stagnation can become if allowed to mature. The giantesses, on the other hand, show us that stagnation can indeed be broken. Spiritual evolution is the result.

Midgard: On the same level of Jotunheim is Midgard. This is the planet Earth. This is the world of new beginnings and the creation of new species. It is the world of physical action, experimentation, happenstance, and growth. Midgard represents the beginning of spiritual awareness. The pursuit for wisdom commences here. Unfortunately, one of Midgard's species sometimes shows a tendency toward stagnation and greed. This is due, in part, to the connection of Midgard to Jotunheim. It is also due to a lack of initiative in bettering oneself with one's given gifts. Midgard is the catalyst that is the result of life being created by Niflheim and Muspellheim in the void of Ginnungagap through the combination of ice and fire. This is where all mortals dwell, and where the Aesir and goddesses come to visit. Midgard is essentially the symbol of new life within the universe.

Svartalfheim: Svartalfheim is the third world on this middle plane. It is occupied by the dark elves and dwarves. Both groups are fiercely protective of their homes, families, and communities. These creatures hide from the light of day, either deep in the forests or far beneath the Earth's surface. They have strong skills and are renowned for their magical and metal-working abilities. The dark elves and dwarves are both credited with having vast riches. This world symbolizes the rewards of hard work through physical labor.

Asgard: On the highest level lies Asgard, right above the spring of Urd. This is the home of the Aesir. Asgard, the realm where many mortals live after death on Midgard, is connected to the two lower groups of worlds by the rainbow bridge, Bifrost. This enables the Aesir and select mortals to travel to and from the other worlds. Asgard is the world of idealism and goals achieved. This is the reward of spiritual strength gained through honorable action.

Vanaheim: Connected to Asgard is Vanaheim, the home of the Vanir and their various halls. Mortals may be chosen to live here as well, after their death. As the Vanir are credited with the fertility, love, and sexuality of Midgard, so too is this realm credited with the spiritual fertility, love, and sexuality of the universe. As Freya is connected with prosperity and magical workings, Vanaheim can also be associated with these attributes.

Ljossalfheim: The third world connected to these two is Ljossalfheim. This is the world of the light elves, who, of course, are the opposite of the dark elves. The light elves are on a spiritual plane, as opposed to a physical one. Their work encompasses advising and helping mortals in quests of a higher, more spiritual nature. This is the world of conscious thought and the ability to see these thoughts develop into positive action.

One obvious implication here is that the concepts of mental awareness and growth belong to the lowest level of worlds, physical action and experimentation to the next, and prosperity and spiritual realization to the highest. This idea is seen in the journey of Balder. He lived on a spiritual plane in Asgard as an Aesir and son of Frigg and Odhinn. He was killed and proceeded to be bound in the mental state of Hel. Upon his release after Ragnarok, he again walked the world of Midgard as a physical being. He then renewed his residence in Asgard. Metaphorically, this can be seen as the ideal of all three realms, for Balder encompasses them all. By the end of his ordeal, Balder actually returns to the beginning of the cycle to become a living god once again.[1]

Yggdrasill is the *axis mundi* of these worlds and springs. We should note the use of the prime numbers three and nine in this myth. This could have been a way for the Norse people to comprehend the infinity of the universe. It would be inaccurate to assume that they thought these were the only planets, because we know they used the planets and stars for navigation—demonstrating exceptional skill. It is totally possible, however, to see the numbers nine and three used metaphorically to describe a concept they could not grasp rationally, much less explain.

Above these worlds lies a vast, rolling ocean of lush green grass. It canopies all of the nine worlds. It is the heavens we can see with our eyes. It also partially hides from our sight the World Tree, Yggdrasill, and all of the wondrous creatures who inhabit its glorious upper and lower reaches.

CREATURES

The creatures of Yggdrasill are very diverse: two swans, a dragon named Nidhogg, serpents (Goin, Moin, Grabak, Grafvollud, Ofnir, and Svafnir), bees, goats, stags (Dain, Dvalin, Duneyr, and

---

1 The concepts discussed under the Springs and Worlds are from my own perceptions, based upon intense meditation and the study of other works. There is no doubt, however, that Edred Thorsson's and Kveldulf Gundarsson's magical and runic writings played a large role in my observations. It was their texts, among others, that initially led me to realize the deeper revelations that Yggdrasill holds. These texts are listed in the Bibliography.

Durathror), a hawk named Vedrfolnir, an eagle, and a squirrel named Ratatosk.

Swans: The two swans have been mentioned previously. They swim in the spring of Hvergelmir and are the ancestors of their species. They represent the beauty of all creation. The swans are also beautiful symbols of perfect duality. They exemplify the genuine balance of female and male. As with positive and negative forces, creation and life are only possible with both male and female. These two creatures show us the perfect harmony, equality, and beauty of true partnership and love.

Niddhogg, Serpents: Near the spring of Hvergelmir, the fearsome dragon Niddhogg continually gnaws at the lowest root of Yggdrasill. Because he embodies death and negativity, he seeks the extermination of all that is alive. Niddhogg is the destructive force that fights the creative ability of this spring. He attempts to eradicate the birth of mental awareness that begins in the realm of Muspellheim. He strives to stop the birth of all new worlds and species. However, Niddhogg obviously does not realize that, if he ever did succeed in this destruction, he would actually be condemning himself to death without the possibility of rebirth. Niddhogg is assisted in his attempts to destroy the Guardian Tree by the serpents, who are, most likely, infant dragons. These serpents, following the example set by their father, are a symbolic attempt at explaining how pure negativity can draw others to it. This is usually the path the weak-of-heart tend to follow.

Bees: Above the realm of Asgard, there is a thick carpet of dew-covered grass from which the trunk of Yggdrasill ascends. Bees hover and feed off of this dew. This action could be seen as destructive, as this removal of dew forces the Norns' to replenish the water supply to Yggdrasill daily. This same activity, however, has a positive side. The bees produce honey from the dew. Called honeydew, this honey is highly prized by the Aesir for the mead it produces. These bees represent diligence and hard work. Through their creation of honeydew, they symbolize how one can achieve rewards through effort. These bees show us that even the smallest or lowest of species has a place within the great web of life.

Stags, Goats: The stags and goats eat the leaves and new shoots of Yggdrasill. This is obviously nourishment for their bodies, although this consumption can certainly be seen as destructive to the Guardian Tree. Without these creatures constantly feeding, the tree would stop producing new foliage, causing Yggdrasill to eventually become stagnant, for the need to nurture would no longer be necessary. This gives added credence to the concept of death sustaining life, for, even as the leaves and shoots are being destroyed to nurture these animals, Yggdrasill is constantly replenishing itself through the growth of even more.

Vedrfolnir: Vedrfolnir is the hawk who sits quietly perched between an eagle's eyes in the uppermost branches of Yggdrasill. While this may symbolize many things, the hawk may simply be the shadow of the larger eagle. This could explain the desire of all humankind to continually better themselves in order to achieve a higher level of life and being. The hawk is obviously close to obtaining this goal, for he does sit at the very crown of Yggdrasill. Vedrfolnir may also indicate the concept of additional sight. The eagle, through the hawk, may be able to view life through different eyes and from different perspectives. The hawk may also be an advisor to the eagle, as Jacob Grimm notes by calling Vedrfolnir the eagle's "hidden counsellor."[2]

Eagle: The eagle is normally considered the greatest of birds. It is independent, large, farseeing, beautiful, graceful, and an expert hunter. Many early religions gave significant value to the eagle, believing it to be a bird of the heavens. This is a very important aspect to consider. The eagle roosting in Yggdrasill is unnamed, even though it is credited with having much knowledge and wisdom. One must reflect on why this animal is unnamed, as all of the other individual creatures of Yggdrasill have been given

---

[2] Jacob Grimm, *Teutonic Mythology*, vol. 2, James Steven Stallybrass, trans., 4th ed. (New York: Dover, 1966), p. 796.

names. It may be that his name has been lost over the years, or it may be that this eagle is all names, or rather, symbolizes the greatest possible achievements of Aesir and mortals. Naming this creature would essentially bind its dimensions, and it is obvious that, on certain levels, this eagle represents idealism and godhood. It also symbolizes light and goodness, for it perches at the top of the tree in full splendor. This eagle may be connected with Hraesvelg, a giant who wears an eagle skin and is responsible for creating the winds of Midgard through the flapping of his wings.[3]

Ratatosk: Ratatosk, the squirrel, is an interesting little creature in the Nordic cosmos. He runs up and down the tree passing supposedly belittling messages between the eagle and the dragon. He is an obvious symbol of duality. Ratatosk represents the constant battle of positive and negative. He is the catalyst that cause these two principles to clash. This squirrel strikes a balance between the eagle and the dragon, not allowing the scales to tip in favor of one or the other.

THE TREE

We have discussed at length the visual and metaphorical description of Yggdrasill—the springs, the worlds, and all of the creatures connected with it. These are all very important aspects of the World Tree, but they should not be allowed to outshadow the symbolic and metaphorical magnificence of Yggdrasill, itself.

It is necessary, for clarification purposes, to visualize the Guardian Tree as described in the mythology. Imagine a massive three-root system thrusting downward through countless miles of dark, rich, fertile soil. Eventually, each huge root tapers to an end, one above the other. At the end of each root lies a calm spring, brimming with pure, clear water. Right above each of these three springs, the three roots plunge separately through three worlds: Asgard, Jotunheim, and Niflheim. The beautiful

---

[3] Snorri Sturluson, *Edda*, Anthony Faulkes, trans., 2nd ed. (London: Everyman's Library, 1992), p. 20.

rainbow bridge, Bifrost, connects these three worlds. Each of these worlds has two other worlds on the same plane, making a total of nine. Above these worlds, the three roots continue rising, seemingly forever. The roots eventually entwine to form an enormous trunk that rises out of a thick, vibrant carpet of grass. Here we are finally able to see the World Tree in all its glory and splendor. The massive branches ascend so far into the heavens that we are unable to see the actual tips of the limbs. The sea of grass extends far past the horizon. Animals abound and bees fly. Dew, originating from one of the springs, drips from the leaves. Yggdrasill is a majestic sight to behold. We will now descend again to the very ends of the roots.

Roots: The roots are literal connections to the nine worlds of the Norse cosmos. Coupled with the rainbow bridge, Bifrost, the roots allow us to travel to different planes on a shamanic level. We may choose to remain in Midgard or become stagnant in Jotunheim, delve into the unconsciousness of Hel or rise to the spiritual richness of Asgard. These roots are always available for us to travel. We have only to discover the hidden doorway within ourselves. This would only be the beginning of such a journey, however.

Grass: If one has discovered the innate ability to navigate through these worlds, one may choose to attempt to climb the roots to the even higher grassy heavens above. This would indeed be a major feat, for the meadow of grass actually separates the nine worlds from Yggdrasill itself. This implies that the worlds and springs are mere diluted images of a grander level of life, just waiting to be discovered and experienced.

Trunk: In the middle of this flowing sea of grass rises the great trunk of Yggdrasill. This is the very strength and backbone of the tree. It is able to endure all hardships, including unimaginable winds and even the horrible cataclysm of Ragnarok. This trunk should not be viewed as merely a pillar of Yggdrasill. We must remember the lessons of the three lower worlds—Niflheim, Hel, and Muspellheim—and the instruction of the bees. Lower and smaller does not necessarily mean negative or devoid of meaning. We know the trunk shields a woman and a man during Ragnarok, so this tells us we should look within. We already know the wisdom that comes from inner exploration of ourselves. This holds true for the World Tree, as well. As the Guardian Tree is infinite, each growth ring found within the trunk indicates a new level of consciousness. While we may never reach the actual core of the World Tree, we can certainly gain much spiritual strength from exploring within, as well as without.

Foliage: The ever-renewing leaves and shoots of Yggdrasill may symbolize a variety of different concepts. Nourishment and regeneration have already been thoroughly discussed. The foliage may be an image of our souls, symbols of planets and stars, species extinct, and species impatiently awaiting creation. It may represent something as minute as a speck of dust, or as vast as an entire solar system.

Branches: The branches are yet another means to achieve a higher level of spirituality. Just as we are able to climb the roots, so too can we climb the branches to the very crown of Yggdrasill. This is what the squirrel, Ratatosk, teaches us. Through the complete balance of positive and negative, we can sit side-by-side with the eagle, overlooking all events and creatures below.

There is one other aspect of the legend of Yggdrasill that is rarely, if ever mentioned—the world from which the Guardian Tree grows. We can speculate as to why this is, but it is doubtful we would find an adequate answer. Nor does this neglect really matter in our exploration. The very idea of the existence of this world opens up another realm of possibilities absent from our previous examination.

The fact that the World Tree has roots and the nine worlds are separated from Yggdrasill by a carpet of grass indicates that there is indeed another, larger world from which both the grass and tree grow. The nine worlds and three springs residing in this world can be seen as seeds in gestation. If this is indeed the case, then the gods, humans, and all other species are also simply babies awaiting adolescence.

Yggdrasill, although described simplistically as a great tree, actually characterizes all that is both knowable and unknowable within the universe and whatever lies beyond. Each part of the tree, from the roots to the leaves, symbolizes different representations of the known and unknown heavens. As the layers are lifted, these same aspects symbolize the Aesir, mortals, creatures, and every other being and substance known to humankind. As more layers are lifted, we can see the symbolism of the mental, physical, and spiritual self, and how one can complement or hinder the other. As the canopy of the World Tree metaphorically shades the universe and its roots support the worlds, so, too, does Yggdrasill metaphorically shelter our lives and our inner goals of wisdom and knowledge. As even more layers are lifted, we can see, from the mixture of opposites, ice and fire, the eventual creation of Midgard and all it encompasses. Yggdrasill is a metaphor for all aspects of life known and unknown, inner and outer. Through its destructive and generative abilities, it illustrates the cycle of life and death and how each is needed to create and nourish the other.

The myth of Yggdrasill is a wonderfully beautiful allegory of the cycles of life on all levels. In it, we can see the many different phases of life: birth, growth, stagnation, thought, wisdom, magic, death, and regeneration. This cycle is easily seen in the way the tree is minutely developed from bottom to top. Even at the upper level of idealism and godhood, the eagle flaps his wings, causing the winds to shake and bend the tree. In essence, this causes the cycle to begin yet again.

TWELVE

MOTHER

Right after the conception of my son, I had a powerful, visionary dream so vivid that I still remember it clearly today, years later. Although I didn't know it at the time, this dream indicated the spiritual journey I would soon be making. Even in my worst periods of despair, this dream offered me the keys I would need to open the gateways to emotional and spiritual enlightenment.

In this dream, I was comfortably perched upon a huge limb of a tree so massive I could not even begin to see the uppermost branches. Seated beside me was my patron god, Odhinn. Interestingly, he kept shape-changing into the character Gandolf, from the famous Tolkien series.[1] I, on the other hand, kept shape-changing into the little hobbit Bilbo. All of a sudden, while these peculiar acts of shape-changing were occurring, I/Bilbo manifested as two beings, myself and a beautiful, baby boy. All three of us, for there were indeed the three of us at this point, were fishing in a circular well far beneath us. This well, located right next to the trunk of the tree, was filled with leaping, orange-red flames. The dream was so peaceful and comforting that I still use it as a meditative tool.

---

[1] J.R.R. Tolkien, *The Hobbit*, rev. ed. (New York: Ballantine, 1966). See also *The Fellowship of the Ring: The Lord of the Rings, Part One* (New York: Ballantine, 1965), *The Two Towers: The Lord of the Rings, Part Two* (New York: Ballantine, 1965), and *The Return of the King: The Lord of the Rings, Part Three* (New York: Ballantine, 1965). All references to the Tolkien series, Gandolf, and Bilbo are from the above texts.

Needless to say, upon awakening from this peaceful interlude, I immediately knew I was pregnant, which I verified a few weeks later. I also knew I was going to have a baby boy, which certainly came to pass. The raging, colorfully intense fire within the circular well totally mystified me, however. I simply had no idea what the well, the fire, or the act of fishing could possibly signify. I had no doubt that these three images were extremely potent symbols of energy, but energy for what purpose? This dilemma weighed on my mind for many months. Eventually, in pure frustration, I was forced to put this question aside for later contemplation.

Many months later, I experienced the most miraculous event of my life, the birth of my child. This experience was twofold: on the one hand, I was overcome with emotion at the young life in my arms; on the other, I began to feel a budding need to know the Goddess more intimately. While I held my baby one night, rocking and crooning to put him to sleep, I considered the existence of a primordial goddess of the Norse Tradition. This thought became a driving desire. As a new mother and a mature woman who had just experienced a wonderful and in some ways, catastrophic life transition, I began to question whether I was indeed in the right spiritual tradition. I was blessed that special night, not only with an insight into the Goddess in the historical framework of Nordic studies, but also with Her wonderful enveloping embrace of love and warmth. Furthermore, I was finally given an insight into what my divinely given dream actually symbolized.

Odhinn, my patron god, gifted me with the spectacular sight of the utter magnificence of the Mother aspect of the Goddess. I finally discovered I was actually cradled deep within Her enveloping embrace, not only in my inspiring dream, but in the reality of my everyday life. I also finally figured out the mystery behind the well, the fire, and the fishing. They were indications of the turmoil I was about to experience, and symbols of the strength and ability the Goddess and Odhinn knew I had within myself to complete this particular journey. These two deities lovingly and trustingly shared this vision with me for my own personal sake, and granted me the ability and desire to share with others who wished to know the truth of the Goddess of the North.

Yggdrasill is indeed the Mother aspect of the Goddess of the North. This was the insight given to me by the Goddess and Odhinn in my prophetic dream, the nudge the Goddess Herself gave me on that lonely night as I contemplated Her existence. While much of this chapter is a discussion of my own perceptions, it is also founded on intense research in the field of Norse studies and in other related fields.

In chapter 10, we examined Snorri Sturluson's claim that all Asyniur were one goddess. We pieced together the many different feminine fragments into a cohesive whole. Why Sturluson did not himself specify or go into more detail on this issue we can only speculate. It is almost certain he did indeed know the answer, but decided to be as vague as possible about it. He may even have thought that a more thorough study of the Norse goddesses was simply unimportant, although this seems doubtful. We must remember that Christianity was fairly new to Iceland, Sturluson's homeland, and the repercussions for practicing heathenism were extreme. As a consequence, he and other notable scholars have left this mystery for us to examine and decipher. Luckily, we have been left a good deal of documentation to verify with our personal perceptions and intuition, allowing us finally to realize an in-depth understanding of the Goddess. This admittedly mind-boggling task will enable us finally to achieve a binding truth of the Goddess of the North.

Needless to say, Yggdrasill is rarely, if ever, discussed as an actual deity, feminine or masculine. While the Guardian Tree is clearly a metaphor for the feminine divine, as evidenced through Yggdrasill's ability to give birth, create, and nurture, the idea that Yggdrasill represents a deity has not been explored at any length. The Guardian Tree has always been viewed simply as a tree. Granted, Yggdrasill is indisputably a sacred tree symbolizing the entire Norse cosmos, and is duly respected as such. We have to question, however, why Yggdrasill has not been thoroughly studied as a deity.

The very name Yggdrasill may mean "Odhinn's horse," as Ygg is another name used to describe Odhinn. The World Tree has, thus, sometimes been interpreted by modern-day scholars as a mere object, and not as a divine being. It also alludes to the

possibility that the greatness of Yggdrasill is due to Odhinn, and
not the World Tree's own magnificence. It is important to note
this name most certainly derives from Odhinn's sacrifice on the
Guardian Tree in order to possess the magical runes. As we have
discussed earlier, Odhinn's magical knowledge was taught to
him by Freya. The myth describing his sacrifice of himself to
himself obviously portrayed an event that happened much later
than the creation of Midgard in the Norse legends. Also, it
is known that Yggdrasill is infinite, whereas Odhinn is not. It is
probable that this naming of the tree with reference to Odhinn
has, in and of itself, precluded any serious research into the
being of Yggdrasill. This may be another example of the displacement of the Goddess by Odhinn, begun by the intermingled Nordic peoples and, later, by the advent of monotheism.[2]
This being the case, Yggdrasill most likely had another name
that has been lost in antiquity, or was previously called the
Guardian or World Tree. This practice of ignoring Yggdrasill's
feminine qualities has been perpetuated by the thought of, and
actual portrayal of, the Nordic Tradition as male-dominated.
This has led many to ignore the feminine in order to concentrate solely on the masculine.

As we can see, Yggdrasill perfectly exemplifies the divine
feminine Mother aspect of all life. From before the creation to
after the devastation of Ragnarok, the Mother Goddess shows us
in exquisite detail the irreplaceable gifts of birth and nurturing.
Even death is simply the logical transformation to rebirth. Audmula, the sacred aurochs, is an obvious extension of Yggdrasill.
Audmula nurses the first frost giant, Ymir, thereby granting him
the unique ability to reproduce completely by himself. Even
through his brutal death at the hands of Odhinn and his two
brothers, Ymir's body is shaped into another breathtaking new
form of existence. During Ragnarok, Yggdrasill is not burned or
even singed by Surt the fire giant's destroying fire. The Mother
protects a group of men and women deep within Herself so that
humankind can again walk the Earth and flourish. It can also be

---

[2] Hilda Ellis Davidson, *Roles of the Northern Goddess* (New York: Routledge, 1998), pp.
147, 182–190.

assumed that She protects the nine worlds and the young gods prophesied to survive Ragnarok.

The tale of Yggdrasill is a resplendent depiction of the illuminating being of the Mother Goddess. The World Tree is not just an illustration of the early Norse people's use of creative imagination, it is a perfect example of their deep spiritual awareness of and reverence for the Mother aspect of the Goddess. This beautiful and radiant vision of Her is certainly the result of many ancient shamanic journeys, kept alive through oral and, later, through written tradition. This intricate insight into the very character of the Mother Goddess, as much as we are able to know Her, is reflective of Her generosity through the gift of these wonderful visions. She is not in any way comparable to the controlling deity with which many of us have been raised from childhood. She does not punish us for breaking certain rules not applicable to our lives. She does not rule our personal fate with an iron, unbending hand. She simply is. She does, however, offer us many irreplaceable gifts.

We have seen, through studying the metaphor of Yggdrasill's three springs, the underlying power of the element of water. These springs represent giving birth and the moisture needed for creation, as well as being the very root of knowledge, wisdom, destiny, and magic. This water courses through our veins, shields us in the womb, quenches our thirst, and gives life to numerous species so we may have life. Water nourishes, cleanses, and provides the habitat for the seeds of dreams to become reality. All we need to do is take a simple sip from this fountain of everlasting benevolence.

The Mother Goddess' three mammoth roots reach deep into a vast world. They are the cradling arms supporting the nine worlds hidden far beneath the surface of this massive world. As these roots cradle the nine worlds, so too do they cradle us. Though our lives often seem senseless, we can always remember that She is with us, ready to support and cheer our next fledgling steps. These roots also symbolize spiritual stairways to higher levels of being. Through both inner and outer workings, we enable ourselves to climb to ever-loftier dimensions.

The Mother Goddess' nine worlds are the literal representation of Her children, therefore they also represent the aspect of the Daughter. These worlds are the very seeds exhibiting Her special essence of Motherhood. They are Her children in all phases of growth. These worlds also show us the incredible power of the Earth, the raw physical power needed to compliment the attributes of water. These two elements are the catalyst that forms the environment in which the seeds of creation are born. Each of these worlds has a different definition, ranging from stagnation all the way to the divine. They symbolize very important lessons for us as humans—lessons we must learn to further our personal emotional and spiritual growth. Through this exploration, the Goddess has given us the opportunity to throw away inner self-made walls and ascend to another realm of being.

The numerous creatures of Yggdrasill are so very diverse, in so many different unfathomable ways, that they could fill an entire set of separate texts. The contemplation of each animal should actually end up being an individual journey, although we will certainly discuss their more notable characteristics.

The pure negativity of the dragon, Nidhogg, and his infant serpents is evident, as they are constantly at work attempting to destroy the Mother Goddess' very being. The stags and goats essentially do the same thing, as they continually eat of Her leaves and limbs. We will eventually realize, however, that without these seemingly destructive creatures, She would indeed become stagnant. Both positive and negative forces are needed to achieve a true balance. Without this constant interplay, She would have no need to create, nor would She have anything to nourish. These creatures may also be a simple metaphor for Her ability to nurture new life. As we know, an infant's prime objective in life is to eat and sleep. It must be nourished to grow to more developed levels.

The unnamed eagle is the exact opposite of the personifications of the dragon, serpents, stags, and goats. He perches in the Mother's highest branches, observing all events, creatures, and worlds below. The eagle represents the positive force, in contrast to the creatures of destruction. He characterizes our souls at their most perfect. He has no need to nourish his physical self from the Mother Goddess' bounty, for he has achieved the immortality we all hope one day to possess. He is content to sit within Her branches. Interestingly, through the flapping of his wings, the eagle is also the catalyst that causes the winds to roar across the nine worlds and shake Yggdrasill's limbs. This suggests that his search for higher realms is never complete. We are just able to glimpse a resting stage, symbolized by both the eagle and the hawk who rests between the eagle's eyes. This implies a period of rest prior to the next journey to reach levels unimaginable to us in this existence. The eagle is a metaphor for air, as seen through his creation of the winds. This demonstrates the Mother Goddess' own control over the element of air, as it is needed, along with food and water, to sustain all of the creatures on Earth.

The squirrel, Ratatosk, is a seemingly insignificant creature in the Norse cosmos, but he is the actual symbol of the balancing center of the pendulum motion created by positive and negative energies. These two forces are represented by the eagle and the dragon Nidhogg. Ratatosk shows us our own true human nature. We, as mortals, tend to spend most of our lives involuntarily fighting these two ideals. We begin a climb to a higher level of achievement and then fall back to an even lower level of what we perceive to be failure. Ratatosk teaches us perseverance, for even when we fall, the Mother Goddess is always there to cradle us, nurture us, lift our spirits, and show us, through our very thoughts and dreams, a new path to climb.

The countless bees dwelling at the grassy level of the Guardian Tree cannot be ignored. The Mother loves and reveres all of Her offspring, regardless of how little or insignificant we humans may deem some to be. These tiny creatures, through their neverending diligence, produce the honey used to make the famous mead of wisdom. Through this symbology, the Mother Goddess shows us that each of our actions has a definite reaction. Something very tiny may have a huge effect on our lives or the lives of others. The Goddess is reminding us never to ignore the small things in life, for each thing has its special place in the undulating folds of existence. The products of any endeavor, no matter how diminutive, will certainly either benefit or hinder another.

Yggdrasill is, in actuality, just the first part of the very essence of our search. She represents the wondrous aspect of the motherhood of the Goddess. She is not only the symbol of the universe, She *is* the universe. Her infinite branches protect the heavens and Her huge roots delve deep into the nine worlds. She shelters and nourishes the various animals dwelling under and within Her great limbs and even tolerates the attempted destruction of the dragon gnawing at Her roots. She produces the fruit of immortality, symbolized by apples, and supplies the Aesir and mortals with the mead of wisdom. Within the springs at the foot of each root, She holds all possible knowledge, wisdom, destiny, and magic available to those who are brave enough to seek. The spaces between Her branches are Ginnungagap, the void of patient emptiness awaiting birth. Her trunk is the womb that protects and nurtures Lif and Leifthrasir, representing the women and men who survive Ragnarok.

The Mother Goddess encompasses all of our lives in all conceivable facets. She is the canopy of the heavens and the bed of earth. She is our nourishment. She gifts us with knowledge and the ability to gain further wisdom, if only we apply ourselves. She shows us that, even through heartrending strife, we can ultimately succeed. She is the void, creation, womb, birth-giver, nurturer, teacher, priestess, life-giver, death-giver, and She bestows upon us the irreplaceable gift of rejuvenation. The Mother Goddess has always been and will always be, throughout infinity. Even when our human shells rest in Her womb, our souls aspire to climb another branch of Herself. Through Her own destruction and replenishment, She shows us Her gift of eternal life.

While we have discovered much through our search for the Goddess of the North, it has been made quite apparent that She is a threefold Goddess. Many comparable traditions tend to see these three aspects as the Maiden, Matron, and Crone. While this particular naming is not applicable to the Nordic Tradition, the aspects of Daughter, Mother, and Grandmother are. Lineage plays a key role in the Norse philosophy—not due to prestige, but due, rather, to respect. It is very important to not only remember, but to honor one's ancestors. Therefore, the use of

Table 5. Humanization of the Mother.

Aspects	Mother
Human Given Name	Frigg
Human Names of Attributes	Fulla, Gna, Hlin, Idun, Lofn, Nerthus, Saga, Snotra, Sol, Syn, Vara, Vor
Daily Phase	Sun
Sun Phase	Day
Season	Summer
Guardian Association	Norns

Mother, Daughter, and Grandmother is representative of the Norse outlook and way of life.

We have already decided, through our previous exploration, that the documentation supports Frigg as the Mother, Freya as the Daughter, and Fjorgyn as the Grandmother. It also must be understood that the Goddess' three main aspects are as follows: Frigg as Yggdrasill, representing all that is knowable and unknowable; Fjorgyn as the big world, portraying Her earthly nature; and Freya as the nine worlds, symbolizing Her humanization. Even so, we must not ignore the seemingly less significant attributes of the Goddess, or else we will not be able to fully understand Her in all of Her greatness.

There are a few other aspects of the Mother Goddess that we must investigate before we can confidently go on to discuss the Daughter aspect of the Goddess of the North. These topics are clearly illustrated in Table 5. We have already hinted at the circular concept of time incorporating the nature of the Norse feminine divine. Through our investigation, we have encountered many different ideas to support this theory. What we now see is a definite circling effect of ideas. The best way to picture these concepts is to imagine a series of plates. As each idea expands, a larger plate is placed above a smaller one, and so on, until the ideas finally expand and contract into one huge vision. This vision will actually be a small plate, which, of course, will begin the cycle yet again.

These concepts begin with Frigg and expand to include her other attributes. These attributes then expand to encompass even more aspects, until eventually, Frigg narrows down again to become the huge neverending spiral that is Yggdrasill, the Mother Goddess Herself.

The very roots of the Mother are grounded deep within the realm of human comprehension, symbolized by the matronly figure of Frigg. She encompasses many of the attributes portrayed by humanity, including, but not limited to, wife, mother, and overseer of halls. As the queen of all goddesses and gods and the wife of the All-Father, Frigg is considered to have extensive power. She is a fitting female figure to be acknowledged as the goddess of mortal women and men. Because of this power, the early Norse people knew she had many other qualities, many of which were incomprehensible to our ancestors. To better understand this side of her, these tribes broke her nature down into various aspects, which they described by individual names. Eventually, these names came to represent less-developed goddesses. These names and associations remained firm in history, and the links showing their derivation from Frigg endured.

One of the more notable of these characterizations is embodied in the aspect of Sol, previously thought of as goddess of the Sun. This characterization shows us an important aspect of the Mother, and explains how the early people humanized the Sun to better understand her. As a representation of the Sun, the Mother incorporates that part of each day when the Sun is at her highest, illuminating the heavens and Earth with bright, vibrant light. This symbolizes the Mother Goddess' maturity, as the Sun has always been viewed by the Norse as a mature female being. It also explains the Mother's ability to provide nourishment to sustain Her various children. The Norse knew that the light of the Sun supported the growth of plants on Earth. Because of this correlation to the Sun, the Mother also incorporates the time we call day, as there would be no such concept without Her enlightenment. It is important to note that the Norse assigned the aspect of day to a male deity with the same name. This can cause confusion. Without the Sun, day would have no life or meaning. Basically, the Mother gives birth to day each morning as she passes the horizon, spreading Her shimmering rays of orange, yellow, and gold. She is the life behind the upcoming day.

From this mature orb of shimmering intense light, the season of summer takes its character. This is the pinnacle of the year, when the Sun and day spend most of their daily cycle within the circumference of our limited vision, lofting high in the sky. Summer is the season of rapid crop growth and eventual harvesting. It is the time of the warming of the waters and the earth. It is the season that allows the preservation of life through the continuance of growth. It should be noted that the Norse acknowledged only three seasons—spring, summer, and winter. They did not conceive of autumn as we do today. Autumn was simply a sign indicating the death of summer and the birth of winter.

The last entry in Table 5 is the group of divine women whom the Norse people named the Norns. These feminine deities control the Orlog, or destiny, of all worlds and the life therein. There are three easily discernible aspects of this Nordic concept: the past, the present, and—the end result of both—the unforeseeable future. These phases are represented by the names of the three primary Norns: Urd, Verdandi, and Skuld.

The attribute of destiny falls exclusively in the province of the Mother Goddess. Destiny is only available to those who have been blessed with the irreplaceable gift of life. The past is our marvelous birth into the realm of the human species. The present incorporates all we have personally accomplished with the extraordinary gifts the Mother has so kindly bestowed upon each one of us. The unknowable future is our continued receipt and cherishing of these sacred gifts, as well as the ability to grow and enhance our lives. This unfathomable future also necessarily includes, but is certainly not limited to, the eventual regeneration we will all experience as the ultimate gift from the Mother aspect of the Goddess of the North.

Regardless of our choice of names or attributes, the result is the same. The Norse people, through their intimate relationship with the Goddess, gave us, their descendants, the answer to our question. We now know that there is indeed a primordial Norse goddess, the Goddess of the North. It is up to us to use Her gift of wisdom and inner contemplation to discover for ourselves what the ancient people knew and that by which they lived. Many documents, artifacts, and myths are lost to us forever, due to the advent of Christianity and the inescapable, destructive forces of nature—which are, of course, the Goddess Herself. Many relevant clues did survive, however, most importantly the glorious allegory of Yggdrasill, which has lived on in our libraries and bookstores, patiently waiting for us to rediscover the truth for ourselves. Our Mother Goddess did not abandon us, but has been content to await our rebirth into Her loving arms.

While the tale of Yggdrasill has been our leading clue into the truth of the Goddess of the North, the Guardian Tree is only one of three main aspects of Her divine being. We will now explore the second aspect of the Goddess—the Daughter.

THIRTEEN

DAUGHTER

The personality of the Daughter is ultimately character-ized by the nine known worlds of Yggdrasill. As stated earlier, these worlds are symbols of the children of the Mother aspect and, therefore, are logically embodied in the being of the Daughter Goddess. These worlds are tiny, infantile seeds of new life within the immense domain of the Mother Goddess. These worlds, as mere specks of life tucked deep in the lowest reaches of Yggdrasill, also represent minute mirror reflections of a higher, unknown state of existence. In this light, we can see the symbology behind the nine worlds in both a physical and spiri-tual sense. They represent the egg awaiting fertilization, the fetus awaiting birth, the infant awaiting childhood, the child awaiting puberty, the adolescent awaiting adulthood, the adult awaiting the golden years, the elder awaiting death, the soul awaiting re-birth, and the soul becoming reborn.

Niflheim: The egg awaiting fertilization. At the foot of the Mother's lowest root lie the three worlds of Niflheim, Muspell-heim, and Hel. To the far north, Niflheim, the world of fiercely cold, misty darkness, is the force that created the foundation for the anticipated creation in the void of Ginnungagap. Therefore, it is in fact a representation of the Daughter Goddess awaiting fertilization so She can continue to evolve to the next plane of

life. This is perfectly exhibited by the primitive world to the
south, Muspellheim.

Muspellheim: The fetus awaiting birth. This evolution is flawlessly represented by the searing flames of Muspellheim, slowly
warming the ice of Niflheim. The moistness that results in the
blackness of Ginnungagap provides the perfect atmosphere for
the beginnings of creation. These two worlds show us the natural
attraction of two opposites, and the perfect balance that, combined, they can achieve. Fertilization occurs and the new life, or
fetus, symbolized on a divine level by the Daughter, begins impatiently to await further growth.

Hel: The infant awaiting childhood. The world of Hel depicts
the actual birth of the Daughter Goddess at this early stage of
what the majority of us view as life. Human infants are unable to
physically realize their thoughts without assistance. This is a
prime example of the adult dream state, for, without awakening
and physically implementing thoughts, dreams will not become
reality unless they are prophetic. And like all newly born creatures, the Daughter is rapidly developing and increasingly ready
to approach the next emerging phase of spiritual growth, which
is represented by the three worlds above Niflheim, Muspellheim,
and Hel.

Jotunheim: The child awaiting puberty. The Mother's second
highest root plunges through the three worlds of Jotunheim,
Midgard, and Svartalfheim. These are the worlds symbolizing
the varying stages of childhood. In this phase, the Daughter is
still fairly impatient. All of us can remember the stagnation we
felt as we waited for the life transition into the eagerly anticipated, wondrously new and exciting world of puberty.

The child awaiting puberty is represented exceedingly well
by the male giant population of Jotunheim, for these creatures are
always at odds with others and even themselves. The giants desire growth, but are unsure of how to attain it. They are unable to
learn that, at this stage in their lives, all they can do is wait, while

looking inward to gain mental, emotional, and spiritual growth to balance their physical state and, in turn, enable further growth.

This facet of the Daughter Goddess' growth—or rather, stagnation—is best described by considering Her long rest in winter, anxiously awaiting Her rebirth into the luscious time of spring. The giants are normally described as living in a harsh, cold climate, so this seasonal metaphor is an apt description of this period of the Daughter's symbolic growth.

Midgard: The adolescent awaiting adulthood. The Daughter Goddess is a perfect characterization of both the mortal souls residing in Midgard and the world of Midgard itself. In this aspect, the Daughter exemplifies the unavoidable trials and errors of this stage, and also the ability to learn from one's mistakes. This example can be proven through the actions of most humans in their continual quest for the betterment of their mental, emotional, physical, and spiritual selves. This ability to utilize our inner mental deductive processes in order to improve all phases of the self ensures a probable favorable outcome for future events.

A good example of one of the myths that portrays this behavior is that of the witch Gullveig and her meeting with the Aesir. As she has the gift of prophecy, it is certain she already knew the outcome of her visit prior to its actual occurrence. Even with the foretold threat of burning, she chose to continue. She knew that the result of this visit would ultimately be favorable to the deities, as witnessed by the truce of the Aesir and Vanir races.

Svartalfheim: The adult awaiting the golden years. The world of Svartalfheim is inhabited by the races of dark elves and dwarves. These magical beings are notorious for their constant diligence and aptitude for magical and physical tasks. This represents the Daughter's and humanity's own preparation for "retirement" through the constant accumulation of wisdom and worldly goods. These creatures teach an additional lesson, however. They crave physical wealth, and will jeopardize anything and anyone to attain it. This world gives a strict warning to us to avoid greed.

To prepare for the future is a positive endeavor, but to hoard wealth and allow greed to overpower love, friendship, and family can trap one in this state of existence.

Ljossalfheim: The elder awaiting death. Through the highest level of these worlds, the third root of the Mother plunges. These are the worlds of Ljossalfheim, Vanaheim, and Asgard. Ljossalfheim is the world of the light elves, the beings who have the ability to guide us on our various spiritual journeys. This is also the realm of the Daughter, guiding our lives toward an ever-higher goal of existence.

Ljossalfheim is the world of meditation, inner reflection, and introspection. This is the time to notice and listen to all inner and outer signs and voices. Ljossalfheim is the world representing the initial dawning understanding that soon it will be time for us to anticipate a rebirth. Through the self-induced acceptance and understanding of this world, the Daughter Goddess helps us to achieve our next spiritual evolutionary state.

Vanaheim: The soul awaiting rebirth. Vanaheim, although the acknowledged Nordic heavenly world of love and fertility, also accurately illustrates the Daughter in Her aspect of the soul in suspension, patiently awaiting rebirth. This is of great spiritual significance, as love and fertility are a great part of rebirth on any level. Both of these attributes are needed to grow in a positive fashion toward the next plane of existence. Many may argue that love is unnecessary, but it needs to be made clear that both self-love and love for one's ever-present surroundings are key to positive regeneration, regardless of which stage of life a person may occupy.

This world's lessons are of great significance to us, for, like Hel and Jotunheim, Vanaheim symbolizes a waiting period. Unlike the worlds of infancy and of giants, however, here the Daughter has matured and truly enjoys Her stay in Vanaheim. She is exhibiting the joy we may feel through patiently waiting, observing, and enjoying our own personal selves, instead of constantly and heedlessly plunging toward the unknown future.

Asgard: The soul becoming reborn. This is the final known world of the Daughter. Asgard is the realm where the soul is reborn into a higher, and as yet virtually unknown, realm of renewed life. This represents for us the very pinnacle of our earthly efforts. This upward, continually moving spiral of the Daughter Goddess, as symbolized by Her steady growth through the nine worlds, actually brings Her back to the very beginning of the concept, as represented by Niflheim. This time, the Daughter is on an even higher, unforeseen level. She is showing us the continual cycle of life, ever striving to attain higher unknown stages. This ongoing process again alludes to the ever-present promise of an infinite, ever-growing afterlife.

Each one of these worlds is the Daughter, all embodying different stages of birth, growth, and even death within the greater cycle of life. This constant unfolding of birth and rebirth is the highest spiritual level of Her divinity that the majority of us can understand in our present existence. The Daughter Goddess' ability to manifest to new stages gives us unceasing hope and guidance. She demonstrates that we also are able to achieve this state of uninterrupted physical, mental, emotional, and spiritual growth. The Daughter also reminds us that growth will never be complete. We will always find ourselves as an infant at each new level of our lives.

Aside from Her obvious metaphorical alignment, the Daughter is deeply rooted in the security of early human perceptions, as we found with the Mother. Much of what the early Norse people found beautiful they named in open admiration and acknowledgment of the Daughter and Her various attributes. In some cases, this naming of objects encompasses the Daughter Goddess' traits of youth and beauty. At other times, it denotes Her seemingly more cruel nature.

The Daughter aspect of the Goddess of the North is the one with which we, as humans, are most comfortable and to which we can usually relate most easily. We know the Daughter Goddess as She is represented by the stunningly beautiful goddess Freya. The Daughter is wild, carefree, exuberant, and very generous with Her gifts. She is blatantly open with Her sexuality

Table 6. Humanization of the Daughter.

Aspects	Daughter
Human Given Name	Freya
Human Names of Attributes	Bil, Eir, Gefjon, Gersemi, Hnoss, Sjofn, Thrud, Wave Maidens
Daily Phase	Moon
Sun Phase	Dawn
Season	Spring
Guardian Association	Valkyries

and is proud of the manifestation of Her glorious body. She is confident in Her ability to utilize all of Her various talents positively, for both good or ill, depending on the circumstance. The Daughter is surrounded by many animal friends, whom She loves and cherishes as a very special, irreplaceable part of Herself. She is continually delighted by the unsurpassed, unequaled beauty of Herself, Her companions, and Her surroundings.

The Daughter is the symbolic representation of all new beings, new stages, and new lives. She is the physical manifestation of all universal creation. Regardless of the powerful characterizations of birth, again similar to that of the Mother, the Daughter Goddess symbolizes much more than simply the active manifestation of creation. She is in total harmony with the Mother. They intertwine beautifully in every possible phase of birth, growth, existence, and death. As they did with the Mother, early Norse tribes gave the Daughter many different human aspects, as exemplified by the numerous human names given to the individual aspects of the goddess Freya.

As noted in Table 6, the Daughter has Her own special place in the darkness of night. She is symbolized by Bil, who is normally acknowledged as the goddess of the waxing Moon. The Daughter Goddess is the promise of the unfailing, upcoming appearance of the Full Moon.

Throughout the beginning of each month, the Daughter spends a few earthly nights slowly patrolling the nighttime skies, basking in the beauty of yet other experiences unfolding under the camouflage of calming darkness. The hooting of an owl, the chirping of a bat, the yapping of a fox, the flutter of a moth—

they all remind us that the Daughter is near, overseeing the creatures of Earth. With the birth of each Waxing Moon, the Norse people knew that the Full Moon would soon be in the offing. They were able to track the year's progress through this continual rebirth of this pale sliver in the nighttime sky. Pregnant women counted these Waxing Moons with joyous anticipation, for after the ninth tiny crevice of light appeared, they knew their labor was imminent and that the anxiously awaited birth was close at hand.

The Daughter also shares with the Mother a special place in the neverending cycle of each day. The Daughter begins each morning anew, shimmering fresh with the glint of dew rainbowed in the dazzling display of a spectacular sunrise. She shines Her sparklingly new, bright light upon all of us from the east. She is the dawn, the new beginning of a brand-new day. She beckons all of us to wake and enjoy the lovely new morning with which She has gifted us. The birds, chirping and singing, are the Daughter Goddess' voice giving enchanting music to Her call. She is telling us to hurry and partake in this glorious splendor of another sunrise, for no two are alike: there is only one today. She is rejoicing with us in the anticipated coming of Her Mother, who as we know, is represented by the full light of day.

Spring is the Daughter's time to flourish in all of Her incomparable beauty. This is Her season, and all within is under Her domain. To humans, the time of spring has always represented youth, love, babies, and flowers, among many other breathtakingly glorious and new things. Spring is the sign to all of the Daughter's beloved creatures that the unbearably long, cold winter has finally passed. This is the season when most animals bear young, when most trees and plants come out of their long hibernation, and when humans begin to plant crops. It is the Daughter who rejoices in these events, and blesses each with prosperity and fruitfulness. Some springs are brutally harsh, with famine and drought the unfortunate result. Even then, the Daughter is still at our side, for otherwise, we and other species would not survive such hardship to create yet another generation of descendants.

The Daughter Goddess is symbolic of all that is new and untouched. She is the buds, shoots, and new plant growth of spring. We hear Her voice in the mewing of baby animals, the twittering of tiny nestlings, and the wailings of newborns. She is the unavoidable call of love, and is in evidence whenever a young or old couple lovingly holds hands for the first time. She is the light shining in their eyes, and is in their thoughts as they rejoice in the new-found feeling of oneness within each other's heart.

The Daughter is not all love and happiness, She has a harsh side, as well. We have discussed at great length the connection of the Valkyries to the goddess Freya. Because of this connection, these feminine guardians are also encompassed within the divinity of the Daughter Goddess. The aspect of the Valkyries challenges us continually to test our prowess, both in the realms of battle, physical and mental, and in the life-giving ability to heal. They show us minutely the unavoidable birth process in both extremes of life. These goddesses are fierce, aggressive, and heartless—but also loving and lighthearted as they explore their surroundings with wild, unsurpassed abandon. They teach us to enjoy each aspect of life, no manner how minute, shocking, devastating, enriching, or life-affirming. These goddesses teach us to meet each new occurrence with an open mind and open arms, but also not to avoid conflict if it is a necessity to protect one's self, kin, friends, and many freedoms. The Valkyries are the Daughter in all of Her magnificent being of birth and rebirth.

As stated previously, the Daughter aspect of the Goddess of the North is the most pleasingly visible to many of us as humans. She touches our lives continually, and is ever a part of our daily routine. She is with us to begin each new day, to watch over us during sleep, to rejoice in a birth, to heal our myriad hurts, to share in our loves, and to play happily in the rain. The Daughter Goddess is the sensual part of our nature who, without reservation, partners with us to enjoy the pure pleasure found in the touch of others. While the Mother lovingly cradles and nurtures us, the Daughter grabs our hand, encouraging us to explore every new experience, whether mundane, new, profane, old, beautiful, or frightening.

GRANDMOTHER

T he Grandmother is the third and final fully developed aspect of the Goddess of the North. The Grandmother is the supporter and nurturer of the Mother, and is always at hand to nestle and sustain Her granddaughter, the Daughter. These three aspects illustrate the very human concept of ancestral lineage, as explained in chapter 10. The Grandmother Goddess demonstrates the need we all feel to remain in constant contact and communication with our own mothers and grandmothers. They are the ones who physically gave us the irreplaceable gift of human life. We can always rest assured that at least one of our many female ancestors will always continue to oversee our well-being and help to guide us in our neverending search for constant growth. As a whole, humans are, in essence, represented by the Daughter, who is always overseen and cared for by the Mother, who, in turn, is continually watched over and counseled by the Grandmother.

The Grandmother Goddess is symbolized metaphorically by the massive, apparently ignored, world from which the World Tree, Yggdrasill, grows and in which the nine Nordic worlds are securely embedded. The Grandmother represents the unknown beginning of what we humans call time. She also characterizes the very beginning of all known and unknown concepts that are prior to all creative actions. The Grandmother is the ancestry behind the Mother and the Daughter. She may actually be viewed as the primordial foundation from which all life has derived.

Even though this huge world is normally not alluded to in any myth, it is obvious that this is the solid indestructible domain of the Grandmother. She lovingly embraces Her cherished Daughter, and Her Daughter's Daughter, and their children, and theirs, throughout countless millennia. It is the Grandmother who gives Yggdrasill the stability She needs to withstand all chaos, including, but not limited to, the terrible onslaught of Ragnarok. The Grandmother's world simply is. Her priority is to nurture and stabilize the Mother aspect, thereby protecting deep within Herself, not only the Daughter, but all creatures, including ourselves.

To the best of our knowledge, the early Norse people never gave the world of the Grandmother Goddess a verbal definition, as they did with Yggdrasill and Her nine worlds. Because of this, we are left to intuit and speculate, using the available historical documentation, on the spiritual importance of this world. It is arguable that we may never know this aspect of the Goddess of the North at this level of life. Some may even deem this personality unimportant, as shown by the unfortunate and sad treatment of many elders residing within our own society. It is also possible that the witch hunts that scar our history are a leading reason why we do not know more of this world and the Grandmother Goddess, since the aged were then severely persecuted. Luckily, we have been left various clues that deny this misinterpretation and that can lead us in the direction of truth.

The Grandmother Goddess' unimaginably large size suggests that the World Tree represents many Guardian Trees, and that the nine worlds represent many groups of worlds, all hidden from our eyes within the Grandmother's vast and infinite grandeur. This is an easy deduction to make, as we certainly cannot expect this huge world to sustain only one tree and nine little minuscule seeds.

What it does suggest, however, is that there are infinite levels of existence of which humanity is unaware. This being the case, it places us as a species near the bottom of this proverbial spiritual ladder. We know today, through scientific endeavor, that

Table 7. Humanization of the Grandmother.

Aspects	Grandmother
Human Given Name	Fjorgyn
Human Names of Attributes	Iord, Erce, Gerd, Giantesses, Hel, Hloydn, Ilm, Nanna, Nott, Ran, Rind, Sif, Sigyn, Skadi
Daily Phase	Night
Sun Phase	Dusk
Season	Winter
Guardian Association	Disir

there are many more galaxies than ours alone. It would be arrogant to assume we are the only "intelligent" species, even within our own world. There is much more to life than what we can physically see and touch. This idea of infinity lends further credence to the theory of the Grandmother's being.

As with the Mother and the Daughter aspects, the Grandmother has Her traditions enmeshed deeply in the Nordic culture. This will probably be the hardest aspect to research, due to the lack of substantial written documentation available to us. We will have to use all of the considerable knowledge we have gained in order to ascertain the truth of the third aspect of the Goddess of the North.

In some distant past, early Norse people must have begun to call the Grandmother by the name of Fjorgyn. Thanks to Sturluson's documentation of the myths, we know that She is the mother of Frigg, and the grandmother of Freya. We know little more than that about the goddess Fjorygn, except that Her name is used as a description of Earth.

This one seemingly insignificant clue, in fact opens up a wide vista of possibilities. Thorough study of it can lead us to a clearer understanding of the Grandmother Goddess. Many legends lived on to give us a glimmer of insight into Her true nature as the Grandmother. These hints are seen in the various stories portraying attributes of different goddesses and giantesses, all linked directly to the earth, winter, night, and death.

It would be wrong to assume that the Grandmother aspect of the Goddess of the North is aloof, only with us as the huge world supporting Yggdrasill and the sparse identity of Fjorgyn.

One of the Grandmother's various attributes is represented, no doubt, by the mature goddess of the night, Nott. The aspect of Nott teaches us acceptance for all that may be different. It is only through age that most humans learn indiscriminate hate, which, nine times out of ten, is based upon simple fear of the unknown. Nott, with her dark skin and hair, shrouded in the darkness of night, is the Grandmother teaching us love and respect for all life. In this cloak of blackness, the Grandmother is in total control of the night and all within its quiet province of soothing darkness. She grants us the time for deep undisturbed solitude and induces the comfort of sleep. Night is the time of the unconscious thought, when dreams begin, forming the very seeds that will shape tomorrow's reality. The Grandmother, in this facet, is like the soft, comforting blanket with which a loved one gently covers us, and the light kiss a parent lovingly bestows on the soft cheek of a small, sleeping child.

The Grandmother also characterizes the death of the sunlit day through Her appearance as the time we call dusk. She appears in the glorious sight of the Sun falling slowly behind the horizon to the west, clothed in wondrously vibrant tones and subtle hues of color. It is probably inaccurate to term dusk simply as death, for even though it does indeed put an end to day, the Grandmother Goddess actually gives birth to the neverending renewal of night. She displays the beauty found in a death as the beginning of a new life. Dusk is the sign that our daily work is finally completed. Sustenance and good cheer are in order. This is the time of relaxation, and our signal to bask in the self-rewarding completion of a good day's work. Eventually, as dusk deepens into night, it becomes the time for rest and restoration. In turn, night will die and a new, glorious dawn will be reborn.

The season symbolizing the Grandmother is winter. Many humans move, to avoid the winds and cold, to a more temperate climate, therefore only experiencing the Grandmother through the gentle and lingering touch of mild breezes and cooling rainstorms. Others of us relish this season, and eagerly anticipate each birth of winter. The Grandmother Goddess is awake and most active in our lives during these long winter months. Her harsh side is evidenced through bitter, blowing winds, wicked

storms of ice, and lovely, softly falling pristine snow. The Grandmother's soothing presence is noticed through the warmth of a
cozy fire, the heavy, protective clothing snuggled close to our
bodies, and the feeling of a warm drink coursing down our
throats.

The thick blanket of snow resting upon the earth's surface
only enhances the subtle beauty of the Grandmother. It is like an
all-encompassing cloak made of the whitest cashmere, floating
slowly open on occasion to give us a brief peek at a withered
blade of grass, the bare limb of a tree, a starkly naked bush, or the
expertly camouflaged den of a rabbit. As the snow flows and ebbs
over the Grandmother's body, ice develops, freezing parts of Her
being into awesome visions of incomparable beauty. Frozen lakes,
rivers, and streams are merely at rest, enjoying their oneness with
the Grandmother.

The Grandmother Goddess was the aspect of the Goddess
that the Norse people reverently praised during the long winter
when food was scarce and a herd of massive aurochs or delicate
deer suddenly appeared in a neighboring valley, deftly foraging
for food. For these gifts of food, pelts, and warmth, the Grandmother was worshipped on the one hand, but sometimes feared
on the other. While She did indeed supply these necessities for
survival, She relied heavily on people's ability to utilize their individual strength and perseverance to see them through Her long,
harsh season of cold, ice, and snow.

Today, many neglect the Grandmother through lack of respect for Her physical visitation during the months of winter. In
reality, this lack of respect stems, not from the dislike of winter,
but from a dread of and dislike for that which is uncomfortable,
old, difficult, or different. Often, these things interfere with our
daily lives and, to the majority of modern humans, this is simply
not acceptable.

People have become too accustomed to flipping a switch for
light, or turning a knob for warmth, or neighboring stores brimming with food for nourishment. Some see winter merely as a
time to complain about the lack of the Daughter's and Mother's
green, while others see winter as a playland. Both groups completely fail to see a season that could be, and often is, fraught

with deadly danger. A simple long-term power outage, an extreme drought, or a natural disaster during the long months of winter can be devastating, if not fatal. This season should not be seen through fear-filled eyes, but should be considered a challenge to show the Grandmother Goddess that we are indeed capable of applying the unique gifts She has so lovingly given us.

In our seemingly distant past, our ancestors spent the winter months sheltered together. This enabled them to take advantage of this precious time to learn the art of entertainment and to fully enjoy each other's company. This is the time when deep friendships were formed, love between a wife and husband deepened, and young children bonded ever closer with each other and their beloved elders. This is when the lore of each tribe was happily shared over a crackling fire, or when sitting at a long table, heaped with food and drink. This is how the Nordic heritage was passed down, when deeper wisdom was accorded those who wished to learn. Winter was the season of the family, and the closeness and interaction benefited all members of this close-knit society. The Grandmother Goddess taught these people to love and cherish their children, spouses, kin, and friends, above and beyond all others. She taught these people by example to love being alive purely for the purpose of enjoying their skill at survival. She also educated them in the need to desire and cherish the special bonds they developed with their loved ones.

The Grandmother is represented in our myths and in our lives by the feminine guardians called the Disir. These divine beings are the deceased women of each individual family line who continue to watch over and guide their many children through the trials and joys of human life. These supernatural women are the actual hands and eyes of the Grandmother at work. As they are our ancestors, so too is the Grandmother Goddess both a Disir and our divine ancestor. While the Disir may not be felt in a dramatic way in our daily lives, their soft touch and proximity constantly reminds those of us who listen of the soft, loving presence of the Grandmother Goddess.

The Grandmother provides humanity with some very specific and necessary messages, if we are willing to watch, listen, and learn. She gives us the very comfortable atmosphere of restful night to dream peacefully, which, in essence, gives us the tools needed to recreate our own, personal reality. This is a wondrous gift, and one not to be ignored. Dreams and ideas, when implemented, are what keeps our species alive and continually evolving. The Grandmother's gift to our unconscious allows each of us to enjoy firsthand the fruits of our labor.

The most important lesson She teaches us, however, is to love, honor, and cherish our children, spouses, kin, elders, and friends. This love and respect is what has kept the human race strong and able to move perpetually forward throughout the ages. It is what has taught us to be proud of our individual heritage, and also of our many predecessors. This is the main reason some of us name our children after the dead we have loved—to honor the memory of their accomplishments and the gift their living has meant to us. Tribes used to work together to protect the community. They looked out for each other, provided food for all, and raised the children. We have lost this life-affirming tradition in the modern age, and the effects of this loss are becoming more and more evident with each passing year.

Today, in the United States, our sense of community is slim. Many do not know, nor care to know, their neighbors. People actively avoid acknowledging a stranger's presence. Doors are slammed shut and curtains drawn at the first sound of an outside disturbance. Homeless people are common in many communities, and most are ignored or even labeled as the dregs of society. Children are allowed to run amok, and some even have weapons that allow them to become fierce predators in many cities. Overgrown or "unsightly" trees are hacked from lawns without a thought for the life dwelling within. Animals are hit by cars and disregarded, not only by the person responsible, but also by many passersby. It is easier to continue on the daily path then to stop and assist an unknown being, be it human, animal, or plant. Instead of our communities and families forming a more closely knit group, we are deliberately and actively doing everything possible to avoid such contact and obligation, thereby creating the very predicament just outlined.

This negative behavior and lack of responsibility is in direct conflict with the teachings of the Grandmother aspect of the

Goddess of the North. For us to truly know Her presence within our lives, we must again desire it. We must remember the art of loving and honoring our family members and friends. We must follow our ancestors' lead, and learn again to keep them always within our thoughts and hearts. This is the door we must once more open in order to fully accept and begin to understand the Grandmother Goddess' lessons, taught within Her ever-loving embrace. Her instructions may be harsh at times, as evidenced by bitterly cold winters, but She always remains beneath our consciousness. The Grandmother is a constant source of security, protection, and comfort.

THE GODDESS
OF THE NORTH

As we have discovered through our intensive study of the primordial Norse feminine divine, there is no doubt as to the existence of the Goddess of the North. She has lain patiently in wait for us to recognize and embrace Her magnificent being and bring Her back into our lives. Her quiet fortitude is similar to that which we have learned to expect from Her aspect of the Grandmother. Unlike the Grandmother, however, the Goddess' calmness has not been merely hidden under a blanket of cold and snow, but would be more accurately described as hidden under the soft linen sheet of modern human misunderstanding, misinterpretation, and ignorance. The Goddess of the North's trust and patience is infinite, as She is certainly infinite. She knows that, eventually, Her call will be acknowledged once again by humanity, or at least by those members wishing to embrace the utter serenity of the pure balance of positive to negative, female to male, and ancient to future. This is what the Goddess of the North offers to us.

We have explored at great length the Goddess' various human-based aspects and Her easily understandable attributes. We have slowly pieced these fragments together to form once again the three main aspects of Mother, Daughter, and Grandmother. This has allowed us to study the Goddess from the perspective of the inspiring Nordic symbolism. It is now time to

Table 8. Aspects of the Goddess of the North.

Associations	Mother	Daughter	Grandmother
Human Given Name	Frigg	Freya	Fjorgyn
Human Names of Attributes	Fulla, Gna, Hlin, Idun, Lofn, Nerthus, Saga, Snotra, Sol, Syn, Vara, Vor	Bil, Eir, Gefjon, Gersemi, Hnoss, Sjofn, Thrud, Wave Maidens	Iord, Erce, Gerd, Giantesses, Hel, Hloydn, Ilm, Nanna, Nott, Ran, Rind, Sif, Sigyn, Skadi
Daily Phase	Sun	Moon	Night
Sun Phase	Day	Dawn	Dusk
Season	Summer	Spring	Winter
Guardian Association	Norns	Valkyries	Disir

put the entire puzzle together to get an idea of the cohesive whole of the Goddess of the North. Table 8 summarizes what we have already discussed in the last three chapters. It can also act as a resource for later discussions by placing what we already know about the Mother, Daughter, and Grandmother side by side, so we can see more clearly the continual intermingling of each aspect with the other two.

A wonderful example of this intertwining is the Grandmother's dark night being replaced by the Daughter's brightening of dawn, and then by the Mother's clarity of day, and then again by the Grandmother's colorful tapering into dusk. These three aspects are constantly enveloping, embracing, and enhancing each other, aptly demonstrating the beauty and magnificence of the Goddess of the North.

Table 8 does not include the mythology of Yggdrasill, for a very important reason. Even though we know Yggdrasill, the nine worlds, and the large unidentified world embody our very search for the Nordic feminine divine, we have yet to explore the inner, more deeply concealed representations of these same metaphors. A search of this magnitude requires some repetition in order to reinforce the knowledge gained. I will, therefore, refer back to Table 8 frequently throughout this chapter to help the reader understand more difficult and challenging concepts.

Table 9. More Aspects of the Goddess of the North.

Associations	Mother	Daughter	Grandmother
Planet Association	Sun	Moon	Earth
Norn Association	Verdandi	Skuld	Urd
Springs of Yggdrasill	Urd	Hvergelmir	Mimir
Worlds of Yggdrasill	Asgard, Vanaheim, Ljossalfheim	Midgard, Jotunheim, Svartalfheim	Hel, Niflheim, Muspellheim
Animals of Yggdrasill	Swans, Bees, Hawk	Serpents, Stags, Squirrel	Dragon, Goats, Eagle
Aspects of Yggdrasill	Sap, Trunk, Branches	Leaves, Shoots	Roots, Grass
Metaphorical Alignment	Yggdrasill	Nine Worlds	Big World

PLANET ASSOCIATION

While we have already seen the parts of day and the daily phases incorporated in the three aspects of the Goddess of the North, we must now delve a little deeper to ascertain the importance of the three main "planets" of both the Norse world and our own. These planets are what create the phases we discussed previously.

Sun: While we know the Sun is not a planet, we cannot assume that the Norse people possessed the same scientific knowledge. We have already proven that the time of day at which the Sun is highest in the sky is indeed an aspect of the Mother. We now must explore this heavenly body a little more deeply from the perspective of our Nordic ancestors.

The Norse people knew the Sun gave life through light shining on the species and on the planet, Earth. Therefore, this association with life-giving can also be aligned with that of birth. As we have already discovered, this gift of giving life makes the association of the Sun to the Mother very strong.

Moon: This particular association is more confusing, as we already know the Daughter is aligned with the Waxing Moon through Her attribute of Bil. We also know that the Daughter is represented by the character of the Moon with reference to the daily phase of the Goddess of the North. In the present context, however, the Daughter holds a deeper meaning. The Moon itself is the symbol of all new life forming and growing in all daily and nightly phases of the Earth. It is the sign of the Sun upcoming, and the growth this light will initiate. This being the case, we find the Moon associated solely with the Daughter.

Earth: The Grandmother is indeed the planet Earth. She is the quiet feeling of comfort beneath our feet. She enhances the heavenly aspects of the Mother and Daughter, by giving them both a place to shine their planetary lights to enable further growth, maturity, death, and regeneration upon Her great surface.

NORNS

In chapter 12, we acknowledged the Norns as a direct representation of the Mother Goddess. The three main Norns, Verdandi, Skuld, and Urd, have additional, more developed characteristics, which we explored at length. We will now find that, on a deeper spiritual level, these same attributes will correlate these three specific Norns individually with the Mother, Daughter, and Grandmother aspects of the Goddess of the North.

Verdandi: Verdandi symbolizes being, the present, and the concept of becoming. This is the constant state of the Mother. The Mother resides in our present; She is our being. Her ceaseless life-giving action, through the giving of birth, is a physical representation of Her continual becoming.

Skuld: Skuld is the characterization of debt, guilt, and the unknown future. These attributes can be seen as symbolic of the Daughter. She is always being reborn into a new level of existence. Therefore, each stage is an unknown future. Her continuance is actually a debt She owes to Her Mother, as we all owe our parents, grandparents, and ancestors for our personal gift of life. It is hard to imagine the Daughter Goddess feeling guilt, but it may be that, in this aspect, the guilt lies in the fact that the death of someone or something must precede a birth, lest stagnation occur.

Urd: The past. There is no doubt that this is another representation of the Grandmother. She holds within Her impressive Self all the infinite knowledge of all past stages of life, within and without the universe.

THE SPRINGS OF YGGDRASILL

We can assume that the three springs of Yggdrasill are characterizations of the Mother. As with the planets, however, we must explore the springs more deeply. This will show us that, on a different level, these springs have even greater symbolic meaning and associations.

Urd: The spring of Urd is the metaphorical home of the three Norns, but its main focus is as the spring of destiny—the destiny of all living things and those yet to be born. Because destiny is the key attribute of this font of water, it is based within the present, for the present always rules the future. As such, even though the concept of destiny implies the future, it is, in fact, the present. Because of this, the spring of Urd falls within the realm of the Mother.

Hvergelmir: At the lowest root of Yggdrasill lies the warm moisture encompassed within the spring of Hvergelmir. This is the spring of creation and the resulting birth process. It is the well of the Daughter. Being at the lowest level of the World Tree, this also symbolizes the continual spiral of the progress of the Daughter throughout the various stages of growth.

Mimir: The spring of Mimir holds within it all knowledge and wisdom. This is the Grandmother's domain, for She holds within Her greatness all memories of all past actions, regardless of where or when they occurred.

THE WORLDS OF YGGDRASILL

While we have discussed at great length the connection of the nine worlds to the Goddess, we have yet to explore their deeper metaphorical implications. We know all nine worlds are individual representations of the Daughter, simply because She is the child of the Mother. However, as with any spiritual myth, we must continually peel back the layers to discover a new realm of thought and meaning.

Asgard, Vanaheim, Ljossalfheim: The three worlds of Asgard, Vanaheim, and Ljossalfheim are the worlds we humans view as symbolizing the strongest sense of spiritual strength. They are the focal point between the mundane and sacred paths of life. They are the inner strength of maturity, but they also retain the needed vigor of youth that enables us to explore still more deeply, and to attain yet undiscovered levels of consciousness.

These three worlds are the Mother, for She is our doorway to achieve the higher level of existence they define. Once we mature from our birth and Earthly lessons, as taught to us by the Daughter, we will become enhanced through a new stage of birth, right into the very arms of the Mother.

Midgard, Jotunheim, Svartalfheim: On this deeper level of Nordic metaphoric spirituality, the Daughter is represented by the worlds Midgard, Jotunheim, and Svartalfheim. These are the newly born, or infant, worlds of the universe. Svartalfheim, populated by dwarves deep in the cool bowels of the Earth, represents the Daughter being born from the cold of winter. Midgard is Her infant and youth stage, as seen through Her manifestation of spring into summer. Jotunheim is Her period of rest, beginning in autumn, patiently awaiting Her continual rebirth each spring.

Hel, Niflheim, Muspellheim: Within the lowest worlds of Yggdrasill, the Grandmother exhibits a passive trait through the world of Hel. We know this is the world of the dream state, and positive things can happen from consciously and willfully turning these dreams and desires into reality. We also know that Hel can symbolize stagnation, due to the lack of initiative concerning dreams. On the other hand, Niflheim and Muspellheim show us a totally different side of the Grandmother. These two worlds show the creative ability the Grandmother has when She chooses to utilize it.

Whenever these three worlds are discussed in a metaphoric light, it is imperative that the space called Ginnungagap be included, as it is an irreplaceable part of this lowest level of worlds.

It is very important to remember that Niflheim, Muspellheim, and Ginnungagap were in existence before the gods were created. These same universal beings certainly could not have existed before Yggdrasill as She is their support. Ginnungagap is the womb, metaphorically, within the myths. The age of Ginnungagap, Niflheim, and Muspellheim leads to a conclusion that this void could have been something else; even possibly another, older, set of worlds. Perhaps these older worlds evolved or exterminated themselves. Either way, Ginnungagap resembles the rejuvenation process associated with the Grandmother Goddess. Conjecture is all we have, as there is no way for us to really know the truth behind Ginnungagap as mere humans.

In the myth of creation, Niflheim and Muspellheim show us the road that death has paved to the splendor of creation on a massive scale. This is the Grandmother at work. While She certainly is noticed within our daily lives, Her focus is on other things as well, including the welfare of the universe itself.

THE ANIMALS OF YGGDRASILL

As with the planets and springs, it is correct initially to assign the various creatures and physical attributes of the Guardian Tree, Yggdrasill, to the Mother Goddess. It is also correct to continue to explore these same attributes to discover other important alignments. As we have just learned, this study of metaphoric layering is a many-faceted jewel waiting to be closely scrutinized.

Swans, Bees, Hawk: The swans are the actual metaphor for creation in the kingdom of Yggdrasill. These two lovely creatures, stately in their security and maturity, slowly swim in the spring of Hvergelmir. They simply enjoy each other and their countless children, grandchildren, great-grandchildren, and so on. They are the physical element of the Mother, in Her shining, glorious motherhood.

The bees represent the Mother Goddess' constant diligence with both the overseeing and the nurturing of all Her myriad offspring. Every effort of these small insects represents an action creating a reaction, as does each action of the Mother.

The hawk is the symbol of success in reaching present goals, and setting new goals for newer and higher realms of spiritual being. He is the actual shadow of the eagle, therefore, he indicates even the Mother's search for loftier levels is never complete.

Serpents, Stags, Squirrel: The infant serpents and the stags have a great deal in common, as the entire focus of their lives is actively to destroy the outer edges of Yggdrasill's awe-inspiring wonder. However, while the "baby dragons" are merely following the example set by their father, the stags are performing this action of destruction of their own accord. Both acts stem from the need for nourishment, so they cannot be seen as completely destructive. They represent the Daughter in Her infant stage, growing to early adulthood.

The squirrel, who is perpetually running up and down the tree carrying messages from the lowest reaches to the highest, is a prime example of yet another stage of life for the Daughter. This is Her inquisitive and maturing stage. While She is curious of all doings, She demonstrates the maturity needed not to get overly involved in a truly negative situation, as represented by the dragon. At this stage, She is ready to progress to the level held by the hawk.

Dragon, Goats, Eagle: The dragon is a perfect metaphor for the Grandmother in Her guise as the destroyer. This is the stage of death, decomposition, and rest that will lead ultimately to the rebirth of a new infant being.

The goats, like the stags, are constantly at work destroying the newly grown limbs and shoots of Yggdrasill. In this light, they can be viewed like the dragon, yet they have one additional attribute. Goats give life-preserving milk. Thus, even though they are indeed destructive, they also give back to other creatures what they have taken. This is the mighty lesson of the Grandmother Goddess, which She strives to teach to all in the dead of winter. If we take, we must give back in order to continue to flourish.

The eagle is at the highest level of all the animals of the World Tree, representing the Grandmother as the matriarch of all living creatures. The eagle sits at the very top, overseeing, sustaining, and nurturing all life below. Even though this journey appears to be complete to us mortals, the beating of the wings implies that the eagle has simply been resting before traversing yet another Yggdrasill, as yet unseen.

THE ASPECTS OF YGGDRASILL

While we discussed the aspects of Yggdrasill—roots, grass, trunk, foliage, branches—in chapter 11, we now must peel back another symbolic layer. The study of these aspects on a different level will further enhance our knowledge of them.

Trunk, Sap, Branches: The trunk and branches of Yggdrasill are the support of the entire tree, soaring above the unnamed world of the Grandmother. Neither branches nor trunk are able to be snapped, although on occasion they groan and shake under pressure caused by great winds. This is similar to the idea and truth of creation and birth never being fully stopped, even in the most devastating conditions.

The sap flowing through the entire World Tree is the lifeblood, not only of the Mother, but of all creatures and worlds connected to Her. This sap is the nurturing milk of the Mother.

Shoots, Leaves: The shoots and leaves of the World Tree are the very items destroyed continually by the goats and stags. Both groups, creature and plant, are characterized by the Daughter, for, even though the shoots and leaves eaten by the animals are thus destroyed, they are reborn. Hence, just like the Daughter, they achieve a different level of life.

Roots, Grass: There is no doubt the roots of Yggdrasill are the symbols of the Grandmother. They reach deep within Her world in order not only to support the Guardian Tree, but also to support and protect the Mother's seeds—the nine worlds. This is a perfect example of the Norse view of the extended family. The worlds are the children of the Mother, nevertheless, the Grandmother is always available to assist in the care of Her grandchildren.

Even though we may view the Grandmother in a fashion shrouded by our modern view of death, this is inaccurate. The grass covering Her massive world is a testament to Her ability to give renewed life after death has occurred.

This is the preliminary introduction to the great story of the Goddess of the North. This book can in no way cover all Her glorious meaning. It is meant rather as a stepping-stone to further personal exploration. As we can see, it will take many lifetimes for us to truly understand Her wonderful self. Figure 15 (pages 180–183) can help to further our understanding of the constant interweaving of the three aspects of Mother, Daughter, and Grandmother, and help us to see the continual upward and downward motion of Her being. While we cannot expect to learn all of Her attributes, this enables us to have a starting point for further study.

The triangle is an ancient symbol of the Goddess in many early cultures (see chapter 19). As figure 16 shows, the Goddess of the North encompasses many triangles within Herself (see page 183). There are so many, in fact, that we would be unable to make sense of the drawing if we placed them all in it at once. This is an additional tool for the individual to use to explore the hidden depths of the Goddess of the North. I suggest that you keep a personal diary and begin your own chart. With each new

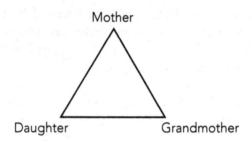

METAPHORIC ALIGNMENT

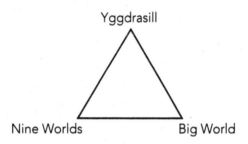

ASPECTS OF YGGDRASILL

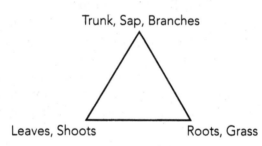

ANIMALS OF YGGDRASILL

Swans, Bees, Hawk

Serpents, Stags, Squirrel   Dragon, Goats, Eagle

WORLDS OF YGGDRASILL

Asgard, Vanaheim, Ljossalfheim

Midgard, Jotunheim,   Hel, Niflheim,
Svartalfheim   Muspellheim

SPRINGS OF YGGDRASILL

Urd

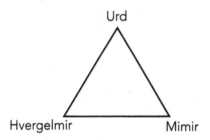

Hvergelmir   Mimir

NORN ASSOCIATION

Verdandi

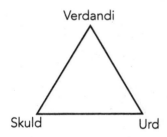

Skuld   Urd

PLANET ASSOCIATION

Sun

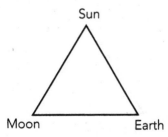

Moon   Earth

GUARDIAN ASSOCIATION

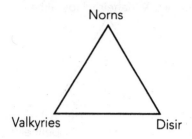

SEASON

SUN PHASE

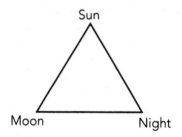

DAILY PHASE

HUMAN NAMES OF ATTRIBUTES

Fulla, Gna, Hlin, Idun,
Lofn, Nerthus, Saga,
Snotra, Sol, Syn, Vara, Vor

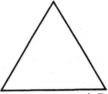

Bil, Eir, Gefjon, Gersemi,
Hnoss, Sjofn, Thrud,
Wave Maidens

Iord, Erce, Gerd, Giantesses, Hel,
Hlodyn, Ilm, Nanna, Nott, Ran,
Rind, Sif, Sigyn, Skadi

HUMAN GIVEN NAME

Frigg

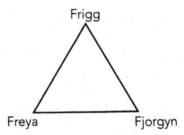

Freya   Fjorgyn

Figure 15. The interwoven aspects of the Goddess of the North.

Mother

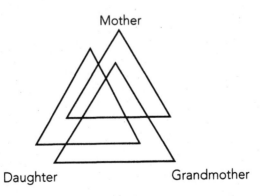

Daughter   Grandmother

Figure 16. The Goddess of North.

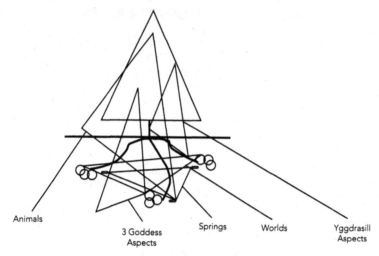

Figure 17. The triangles of Yggdrasill.

evolution of thought, you can chart your progress, and you will be able to look back upon what you have already learned. Old lessons will always show us new ideas, as we have discovered throughout our search for the Goddess of the North.

PART FOUR

PAST TO PRESENT

Our old ancestors were a hardy, conservative race, and tenaciously held by the treasured relics of their former beliefs and customs long after they had been shattered by the onset of Christianity.

—W. WAGNER, *Asgard and the Gods*

SIXTEEN

WOMEN IN NORSE SOCIETY

In any serious discussion of the Northern primordial goddess, it is necessary to explore and study the role of women in Norse society. By studying the actions and attitudes of a specific culture, we can learn not only the value these early people placed on their personal spiritual faith, but also how certain members of their society were viewed and treated. This particular investigation will give us another valuable insight into the being of the Goddess of the North.

In most of northern Europe, Nordic women had the legal right to own property in their own names. Often they were able to choose the husbands they desired, instead of being forced to wed to further another's economic or politic goals. The normal conception most of us have of early Nordic women is with a girdle and a ring of keys to her property, minding her home and tending to her children. It is indeed true she was the *sole* ruler of her home, but this was by no means her entire function within the society.

Not only was the Nordic woman a great-grandmother, grandmother, mother, wife, and daughter of the community, in many instances she also held major spiritual and political positions within that community. In such roles, she had a strong voice in decision making. Norse women were known to march to battle and fight side by side with their fellow male warriors. They were also often seen on the outskirts of the battle, creating powerful spells of protection and victory for their chosen warriors.

Most important, Norse women either held exclusively or shared equally with a small, select group of men positions pertaining to the healing arts, and magical and divination abilities. The women who practiced these specialized and sacred skills were normally given a variety of respected titles, including volvas, seeresses, prophetesses, shamans, shape-changers, spae-wives, and Mothers. Not only were these women a tremendous influence within their communities, they were often called upon by village leaders to assist in insuring victory in upcoming battles, the fertility of crops, safety on sea voyages, and health and well-being. It was very common for a group of these women, called Mothers, to travel to surrounding areas lending their services to various settlements. H. R. Ellis Davidson notes, "It was the custom . . . of the Germans to regard women as endowed with the gift of prophecy, and 'even as goddesses.'"[1]

These women worshipped the feminine deities Freya, the Norns, and the Earth Mother, Frigg. They were also often seen as divine aspects of these goddesses. Although the Norse, in later years, were deemed a patriarchal society, it is interesting to note the deep-seated respect and reverence they held for both their women and their goddesses. This is a strong indication that this culture was originally a matrilineal society. Knowing the Nordic myths as we do today, this forces us to acknowledge the possibility that many goddess myths were either lost or changed in the later transition from polytheism to monotheism. It certainly strengthens the probability of a primordial goddess becoming fractured into small, seemingly insignificant roles, adding even greater emphasis to our previous premise. The role Norse women played in their society is of prime importance to reenforce the existence of the Goddess of the North, and to show that women were not always considered inferior. Instead, they were equal to their Nordic male counterparts.

---

[1] H. R. Ellis Davidson, *Gods and Myths of Northern Europe* (London: Penguin, 1964), p. 121. In this particular quote, Davidson is referring to a source of her own, i.e. "Tacitus in his *Histories* (IV, 61)."

As this particular book is focused more on the feminine divine than the human woman, we will only explore those roles held by early Nordic women that specifically pertain to this study. There is quite a bit of documentation readily available concerning these feminine ancestors of ours. In order to retain our present focus, however, we will rely heavily on the reader's desire to further educate herself/himself in this area of history.

Healer: As stated previously, talented women of the early Norse realm were often practitioners of the art of healing. While there were certainly men who also had this aptitude, it was predominantly a trait in women. Healers would be called upon to assist with many ailments, both physical and mental. They were normally present for childbirth, ready to assist both mother and baby if necessary. Healers had ample herbal knowledge, which they used wisely in their profession. Many of these women also utilized runic lore, which served to enhance their exceptional healing techniques. Often, women who were healers were also further gifted by the community with the title of spae-wife.

Spae-wife: The Nordic spae-wives, usually healers, possessed a tremendous amount of extended runic knowledge. They were extremely well-versed in all areas of the magical arts, and could perform both good and bad actions through their considerable talents. Many of the battle spells were created by them, and they ensured many a victory with their skill. Along with this wondrous and sometimes terrifying craft, spae-wives might also be shamans and even shape-changers.

As shamans, spae-wives had the power to mentally traverse the different dimensions of life. Through the magical act of donning an animal or bird skin, these women were able to intensify their shamanic ability to shape-change—that is, take on the appearance of a chosen creature, utilizing its inherent abilities for their own and others' gain.

Spae-wives may well have been the original students and, later, teachers of rune lore. This may also have included learning the mysteries of the World Tree, Yggdrasill. Thankfully, these wonderful women succeeded in passing this knowledge down to us, their descendants. Many spae-wives may have used an additional title, that of the volva.

Volva: These women may have encompassed all the talents above, but they were specifically known, revered, and sought after for their prophetic abilities. Every Norse community either had a respected volva or was able to contact one from a neighboring village. The volvas' talents were greatly desired and many a person—queen, king, and warrior—successfully made pertinent decisions based upon these exceptional women's remarkable foresight.

Volvas, through the use of sacred animal skins and flawlessly focused, spiritual vocal chanting, were able mentally to leave their bodies (astral projection) and roam to other realms. In their travels, they communicated with divine beings and the dead existing in other phases of life. The volvas, upon returning to their physical bodies, passed these messages to questioning mortals. This unique talent is called *seidhr*.

While this list does not include every position Norse women held in their communities, it does give a glimmer of the conditions under which they lived. As we can clearly see, women obviously held a high level of respect and equality in Nordic society, unlike the common view portrayed today. Unfortunately, many see the Norse tribes as almost mythological groups of people, crueler to their women than what is readily and easily evidenced in later history. Nothing could be further from the truth and we, the descendants of these strong and talented women, are now taking back our place in today's society. We owe this to our ancestors' legacy, for their blood, both female and male, still courses through our veins.

SEVENTEEN

WITCH HUNTS

We human beings have the unique ability to hate something within or without ourselves. This hatred can be focused on a variety of issues—race, sex, religion, to mention a bare few. While anger can be used in a constructive manner, hate does little more than tear the fabric of society and culture apart. Hate also implies the inability to use divinely given gifts, such as thought and exploration. Only those who *wish* to remain truly ignorant choose to stay in the stagnate state that hate causes. Because of this, it is important to study early history. Hopefully, we can learn from the mistakes of the past, as most heartrending tales center around the concept of hate.

The European and New England witch hunts of the Middle Ages are certainly two horrific examples of murder we can study to understand the degradation and suppression of women. These catastrophic events certainly reenforced recent views toward women, with a special emphasis on northern and western European areas. These biased views have remained in effect in this country until the last century for many people, and even into today for others.

The witch hunts of Europe were much more extreme, both in number and violence, than in the colonies of the United States. This is not to imply that the author believes the crimes committed in this country had fewer far-reaching affects. As this

book focusses on the Norse, however, the concentration of this
particular study will remain in Europe.

The net result of the European witch hunts was hundreds of
thousands of brutal and useless deaths. While some men were
tried and put to death in the midst of this terrifying religious
outrage, the focus of the witchhunts was primarily on women.
Not only is this a remarkable fact, but a frightening statistic for
women. Even more appalling is the fact that elderly women were
scrutinized and persecuted more than any other group during the
European witch hunts.

For whatever academically debatable reason, the elders of
the early Catholic Church came to a decision that witches and
witchcraft were offensive and dangerous to the masses. While
the modern reasons and excuses for the Medieval injunction
against witches and witchcraft vary, it is clear that this blatant
discrimination was caused by fear of competition between the
suspected worship of the Goddess and the ordered worship of
the newly enthroned male monotheistic god. Regardless of the
reason for this outrageous ruling, the laws were enforced. It became a punishable act to be named a witch or to be thought to
practice the once-sacred arts of witchcraft.

From the very early years of Christianity, many of the followers of this new faith devoutly believed it their duty to spread
their faith. The early missionaries, often accompanied by warriors and armies, eventually traveled to the societies of northern
Europe. Through various means, some bloody, natives were con-
vinced, and often forced, to convert to the new faith. The unfortunate result of this religious invasion was the control the
followers of this new faith eventually gained over the native tribal
governments.

For a great many years, centuries actually, the early Church
continued to strengthen its hold over northern and western Europe. Feudalism became the norm, with the Church elders
choosing and then supporting the kings of each kingdom. The
Church had so much control over these kingdoms that they
could, and did, displace these kings if they were thought to be
disobedient to the wishes of the Church. The Church would
then anoint another leader more to their liking, one who would

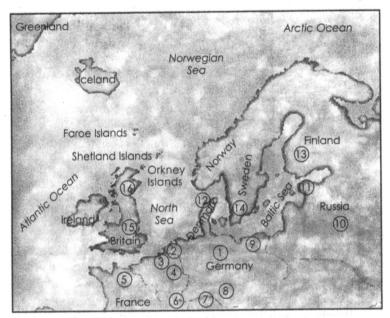

1. Germany: 10,086 + killed. In SW Germany, out of 1,280 executions, 82 percent were women;
2. Netherlands: 238, 93 percent killed were women;
3. Belgium: 144 killed;
4. Luxembourg: 355 killed, 79 percent were women;
5. France: 13,600 + killed. In Lorraine, out of 3,000 + executions, 80 percent were women;
6. Switzerland: 328 killed;
7. Austria: Approximately 1,500 killed;
8. Czechoslovakia: Approximately 1,000 killed;
9. Poland: Approximately 15,000 killed;
10. Russia: 10 + killed;
11. Estonia: 65 killed, 44 percent were women (percentage is highly unusual);
12. Denmark: Approximately 1,000 killed;
13. Finland: 115 + killed;
14. Sweden: 200 + killed;
15. Britain: Approximately 1,000 killed;
16. Scotland: 1,337 + killed.

Figure 18. Innocents slaughtered. This map indicates the witch hunts in northern and western Europe. The actual sites of the executions are not marked, but rather the countries in which they occurred, using modern country borders. The majority of those executed in the European witch hunts have been proven to be women. Areas where accurate gender records were kept are noted above. This map shows executions from 1500 C.E. Prior, there were 490 + executions throughout Europe, 71 percent of which were women. From Anne Llewellyn Barstow, *Witchcraze: A New History of the European Witch Hunts* (Sans Francisco: Pandora, 1994), pp. 179–181, and Robin Briggs, *Witches and Neighbors: The Social and Cultural Context of European Witchcraft* (New York: Penguin Books, 1996), pp. xi–xiii.

be more easily controlled. The Church eventually grew to completely control the religious, political, and economic environment during this Dark Age.

In later years, the leaders of the Church became deeply incensed with the thought of witches and witchcraft. This "sin" had never been truly ignored, but it had been conveniently overlooked. During this particular period of the Middle Ages, the uncovering of witches and the practitioners of witchcraft became the Church's primary objective. People were literally dragged before courts on charges of witchcraft, many completely ignorant of what had caused their arrest. To the Church, witchcraft included the willful working of spells, positive or negative, as well as the benign use of herbal lore, healing abilities, and even midwifery. The persecution was so intense and the death toll so high, that people actually started accusing friends, family, neighbors, and even strangers of practicing witchcraft, presumably to show the Church that they themselves were innocent of these crimes.

People, especially women, were accused and then thrown into filthy jails to be raped, tortured, tried before a biased court, hanged, burned, or drowned. They were cut and poked with long needles. They were violated in indescribable ways. Even pregnant women were murdered. Elders of the communities, so long revered by the natives, were scrutinized by the Church, due, most likely, to their age and "dependency" upon their society. These grandmothers and grandfathers also became innocent victims, leading to a pervasive dislike, disdain, and distrust of the aged that we can still see today. Accused men were also cruelly treated. In some instances, their genitals were removed, and in other cases they were brutally impaled. This points to an overt, yet conscious, display of "lowering" these men to the feminine level.[1]

Although this reign of terror lasted for a very short time in the history of humanity, it left an incredibly lasting negative impact upon our present-day view of women, magical activity of any kind, and even the very concept of a female deity. This tiny second in history was the actual cause of the temporary fall of the Goddess from humanity's thoughts. The Church succeeded in

---

[1] This insight was pointed out to me by my professor, Dr. Theresa Smith.

terrifying the people so much, that, for self-preservation, it became second nature for the masses to view anything of the female sex as evil, dirty, and sinful.

Even today, when one mentions the practice of magic and/or the worship of the Goddess in an open fashion, many people are appalled. This fear has been deeply and deliberately ingrained in our culture. It is automatically assumed that the worship of the Goddess equates with such " evils" as "devil worship." Women still suffer the torment of the legacy of inadequacy left behind due to the early Church's negative activities in the witch hunts. Because of this event, hundreds of years ago, women today find themselves striving to be viewed and accepted as equal beings, not mere sexual, dirty, inferior-minded companions of men.

Heathens and pagans of the modern world have many superstitions to overcome. Luckily, many members of monotheistic religions are open to alternative faith choices. The road, however, has only been partially paved. We have yet to establish a firm, strong path, nor have we succeeded in reaching the gate. The biggest hurdle we have to overcome will continue to be the false and superstitious views of others. This bias against Goddess worship makes many of us fearful and uncomfortable. Many of us to remain solitary and isolated in our personal faith. It is imperative for us to be more open about our chosen faith. This does not, however, mean that we condone proselytizing. If asked, we simply need to learn to be open and honest. Only education will stop the repetition of historical horrors for ourselves, our children, and our grandchildren.

THE GODDESS
REMEMBERED IN
FOLK AND FAIRY TALES

Even though many of our ancestors were subdued during the early monotheistic conversion period, and later during the European witch hunts, these strong people still retained much heathen lore. Through the tales they shared with each other and their children, they managed to save much of this lore for our use today. In many instances, these stories became Christianized or "watered down," but the essence of the Goddess has remained deep within these writings throughout the ages. We will by no means discuss the hundreds of various tales available, but we will study a select three in order to explore the inner workings of the feminine divine.[1]

THE THREE SPINNERS

There was a woman who had a daughter who refused to assist in any household work, even the fine and respected art of spinning

---

[1] These three tales are paraphrased from various translations of Grimm's selection of folk and fairy tales. They, along with other suggested texts of folk and fairy tales, are listed in the bibliography. See particularly Hilda Ellis Davidson, *Roles of the Northern Goddess* (New York: Routledge, 1998), pp. 99–113, 187. Davidson has some interesting input concerning fairy tales, and this text studies two of the stories discussed in this chapter, "The Three Spinners" and "Mother Holle." See also Jacob (Jakob) Grimm, *Teutonic Mythology*, vol 1., James Steven Stallybrass, trans., 4th ed. (New York: Dover, 1966), chapter 13, pp. 250–315. Grimm did extensive study of the goddesses within fairy tales. This section of his text is a must for fairy and folk tale research.

flax. The mother tried everything in her power to convince her daughter to help, but to no avail. One day, the woman lost her temper and started to spank the daughter soundly. The daughter, shocked at this unusual and hurtful treatment, began to cry so loudly that she could be heard clearly from the road. By chance, a queen was passing by at the very same moment. She stopped to inquire about what the girl could have done to anger the woman so.

The mother, afraid to tell the queen the truth about how lazy her daughter was, chose instead to say that her daughter insisted on spinning all the time. The poor mother said she could not afford all the flax the girl was going through. The queen was amazed, and said she loved the sound of spinning. She offered to take the daughter to her kingdom and give her a job spinning flax.

The woman, not wishing to offend the kind and gracious queen, agreed. She helped her daughter gather all of her meager belongings. The relieved mother stood at the side of the road and waved good-bye as she watched her daughter riding next to the queen, until they finally disappeared over the horizon.

Upon their arrival at the castle, the queen showed the young girl to her new rooms, which were filled to overflowing with the best flax in the kingdom. Considering the information the queen had received from the girl's mother, she assumed the girl could have it all spun within three days, and assured the girl she would visit at this time to see the finished work. As an additional reward, the queen promised the girl that, if she were indeed able to spin all of the flax within three days, she would be given the opportunity to marry the queen's son. The girl was terrified, for she knew absolutely nothing about spinning and, instead of attempting to teach herself, she sat and cried for the entire three days.

When the queen appeared as promised, she was shocked that no work had been started, much less completed. The girl told the queen she was homesick, which the royal lady accepted. Regardless, the woman went on to say she expected some work to commence immediately, and she would be back on the morrow.

The young girl again set to wailing, wringing her hands with fear. All of a sudden, three tremendously ugly women showed up outside her window, and offered to spin all of the flax if the girl agreed to a promise. She was overjoyed, and promptly agreed. The women made her swear to invite them to her upcoming wedding, or else she would suffer from bad fortune. She was also to introduce them as her cousins and allow them to sit with her at the marriage table. She found no problem with this oath, so the women commenced to spin all of the flax in the rooms.

The queen came in the next day and was astounded at the sight of all the spun flax. She could not think of a better bride for her son than this hard-working young girl, so arranged that the marriage be held immediately. The girl shyly requested she be able to invite her cousins, and the queen kindly granted her wish.

On the night of the wedding, the royal family was seated around a vast table with the new bride in their midst. Some visitors came to the door and announced they were the young girl's cousins. They requested admittance to the festivities. The three women were, of course, granted this request, and made their way to the places set for them next to the young maiden at the marriage table. The girl introduced them to both the queen and her new husband, mentioning that they were her beloved cousins.

Both the queen and son were shocked at the hideous appearance of these women, as the three were incredibly ugly and each had a severely malformed feature. Even so, the queen and prince were polite people and made no mention of it. They treated these three women as part of their new family.

Finally, the new bridegroom could no longer hold back his curiosity at the physical appearance of the three cousins, so he asked the first how her foot came to be so wide. She replied that it was from treading. He looked askance and asked the second how her lip came to be so huge and drooping. She replied that it was from licking thread. Appalled, he asked the third how her thumb came to be so flat. She answered that it was from winding thread.

The bridegroom looked again upon his lovely new bride and made a proclamation to all to hear. His new wife would never be asked to spin flax again.

This particular tale shows the ancient beliefs and practices of the native Norse. The young girl in the story is said to be lazy, as she is not willing to even learn to spin flax. While this occupation was certainly an esteemed talent, not all Nordic women excelled at this art. The thought of laziness was surely a later insertion, for with the Norse, this young girl would have found another talent to better herself, others, and ultimately, her community. Just as important, she would have enjoyed it, making her talent that much stronger.

This underlying theme of talent comes out slowly with the initial meeting of the three ugly women and the girl. They offer their assistance to her if she agrees to an oath. The Norse took oaths very seriously. To break an oath was an act of dishonor, and would often be seen as a cowardly move showing a lack of a strong inner character.

In this myth, the girl does not break her oath, thereby proving herself honorable. The women had promised her a great reward for keeping her oath, and they delivered as promised. This young woman, who hated to spin flax, ended up in a position more fitting to her and her individual talents. She became a princess of a kingdom, with the opportunity of becoming a queen in the future.

It is obvious that the three women in this tale are recent, twisted versions of the Norns, spinning destiny to assist humankind in their daily lives. The words of the Goddess are strong throughout this myth, and even time and history cannot destroy Her story.

MARY'S CHILD

There was a couple who lived in a vast forest. They made their living cutting and splitting wood for fuel. Times were extremely hard for them. As a result, they eventually ran out of food for both themselves and their young child, a beautiful little girl. For many a night and day, they tried to provide for her, but to no avail.

The man was working in the woods one day when, suddenly, a woman appeared before him. She was very beautiful and wore a glimmering halo. She told the man that she knew of his many troubles, and offered to take his needy child as her own.

She identified herself as the Virgin Mary. The man returned home and relayed the story to his wife. They discussed the offer at length, and eventually came to a heartrending decision. Finally, with tears and shame, they decided to take their beloved child deep into the woods. They left her there, trusting the Virgin Mary to keep her promise to retrieve and care for the little girl.

The toddler, alone and frightened, huddled at the trunk of a tree, calling in vain for her mother and father. All of a sudden, through tear-drenched eyes, she saw before her a beautiful woman surrounded by a golden light. This woman smiled at the sad little girl and announced that she was the Virgin Mary, and that she would take the child to her home in the heavens. She then grasped the little girl's hand, and they flew up into the sky. The Virgin Mary introduced the child to all of her many other charges, young angel children. They all got along famously and spent their days happily playing, eating, and sleeping, as all young children are wont to do.

One day, the Virgin Mary called the girl—not so little anymore—to her side. The woman was going on a journey, and wished to entrust the youth with the thirteen keys to the doors of the heavens. She informed the child that she could look within each of the first twelve doors, but the thirteenth was not to be touched, or she would live to regret her curiosity.

The girl and her companions, the angel children, had a grand time opening the twelve doors and marveling at the many miracles before their eyes. This entertainment was not enough for the girl, however. She adamantly wished to see what lay behind the forbidden thirteenth door. The young angel children cried out that they would not disobey the Virgin Mary, and refused to partake in opening the door.

The girl could not stop thinking of the thirteenth door and the mysteries that obviously lay behind it. She tried to put it from her mind, but even in her dreams it tempted her. Finally, one day when she was all alone in the corridor leading to the forbidden door, she thought to herself that, without any witnesses, no one would ever know if she took a quick look. Satisfied with this idea, she quickly unlocked the door and peeked within.

Blindingly bright light streamed from the door, shining from the Holy Trinity. The girl gasped at the beauty and, before she considered her actions, quickly stuck her finger into the light. Her finger immediately turned to gold. The girl slammed the door shut and ran down the hall toward her room. After she calmed herself from this frightful occurrence, she became certain that she could still hide her disobedience from everyone, including the Virgin Mary.

The Virgin Mary finally returned from her long journey, and joyously greeted all of her young charges. She then requested the return of her thirteen keys from the girl. She asked if the girl had looked into the thirteenth room and the girl replied that she had not. The Virgin Mary, suspecting deception, laid her hand on the girl's chest and felt the young heart thumping with anxiety. She again asked the girl if she had opened the door, and again received a negative reply. The Virgin Mary then saw the girl's golden finger, and asked for the truth for the third and final time. The young maiden again replied the she had not opened the door nor looked into the room.

The Virgin Mary told the girl she would be punished for her sin, and immediately removed her from her glorious home in the heavens. She brought the girl to a clearing totally surrounded by thorn-filled bushes deep in a forest. She then took away the young girl's ability to speak, and abandoned the maiden to fare as she could. The girl, terrified, did not know what to do, but refused to admit her wrongdoing. She found shelter in a hollow tree trunk, and discovered how to sustain herself with the fruits, nuts, and roots she discovered in the clearing of the forest.

The young girl lived in this solitary state for a long time. So long, in fact, that her only set of clothes disintegrated from her body. However, her hair had been steadily growing this entire time, so she found herself thoroughly covered in a long cloak of soft, warm hair.

One day, a young king happened to be hunting near the woods. The deer he was tracking ran deep into the forest. Not to be deterred, the king immediately followed. Instead of discovering his four-footed prey, he found the young girl, now a young woman, huddled near her hollow tree, completely draped in her shining hair. The king asked her name, but soon realized she was unable to speak. He asked her gently if she wished to return with him to his kingdom, and she replied in the affirmative with a nod of her head.

The lovely young woman became quite happy in her new home. Love soon developed between her and the king, and they happily married. Within a year, they had their first child, a little boy. Right after the birth, the Virgin Mary appeared next to the woman's bedside and asked her if she was now ready to admit to her sin of opening the thirteenth door. The woman refused and, as further punishment, the Virgin Mary took the newborn infant with her up to the heavens.

All the people in the kingdom were crushed at the disappearance of the young prince. They did not know what had actually happened to the babe, nor was the queen able to tell them. They started to wonder about the nature of the woman, and their trust for her lessened. The king, however, continued to love her deeply, and they had another son a year later.

Again the Virgin Mary appeared, and requested that the woman tell her the truth about the thirteenth door. Again the woman refused, adamant that she had not committed such a great sin. And again, the Virgin Mary disappeared with her second newborn son to the heavens. This unexplained loss of a second child created much havoc among the people, for they still did not know the truth. They were sure the young queen must be involved in some evil doings. The king still retained his trust for her and they had another child within the year, this time a little girl.

As with the past two royal births, the Virgin Mary appeared, demanding the truth so the queen could be absolved of her sin. For the third time, the woman refused. The Virgin Mary even took the queen for a quick visit to the heavens, so she could see her two little boys happily playing with the angel children. Even knowing the probable result of another lie, the young queen still refused to tell the truth. Her third baby was taken, just as the previous two had been. This time, the king could not hold back the angry people, and the queen was prepared to be burned at the stake.

The queen, missing her babes and fearful of death, humbly regretted not ever telling the Virgin Mary the truth about the thirteenth door. All of a sudden, she discovered her voice had returned and she cried out for all to hear that she had indeed opened the heavenly door. Rain appeared in the skies and drowned the flames beginning to lap at the queen's feet. The Virgin Mary appeared with the three royal children in tow. She handed them to the queen and broke the spell of silence forever. The people, understanding now what had transpired, took their queen from the stake and rejoiced. The young queen, king, and their three children lived happily ever after.

This myth is based directly on ancient beliefs involving the goddess Frigg. She was known to watch over children and take deceased, dying, and needy children to her great hall in the heavens. There she tenderly cared for them and allowed them to play around her in her daily activities. They assisted her in watering the fields, which actually means they were her companions in causing rain to fall to the Earth.

While the concept of sin is alien to the Nordic culture, the concept of honor is not. The young girl lied to a goddess, which is one of the greatest acts of dishonor the Norse people acknowledged. For that, she was swiftly punished. Again, the Norse do not accept the idea of redemption, but rather expect one to be responsible for one's actions. In this case, to be responsible was to admit the wrong done and offer either to physically repay or to repair the damage to the person wronged. For the goddess Frigg, the only repair she required for this wrongdoing was the truth. At the moment the young woman admitted to her lie, she was immediately absolved of her past lies. The connection between her and the goddess was renewed, and strengthened.

MOTHER HOLLE

A widowed woman had charge of two young girls. One of these, her daughter, was ugly and lazy, while the second, her stepdaughter, was very beautiful and responsible. The woman lavished time, love, and gifts upon her daughter, but jealousy drove her to hate the other. She forced the stepdaughter to do all the housework and kept her constantly busy spinning flax when she was not cleaning.

When this young girl would spin the flax, she would sit by a well in the yard and spin for so long that her fingers would bleed. This ready access to water allowed her to clean the blood from her hands and spindle, so she could get back to work as quickly as possible. One day when her spindle became covered in blood, she dipped it into the well to rinse it off and accidentally dropped it. Shocked, she watched it slowly sink to the deepest reaches of the well. The poor girl was mortified at what she had done, and went immediately into the house to tell her stepmother.

The stepmother was furious and ordered the girl immediately back to the well to retrieve the spindle, regardless of the consequence. The girl made her way slowly back to the well, attempting to devise different ways of getting the spindle back. No matter how hard she thought, she could not come up with any way other than to jump into the well after it.

This was a scary proposition, but the beautiful young girl was brave at heart, so she stood resolutely at the edge of the well, tightly closed her eyes, and jumped in. The well was very deep, and the poor girl could not hold her breath long enough to reach the bottom. She continued to try, but soon ran out of air and drowned in the well.

All of a sudden, she woke from her death-like sleep and looked around her in wonder. She was sitting in the midst of a beautiful, flower-filled valley with the Sun streaming brightly down upon her. She was unsure where she was or what to do, nor did she know which direction to take to get back home. She did not realize she had drowned. The young girl got up and began to walk, meandering toward the outskirts of the valley.

On her journey, she discovered a baker's oven. There was bread cooking within. The bread was mournfully calling to anyone within hearing distance that it was done being cooked. It would burn very soon unless some nice soul kindly removed it. The girl immediately opened the oven door and took the bread out. She could not bear to hear fear or pain in another's voice, regardless of who or what was making the sound. Once she felt confident that the bread was cooling properly, she continued on her walk.

She again heard a voice, this one filled with anguish. She followed the sound and came upon a tree filled with ripe apples. The tree begged her to please shake it so the apples would fall off. The weight was unbearably painful and she needed help to bear her children. The girl, full of understanding, promptly shook the tree until all of the apples fell to the ground. She then gently picked them all up and put them in a mound next to the trunk of their mother. Satisfied with her work, the girl continued on her journey.

The poor girl walked and walked, and soon began to tire. No matter how far she looked or how much she thought, she could find neither her way home, nor any shelter for the night. Eventually, when she was ready to just sit down and sleep, she came across a tiny house. She stood in the clearing in front and saw an aged woman staring back at her from a window. The old woman's appearance was frightening, for she had very big teeth. The girl turned around in fright and began to leave the clearing. Just then, she heard the woman calling to her, asking why the maiden was leaving.

The old woman's voice was so kind that the girl lost her fear. She stayed and chatted with the elderly lady. After a time, the woman offered the young girl a job cleaning the little home. The woman promised a good reward for work well done, and had specific instructions concerning the care of her bedclothes. She insisted they be flapped in the air until the feathers flew, claiming that this is what created snow on Earth. She also expected the bed to be neatly made. She then gave her name to the young girl. She called herself Mother Holle.

The aged woman was so nice to her and treated her with so much respect that the girl agreed to work for Mother Holle. She did her work very well, and the old woman was very happy. She treated the girl kindly, making sure she had food and shelter, and was never mean to her in any fashion. Regardless, the girl dreamed of going home. Her wish became so strong that she became despondent. She finally approached the kind woman and requested her permission to return home.

Mother Holle, kind as always, understood the girl's desire and was so content with the girl's honorable decision that she offered to return the girl to her home herself. The woman grasped the girl's hand and showed her a previously unnoticed door.

Mother Holle opened this door and bade the girl go through it with her best wishes. The girl did as she was told, and found herself completely covered with gold. Mother Holle told the stunned girl that the gold was her reward for a job well done. She also gave her the long-lost spindle. Mother Holle smiled upon the girl as the door slowly closed.

The girl looked around and discovered she was very close to home! She took off at a run for the house, passing the well on the way. Sitting on the edge was a rooster, calling to all who could hear that the young girl had at long last returned home and was covered with gold. She entered her house and found her stepmother and stepsister, both of whom were amazed at the gold the girl had acquired. She related her entire story, and the stepmother became greedy. She felt her blood daughter should have the same good luck, and decided to recreate the situation so the other girl could benefit.

She told her beloved daughter to go spin flax by the well until her hands bled. The daughter was too lazy for that much work, so she stuck her hand in thorns to make it bleed. She covered the spindle with this blood and then threw the instrument into the well. Not afraid of truly drowning after hearing her stepsister's story, she jumped right into the well. Drowned, this girl woke in the very same valley in which her stepsister had previously awakened.

She began to walk, following the directions given by her stepsister, and soon came across the bread oven. The bread within was again crying for release, but the girl ignored it, as she did not wish to get flour and dirt upon her. She continued walking and soon heard the same apple tree crying for assistance. The girl was so skeptical, however, that she refused to help. She thought the tree was playing a trick on her, hoping to drop the apples upon her head. Soon after, she found the tiny house of Mother Holle. She was offered the same job her stepsister had been offered. This girl, of course, agreed to take the position, as she wanted as much gold as her stepsister had earned.

On her first day with her new job, the lazy girl worked very hard. On the second day, her real nature began to surface. By the third day, she fought even trying to get out of bed. She refused to make Mother Holle's bed as directed, nor did she shake the linens enough for the feathers to fly, thereby depriving Earth of much-needed snow. Mother Holle was disgusted and told the girl to return home. The young girl was very happy with this news, for she knew she was ready to receive her reward.

Mother Holle took her to the same door she had used previously, and told the lazy girl to walk through. Instead of gold, however, a huge pot of tar rained down upon her head. The girl found herself close to home and mortified. As she approached the house, the same rooster that had greeted her stepsister announced to all within hearing that the lazy girl had returned, covered in tar. Because she would not change her selfish nature the girl lived her whole life covered with tar.

This is another tale directly connected to the goddess Frigg. Mother Holle is another name for this Norse goddess, and the metaphor of shaking out linens to create snow appears elsewhere. The appearance of the goddess has changed over the years from beautiful and stately to old and ugly. In the modern era, old and ugly are commonly seen as traits of elderly women. In the not-too-far-distant past, old was not necessarily related to ugly nor was either considered a negative feminine attribute.

In this particular myth, Mother Holle is seen to reward good work and punish poor or incomplete work. Frigg has always been acknowledged as the goddess of the home, among many other attributes. This story is a fitting example of her control over this particular domain.

Not only did Mother Holle reward and punish in regards to work, she also took into consideration the treatment of the bread in the oven and the apple tree near her home. This is a very telling part of the story, as compassion and understanding are strong aspects of Frigg's divinity.

Figure 19. Freya among the Dwarves (from Dr. W. Wagner, *Asgard and the Gods*, New York: E. P. Dutton, 1917, p. 265).

This particular tale hints strongly at Frigg's role in listening to oaths. The first girl honored her oath through her promise to properly maintain Mother Holle's home, linens, and bed, whereas the second girl did not honor her oath, nor did she ever have any real intention of doing so. Mother Holle rewarded the first girl with gold, a metal sacred to this goddess. She also permanently punished the other with tar, as she knew, through her divine gift of prophecy, that the other girl would never allow her inner self to grow.

In all three of these tales, we see the use of certain numbers—three and thirteen. These, among others, are sacred numbers in the Norse worldview, and their spiritual worth has never been undermined throughout the years. These numbers will be discussed at length in chapter 19.

The folk and fairy tales of northern and western Europe are key pieces of evidence in understanding the underlying thoughts and practices of the ancient Norse. Much information concerning the Goddess of the North lies hidden in the words of "children's stories." When reading them, we should always keep in mind that these myths were not always for children, but were, in fact, a large part of the oral tradition the Norse passed down to their descendants. It is only in relatively recent years that these myths were deemed fit only for children, and called folk and fairy tales.[2]

---

[2] Jakob and Wilhelm Grimm, *Grimm's Tales for Young and Old*, Ralph Manheim, trans. (New York: Anchor Books, 1977), pp. 1–2; Jacob (Jakob) Grimm, *Teutonic Mythology*, p. 267.

NINETEEN

SPIRITUAL SYMBOLS

All faiths have their own individual spiritual symbols, and the Norse Tradition is no exception. Many texts devoted to the study of the Norse discuss various spiritual attributes that will not be explored in this chapter because they are male-oriented and are not relevant to this research. However, many supposedly male-oriented symbols *are* mentioned here, but with different interpretations. It is not unusual to find variant meanings for ancient symbols.

Since this book focuses on the female divine in Norse mythology, the reader may notice topics throughout this chapter that are neglected in other Nordic writings. This again is not unusual. The lack of available available historical documents treating the Norse goddesses has made discussion of and interest in them rare, leading to an unfortunate lack of knowledge concerning Nordic feminine sacred symbols.

Animals, birds, and insects—all creatures—play a huge illustrative and spiritual role in most religions. They appear as metaphors for various mundane and divine concepts. By observing their behavior and exploring their meaning, we are able to learn much about our own lives, and, in many cases, glean messages from a higher spiritual level. In this section, I have relied heavily on Jacob Grimm's list of symbolic creatures in *Teutonic Mythology*,[1]

---

[1] Jacob Grimm, *Teutonic Mythology*, 3 vols., James Steven Stallybrass, trans., 4th ed. (New York: Dover Publications, 1966).

with Ted Andrew's *Animal Speak*[2] as an essential counterpart. These sources are a must for any reader interested in the symbology of the Goddess and Her creatures. (See figure 7, page 76.) Other highly recommended texts focused on Nordic animal symbolism have also been used, and are outlined in the bibliography.

BIRDS

Cuckoo: This bird has always been associated with the gift of prophecy. For this very reason, the cuckoo is symbolic of the feminine. Only the female Norse deities have the gift of prophecy, although the god Honir is reputed to acquire this talent after Ragnarok. Legends surrounding the cuckoo vary, but the bird's antiquity in early Nordic lore is unquestionable. The cuckoo's song must be noted carefully, for it can have various meanings. Strife, luck, death, and spring can all be heard in her call. When you hear the cuckoo, you must become objective about your life and goals. The cuckoo is always a symbol of impending change, be that the coming of spring or something more personal. This bird's gift of prophecy is a spiritual extension of the Goddess, advising us to look inward toward the feminine intuition for our personal resolution.

Legend tells of the cuckoo turning into a hawk at the beginning of autumn. This correlates with the theme of continual growth through change characteristic of the Goddess of the North.

Eagle: The eagle is normally considered a masculine bird, reigning supreme and magnificent over all other feathered creatures. This beautiful bird is symbolic of nobility, strength, energy, regeneration, introspection, protection, prophecy, health, wisdom, spirituality, and creative ability. The eagle can also be representative of the Sun, winds, and storms.

The eagle is able to visit other realms of existence, often as a guide for mortals. Through this bird's association with the

---

[2] Ted Andrews, *Animal Speak* (St. Paul: Llewellyn, 1995).

Figure 20. "Sacred Animals." A beautiful depiction of a few of the many spiritual creatures of the Norse Tradition. (From the author's collection; painted by Ingrid Ivic.)

Valkyries, it is also associated with death. As the eagle sits at the very summit of Yggdrasill, otherwise known as the Mother Goddess, he displays a strong feminine side.[3] This eagle of Yggdrasill was in existence long before the god Odhinn, even though it is considered by some to be his familiar.

This thought leads us to a more profound meaning. The eagle is an actual representation of all three aspects of the Goddess of the North. The eagle, calmly perched in the uppermost branches of Yggdrasill, is the Mother. Through its prophetic ability, it symbolizes the future, which falls in the realm of the Daughter. Through its strong association with death, it is symbolic of the Grandmother. (See chapter 11).

---

[3] Ted Andrews, *Animal Speak,* p. 138.

Falcon: Kveldulf Gundarsson says, "The falcon shares many characteristics with the eagle, though it is usually feminine. . . ."[4] The falcon, as the direct feminine counterpart of the sometimes masculine eagle, shares with her larger cousin the highest rank of respect attained by birds among the early Nordic peoples. The falcon is a quick and expert hunter. She is also credited with mental speed, agility, and grace.[5] The falcon is not a migratory bird, so we can assume her spiritual strength is available to us year round. She connects the elements air and earth, for, while she rides the winds of air, she finds her nourishment and shelter on the Earth.

The falcon is the only raptor generally associated with any of the goddesses. Both Frigg and Freya have falcon skins, which is another way of saying they have the ability to shape-change into the physical body of a falcon. This allows us a fundamental insight into the very being of the goddesses Frigg and Freya, indicating that the attributes of the falcon are also a significant part of the lessons of the Goddess, Herself. She is teaching us to shed our fears and soar, never fearing the unknown future.

Hawk: This creature is also a key figure of Yggdrasill (see chapter 11). The hawk is the messenger of the divine. If you see this bird, listen to and watch closely for her message. It is imperative to try to understand what she is communicating; it will lead to a more productive and positive future.

Magpie: The magpie has a piercing song, and Nordic legend tells us that her call can warn us of possible danger. She is associated with the goddess Skadi.[6] The magpie is actually a very pretty bird, with unusual black and white coloring. Her call can tell us many positive things pertaining to future events. Two of these birds together indicate that a good relationship is in the offing, or that a present relationship is stable and full of happiness.

---

[4] Kveldulf Gundarsson, *Teutonic Magic: The Magical and Spiritual Practices of the Germanic Peoples* (St. Paul: Llewellyn, 1994), p. 264.

[5] Ted Andrews, *Animal Speak*, pp. 159–161.

[6] Jacob Grimm, *Teutonic Mythology*, p. 675.

Raven: This wonderful bird is viewed inaccurately today as a harbinger of death, a thief, and a being with "evil" intent. Nothing could be further from the truth. While this creature certainly can be associated with death through its relationship with the Valkyries, the raven actually helps with the regeneration process. The raven is, therefore, a bird of creation. The color black is a known symbol of creation, as evidenced by the void of Ginnungagap.

This bird has many attributes, including wisdom, protection, healing, and prophecy. The raven is able to guide us throughout all realms and is a strong representative of magic. Any of us who are interested in delving into the Nordic runic and magical arts will do well with the raven by our side. As with the eagle, the raven is often thought to be an animal of Odhinn because of his two raven friends, Thought and Memory. This is simply a hint to all of us that nothing can be purely female or male. Balance is necessary in all thought and action for us to truly achieve equality on any level.

Swallow: Swallows are the bringers of both spring and good fortune. To have a swallow's nest on your roof or in your barn is always a sign of positive things to come, but to displace this nest is to openly invite disharmony upon yourself. Swallows have the endowments of prophecy and wisdom.[7] While the majority of the Norse goddesses have these attributes, swallows are bonded most closely with the Norns, Frigg, and Freya. As such, these tiny birds were sacred to the Norse. In the centuries following the Nordic reign, these little birds were given a negative reputation and became associated with witchcraft. Today, many people still see swallows, wrongly, as bad omens.

Swan: As we know, two beautiful and graceful swans swim in the well of Hvergelmir at the foot of Yggdrasill's lowest root. These creatures are very important in the study of the feminine Norse divine. They symbolize the complete balance and harmony of female and male and represent birth and creation.

---

[7] Kveldulf Gundarsson, *Teutonic Magic*, p. 262.

Valkyries are known to wear swan skins on their Earthly travels. Many times, these goddesses remove their swan skins to swim in rivers and streams. If a person happens to come across this skin and take it, the Valkyrie is bound to Earth until she recovers it. The female swan also shares the Valkyrie's attributes of protection and guardianship.

The swan is said to represent music. Her song tells us to utilize our mental abilities to discover our innate sixth sense. The swan's call may also announce that a true relationship is in the offing, or that a present partnership is strong. The swan is a powerful representation of monogamy (see chapter 11).

Titmouse: The tiny titmouse was special to the Norse people as a bird of much wisdom. She has the ability of prophecy, as do most birds. If you see a titmouse, observe her actions and compare them to your own. The bird is indicating a change of some type.

ANIMALS

Bear: The bear is a wondrous creature—beautiful, immense, and strong. She is both a hunter and a gatherer. She hibernates in the winter, as the Earth rests, covered under a deep blanket of snow. The bear is usually an aloof creature, unless it is mating season or she is rearing her cubs. The female bear does not share the responsibility of nurturing her cubs with any other bear, especially not with the male. Males are so concerned with territory that they have actually been known to kill their own cubs on occasion. For this reason, the female bear will not tolerate any intrusion or act of aggression near her cubs. She will attack and possibly kill whomever she sees as a threat. She is fiercely loyal and protective of her babies, and has the strength of two bears when provoked.

When she is not rearing cubs, she is completely solitary. The bear is perfectly content with her own company and thoughts. She teaches us not only to protect our young at all costs, but to enjoy our own unique selves. She shows us how to explore our conscious and unconscious thoughts privately and thoroughly, and to relish the ability to do so. The bear is associated with the Goddess. It is also possible that the term "cat" has been misinterpreted in Nordic lore and that the bear is actually the creature that pulls Freya's cart.[8]

Cat: The cat has been seen for centuries as a mysterious, solitary creature. The witch hunts in Europe and North America have contributed to the superstition, still alive today, that these animals are "evil." This unfortunate view of the cat is a perfect example of the new philosophy of monotheism displacing the older, more Earth-centered philosophy of polytheism. A cat's behavior can be quite unsettling at times, and, in many cases, totally bewildering. Instead of learning understanding, new faiths have taught, possibly inadvertently, intolerance of the unknown. While the polytheist's goal is to seek enlightenment from all sources, the modern norm has been to "demonize" the unknown. The cat is just one creature unfairly thrust into this category.

The common house cat is a wondrous creature. She is our gateway in contacting the natural world. She teaches us how to keep our true nature at the forefront of our daily lives. The cat does not conform to anything. Ever. She simply is who she is. She plays, hunts, sharpens her claws, cuddles, and observes unknown objects on walls. She can be arrogant, loving, independent, and enjoys solitude just as much as companionship. She has fierce sexual desires and, if left to her own devices, will be flamboyant with her favors. Even in old age, the cat shows her eternal youth by playing with a string or small toy. She can be a fierce predator and is able to defend herself quite efficiently with tooth, claw, agility, and thought. Her nature will not change, nor will she ever lose her wild essence, which is so loved by many humans. The cat is the wild beast who chooses to coexist with us.

The cat is known for intuition, magical abilities, the mysteries of life, freedom, and even healing. She is associated, first and foremost, with the goddess Freya. Any of us who have an affinity for cats, or are being called upon by a cat spiritual guide, should look to the Daughter Goddess, for She is beckoning.

---

[8] Jacob Grimm, *Teutonic Mythology*, p. 669.

Cow: As discussed in chapter 4, the cow is a sacred creature to the Norse. She is of the aurochs species, now sadly extinct. These creatures were aggressive, hardy, could survive in brutal conditions, were protective of their young and exceedingly dangerous to hunt. The aurochs had a strong herd sense and were revered by the Nordic peoples. To be called by the aurochs is powerful and best not ignored. Her call is one of Earth and the heavens. With the aurochs as your guide, balance, coupled with the previously mentioned attributes, waits for you to employ it. Even though the aurochs is extinct, other species of cattle and bison are not. The aurochs blood is still alive, both physically and spiritually.

Deer: The deer can probably be called the most gentle of all undomesticated species. They are beautiful and graceful creatures, quick to run at the slightest hint of a threat. If a deer comes into your life, either in physical or spiritual form, she is saying to accept things as they are. There is a reason for this need for acceptance, which may or may not be evident. This message comes from a higher power. Dolfyn and Swimming Wolf say, in *Shamanic Wisdom II*, "To encounter Deer is to behold the soul of Earth Mother in Her most gentle aspect . . . ,"[9] For further information on deer, see chapter 11.

Goat: The goat is a stubborn and tenacious creature. Whatever she wants, she gets. She may have to push offending obstacles out of her way, jump over them, or even run over them, but she will succeed. The goat is revered for her wisdom in deducing the best possible solution to a problem. She also has the spiritual characteristics of sexuality and of being securely grounded in the earth (see chapter 11).

Horse: A more magnificent creature than the horse is not to be seen. She has speed, agility, and endurance. Her hoofs and teeth can be used to defend herself and her foal. The horse has enormous power and stamina. While most scholars associate the horse with the gods of the Norse, the feminine association has,

---

9 Dolfyn and Swimming Wolf, *Shamanic Wisdom II* (Oakland: Earthspirit, d/b/a Sacred Earth in California, 1994), p. 44.

inexplicably, been overlooked. The Valkyries ride horses on their airborne flight over land and sea. These goddesses are as one with their mounts in battle, no matter how bloody it becomes. Hel rides a three-legged horse on her visits to Earth, and the nine Wave Maidens of the sea are often referred to as steeds. Sol, Nott, and Bil all ride in horse-drawn chariots in their daily and nightly travels through the heavens.

Horses are associated with psychic and magical abilities. They can assist us in shape-changing, and can also guide us in our mental travels through other levels of life. Horses are wise and can teach us much about ourselves and others. Most of all, the horse is the sign of freedom, victory, and power.

Pig: The pig is a fascinating creature—intelligent, possessive of her young, and extremely aggressive if necessary. Pigs have long been a source of food, even before some species of pig were domesticated. Wild pigs are extremely crafty and ferocious. They are not a creature to take lightly, for they have the ability to maim and even kill a grown human.

The pig has long been symbolic of the goddesses throughout Old Europe. It is possible that the pig is a representation of corn. This symbology, and the sacredness of the pig, is seen in various early European cultures. Archaeologists have recovered stylized figurines of the Goddess wearing pig masks.[10]

Pigs, both sow and boar, are symbolic of the goddess Freya for all of the above reasons. Freya is a goddess of fertility, hence the similarity to the sow. The boar is also associated with Freya, as she has the ability to shape-change her lover Ottar into a boar.

Snake: In his studies of the snake, Jacob Grimm discovered that, to the Norse, the male snake was a representation of the dragon, a symbol of greed. The female snake represents friendly, protective house spirits.[11] This quality bonds the snake with the Valkyries, Disir, and Norns, as they too are protective, female guardian spirits.

---

[10] Marija Gimbutas, *The Gods and Goddesses of Old Europe 6500–3500 B.C.* (Berkeley: University of California Press, 1982), pp. 211–215.
[11] Jacob Grimm, *Teutonic Mythology*, pp. 684–691.

The female snake has various attributes, including sexuality, life, death, and regeneration. She shows us the polytheistic belief in the neverending cycle of life, for even through death, a new life is always born. This also can be seen from a magical perspective. For us to perform such a powerful act, we must renew ourselves, shedding old worries, tensions, and anxieties. To have the snake as a personal guardian shows us that this creature's attributes are available if we learn to shed the past and forge ahead into the future (see chapter 11).

Squirrel: Squirrels are wonderful creatures to watch. They play, run about, race through trees, and are constantly gathering food for the upcoming winter. They are incredibly social, and it is not surprising to see groups of them living in a suburban backyard. The squirrel teaches us a valuable lesson. Gathering is always necessary, but hoarding leads to imbalance. The squirrel shows us how to share our wealth—physically, mentally, emotionally, and spiritually. Dolfyn and Swimming Wolf state in *Shamanic Wisdom II*:

> The ancient Germanic peoples held the Red Squirrel to be sacred. Red Squirrel gives away her territory to her young, leaving her offspring a place to live and a way to eat, and truly these things are a precious legacy.[12]

As we can see, the squirrel can be a great teacher in the realm of the family. It is no wonder she was loved so much by the Nordic peoples. Ratakosk, the squirrel of Yggdrasill, exemplifies pure balance, acceptance, and love of diversity (see chapter 11).

Weasel: The weasel is a wily creature—aggressive, protective of her territory and young, ferocious in a fight, and an intelligent and crafty hunter. She has no fear, and will use her opponents' fear to benefit herself. She shows us how to think and act quickly, and to be aggressive if need be. She is also quiet, which teaches

---

12 Dolfyn and Swimming Wolf, *Shamanic Wisdom II*, p. 116.

us to listen for the hidden message. The weasel is associated with the goddess Freya.

Wolf: In Nordic lore, the wolf is of tremendous importance, although she is normally viewed as both male-oriented and as a companion of Odhinn. Wolf-skin wearers and berserkers are common in legend and these gifted people were not to be taken lightly. Berserkers were incredibly fierce warriors who rarely fell in defeat.

Regardless of these characterizations, the feminine aspect of the wolf cannot be ignored. Wolves are linked with the Valkyries in their visit to battlefields both during and after battle. This gives the wolf associations with both death and rebirth. The Nordic myth of the giantess Hyrrokkin, lends further credence to this.

Hyrrokkin was asked to assist the goddesses and Aesir in their attempt to push the ship carrying the dead body of Balder out to sea. Hyrrokkin immediately came riding a wolf and using snakes for reins. She then pushed the ship easily out to sea. The association between Hyrrokkin and her mount shows us the role of the wolf in death as a guide. The wolf leads and assists the soul to the next stage of life.

The behavior of the wolf teaches us many lessons. She is intelligent and exceptionally loyal to her pack. She teaches us to protect, guide, and love our families. Some cultures see the wolf as being a guardian and teacher of intuitive, psychic, and magical powers.

INSECTS

Bee: The bee, as do many birds, heralds the coming of spring.[13] She is constantly busy pollinating flowers, building her hive, and feeding and protecting her queen. The bee lives in a huge community, performing a set function throughout her life, be it as queen, nurse, drone, or worker. Through the act of pollination she teaches us the importance of gathering. She also teaches us

---

[13] Dolfyn and Swimming Wolf, *Shamanic Wisdom II*, p. 27.

the art of creation through her ability to create honey. Above all, she teaches us respect and reverence for the divine by diligently caring for and nurturing her queen.

The bees' acceptance of their fate is a simple lesson for us all to accept our present. This in no way insinuates an acceptance based on lack of participation, however. The bees are simply telling us to enjoy each minute of every day, without constantly trying to change what is already in place (see chapter 11).

Beetle: According to Jacob Grimm, the little goldbeetle is a Norse feminine spiritual symbol. He states:

> In spring the girls let her [the goldbeetle] creep about on their hands, and say, "she marks [foreshews] me bride's gloves"; if she [the goldbeetle] flies away, they notice in which direction, for thence will come the bridegroom. Thus the beetle seems a messenger of the goddess of love; but the number of the black spots on his wings has to be considered too: if more than seven, corn will be scarce that year, if less, you may look for an abundant harvest. . . ."[14]

As such, the beetle represents love, fertility, and crops. This would align her with the Daughter, as these attributes are Hers as well.

Butterfly: The butterfly is one of the most beautiful of all insect species. With vibrant colors and fragile wings, her flight is an intricate dance of joy showing delight in her surroundings. While the butterfly is certainly one of the smallest creatures we will discuss, she has profound lessons to teach. She is the embodiment of all cycles of life—birth, maturity, death, regeneration, and rebirth. The butterfly begins as an egg. This is symbolic of our own birth and early childhood. The egg hatches into a caterpillar, which is a representation of our middle and late years. As she

---

[14] Jacob Grimm, *Teutonic Mythology,* p. 694.

gets older, the caterpillar begins to spin a cocoon, preparing for her death and regeneration.

This spinning of a cocoon is much like us preparing for our retirement years and our own inevitable deaths. While many of us fear this stage of life, however, the caterpillar teaches us that this is not the end. Death is merely a period of regeneration. The caterpillar is soon reborn as a higher form of life—this being the magnificent butterfly. This insect's life gives us hope and faith, for she is a representation of the divine and the assured continuance of our existence through regeneration. Since the butterfly is associated with the goddess Freya, she is closely aligned with the Daughter Goddess.

OTHER SPIRITUAL SYMBOLS

There are other symbols important to the Nordic faith, but the ones following are strictly connected to the Goddess.

Apples: Apples are the most sacred of all fruit in the Norse worldview. Apples are believed to give youth, vitality, health, and even immortality. These gifts are offered not only to gods, but to mortals. The apple tree is also revered, and many modern runic magicians use a branch from this hallowed tree for their workings.

Gold: Gold has long been prized for its beautiful color and maleability. Because of these special characteristics, gold eventually became a metal used to measure material wealth. Gold's greatest significance in the Norse legends, however, lies in its connection to the goddesses.

The goddesses Frigg, Freya, and Gefjon all loved gold so much that they traded sexual favors for a golden necklace. Freya, on the yearly search for her husband, Od, cries tears of gold throughout the countryside. All the goddesses and Valkyries have hair described as golden, and Sif's hair is especially compared to golden fields. Ran, the goddess of the sea, decorates her hall with the gold from dead voyagers. All of these examples lead to the conclusion that gold has a many-layered meaning and is not merely a pretty metal used for adornment or to gauge wealth.

Gold, through its color, is symbolic of many things. Most notably, gold is characteristic of the Sun, fertile fields, and grain. Gold is unique in that it combines all four elements within itself. The element of fire is obvious through its association with the Sun. The element of water can be observed through the very softness gold exhibits when molded. The element of earth is seen, as gold is found deep within the Earth. Because the Sun is in the heavens, and the goddesses have the attributes of air, so gold also has air attributes. This is a powerful metal, one that enhances the ability to tune in to all elements and aspects of the Goddess of the North.

Drinking Horn: The drinking horn is a highly sacred tool in the Nordic ritual. While it used to be made strictly from an aurochs horn, today any drinking cup, be it horn, glass, stone, or even plastic, is acceptable. The drinking horn, regardless of source, was once part of another being. This use of different materials shows us the constant renewal of life, and the liquid the horn holds is symbolic of the water of the springs of Yggdrasill. As we know, these springs hold a variety of meanings, including creation, birth, death, reincarnation, magic, knowledge, and foresight. To take a drink from the sacred horn is to receive a gift directly from the springs of Yggdrasill and the Goddess of the North.

Keys: In the Norse myths, Frigg is said always to wear a set of keys on her girdle. In imitation, Nordic women did so as well. Initially, these keys may be seen as a symbol of female subservience—of Frigg and her worshippers being confined to the home. This is far from the truth. These keys symbolize the fact that Frigg and her followers are in total control of their *environment*, and all that it may encompass. Frigg controls three halls: her own, the goddesses', and Odhinn's. She oversees and controls all aspects of these halls, both inner and outer. This outer influence was well evidenced in Frigg's manipulation of Odhinn in the myth concerning the two warring mortal tribes.

Keys symbolize the opening of all doors in both the mundane and sacred areas of life.

Spindle: The spindle is symbolic of the yearly cycle. The flax seed is planted and nourished, then it sprouts into a seedling, and eventually grows into a mature plant. At this time, the plant is harvested and, through the use of the spindle, the flax is given a new, different life. The spindle is directly related to Frigg and the Norns, both being aspects of the Mother. On another level, the spindle is the promise of constant renewal, birth, maturity, death, and regeneration, thereby making it a symbol of all three aspects of the Goddess of the North.

Thorr's Hammer: Thorr's hammer holds special significance in all the Nordic myths. It was sacred to the early Norse people, and is still hallowed by both Norse polytheists and Asatru. The hammer is a symbol worn proudly to portray one's deep affection for and honor of the Goddess and the gods of the Norse Tradition. Thorr's hammer demonstrates the equality of the sexes for which we strive in the modern age.

As a god, Thorr represents both the Aesir and the Vanir. His father is Odhinn and his mother is Iord, another name for Earth. While Thorr certainly displays warlike tendencies, always battling enemies, he does so, in most instances, to protect his kin. His behavior could easily be likened to a female bear protecting her cubs. Aggressive, certain of victory, and undaunted by the size or number of the foe, Thorr, unlike other members of the Aesir, fails to be intimidated, coerced, or threatened. Thorr is also unique in that he represents fertility, a virtually unheard of concept among the Aesir race of gods, as fertility is almost universally a feminine divine trait. Thorr's hammer characterizes lightning and rolling thunder, indicating that rain is certain to follow, allowing fertilization of the Earth.

Thorr is the son of the Aesir and the Goddess and, as such, is gifted with both female and male traits. For those of us striving to achieve true balance, a hammer talisman, along with another sacred emblem of the Goddess, is a good tool to wear and contemplate.

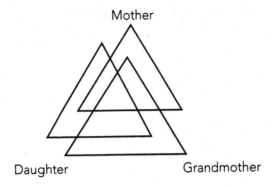

Figure 21. The Valknut.

Valknut: This symbol, long associated with death and the god Odhinn, has a dual meaning with regard to the Goddess. The valknut is made up of three interwoven triangles. The triangle is an ancient sign of the feminine divine, and the use of three triangles knitted together hints strongly at the valknut's feminine aspect, representing the Mother, Daughter, and Grandmother aspects of the Goddess. The valknut indicates a complete unit of one, comprised of three fully developed triangles (see figure 21, above). The number nine, highly significant throughout Nordic lore, is also found in the valknut, the points of all three triangles totaling nine.

The valknut represents countless concepts to the Norse— the three phases of the day, Moon, season, and year; the three sets of nine worlds; the three springs of Yggdrasill; the nine animals of Yggdrasill; the Mother, Daughter, and Grandmother— the list goes on indefinitely. For this reason, solitary exploration of this sacred image is of great benefit to the seeker.

NUMEROLOGY

Certain numbers are very important in the Nordic myths. Normally, it is assumed these special numbers are indicative of runic and magical lore. While this is certainly true, these numbers hold a deeper, more divine meaning. When meditated upon, truly understood and utilized, these numbers will greatly enhance any spiritual, magical, or runic working.

One: This is the primal number of the Goddess, the inner self, and the individual. The number one is indivisible by any other number or force.

Three: There are three roots of Yggdrasill, three springs, three groups of worlds, three phases of the Moon, three phases of a year, three phases of a day, etc. Most important, there are the three aspects of the Goddess of the North—Mother, Daughter, and Grandmother.

Nine: There are nine Wave Maidens, nine worlds, nine animals of Yggdrasill, and many other instances of the number nine throughout Nordic myths. This number is also directly related to the Moon cycles of a woman's pregnancy. While it is known that there are actually ten Moons to a human pregnancy, it is also a fact that, after the ninth Moon, childbirth is not only imminent, but safe for both mother and infant.

Thirteen: This is the number of the yearly cycle of Moons. One can also correlate this number in various ways to Yggdrasill—for example, one tree, three springs, and nine worlds equaling thirteen. This sacred number symbolizes the constant birth, growth, aging, death, and rebirth characteristic of the Goddess of the North.

While an entire book could be written about the spiritual symbols of the Norse Tradition, the purpose here is to give a brief description, without compromising the reader's own intuition concerning the symbols. Two of the most valued concepts of heathenism and paganism are the acceptance of diversity and individualism. This diversity and individualism pave the way for personal interpretations, teaching each one of us to be unique. Any spiritual insight that is divinely inspired is always correct. We are all of the Goddess. Therefore, no sign She gives us personally can truly be called incorrect.

THE GODDESS TODAY

It is an indisputable fact that our northern European ancestors worshipped the Goddess. It is also a fact that She had a divine male counterpart—husband, lover, and son. While we have not discussed this aspect, it is certainly implied by the many Norse myths we have studied. The role of the God will be studied in a later text, but it is important to note the duality of the divine figures worshipped by the Norse. Even though the emphasis of this book is on the feminine, we do not wish to make the same mistake made in the past by perpetuating an imbalance of the sexes. Our goal here is to seek the equality which is our right, and to restore the Goddess to the proper and much deserved place She held in our early history.

The Goddess of the North is not an aloof deity. She does not wait in the wings observing our every move, weighing the positive and negative of our actions. She does not judge the outcome of our lives, nor does She reward or punish us with the promise of either a utopian or an infernal afterlife. Our participation in the next level of existence is based upon our individual goals and achievements. As we move into the next phase of life, we hold within ourselves the gifts and abilities to venture closer to, or farther from, the Goddess.

The Goddess is incorporated into every facet of our lives—our shelter, food, clothing, children, and family. Her involvement and support is limitless. The fact that She does not use fear as a tool of worship should be considered a blessing, but because of this, She does indeed place a great responsibility on our shoulders. She expects us to use our talents to enhance our lives and the lives of those around us—not only humans, but all species and beings, animate and inanimate. This, then, is our goal—to cherish, revere, and enjoy all of the Goddess's wonderful creations. To become a friend to all—be it neighbor, squirrel, or tree—is a requirement and the very foundation of our continuing future.

To accomplish this task, we must learn to view our actions, thoughts, and lives through new eyes. Recycling is a requirement, not a choice; purchasing products that are safe for the environment is a necessity; boycotting products made from endangered species is a must. Within the parameters of protecting the environment—i.e., the Goddess—we, as consumers, have the upper hand, as long as we choose to utilize it. Manufacturers will not produce what we will not purchase. It is simply not profitable.

These are only a few of the steps we can take to acknowledge, remember, and worship the Goddess. It is hard for us, at times, to remember that every single item within our lives is of the Goddess, as She *is* the Earth, the universe, and so much more. This very book is made from materials grown and harvested from the Earth. The clothes on our backs, the carpet at our feet, the chair on which we sit—everything is of the Goddess and, in that sense, is sacred. It is hard for us to remember that our trash, packed away in a can to be removed to an unseen place, is also a part of the Goddess, rejoining Her through decomposition. This concept of everything having a meaning, a soul, and a purpose is called animism. It is a large part of the Nordic Tradition. Everything is sacred and has life, for everything is of the Goddess.

We are fortunate to have so many authors and practitioners of heathen and pagan traditions today. These people have kept alive the essence of heathenism, paganism, polytheism, and animism for others to learn, nurture, and eventually teach. While our society, politically, does not condone discrimination against religious preference, it is an unfortunate truth that, within our culture, such discrimination does exist. We, as members of this society, have an obligation to ourselves and to our children to perserve our religious freedom. We must not allow it to be suppressed, or we will be thrust back into the Dark Ages.

To achieve the balance of feminine and masculine, and to protect religious rights for ourselves and our children, we must be willing to be more vocal. We must be willing to talk to, listen to, and educate those of other faiths. Only in this way will we be and able to publicly retain and share our faith. Secrecy and silence are no longer the path to the wondrous myths, legends, stories, and beauty of the Goddess.

Another challenge facing heathens and pagans today is educating our children. We question how to raise them with proper reverence for nature, the divine, and each other, and with positive goals for their future. Today's children are in dire need of the Goddess. Many run wild, in packs, and prey on innocents. They have little or no supervision, and it has become the custom to blame the educational system for this lack of restraint. Many children are "latch-key kids," expected at a young age to fend for themselves after school while their parents work. Others are left at daycare centers to be raised by people other than family members or friends.

In the past, children were raised by the tribe. They were not left to their own devices. Creativity and other skills were applauded and directed with loving care. Children were a part of every meal, ritual, and celebration enjoyed by the tribe. Mothers, fathers, grandmothers, grandfathers, aunts, and uncles were all directly involved in the raising of each child. To have a child was a direct blessing from the Goddess, and each child was cherished as a precious new member of the community. The naming of a child required much care and contemplation, for the name would draw protective spirits to the child—including those of the dead, if a child were named after a deceased person. Children were taught to respect themselves, their deities, kin, tribe, and community, and to put these interests first and foremost over any other material concern. Children were shown the Goddess and all of Her splendor firsthand, and knew Her intimately throughout their lives.

The difference in the two scenarios of childrearing is huge, and the reasons for it are many. First, the need for money to survive in the modern society is overpowering. Many people have no choice but to work outside the home, and most households need at least two incomes to survive. Second, it has become the norm for extended family members to live far apart. As communication systems have evolved, the need for adults to see each other on a daily basis has diminished. Third, the ability and/or desire to instruct children on the issues of morality and ethics has been compromised to an alarming degree. Parents don't have the time to do this and, as other family members and close friends are usually not available to fill this gap, the brunt of this task has fallen to other sources. Most of these people—teachers, clergy, neighbors, daycare providers—are unable and, understandably, unwilling to meet this fundamental need of our youth.

The same influences that are creating havoc among our children have been responsible, in recent years, for our questioning and abandoning current faiths and searching for the path of our ancestors. The desire for financial gain, to the detriment of family, cannot be blamed solely on monotheism, but it is, indeed, a fact that a society does base many of its goals and desires on accepted spiritual teachings. And while there is certainly nothing wrong with aspiring to gain financial independence, we must each question whether the material goals are truly a necessity. If so, we must then decide if the particular goal we have in mind is deterring us from other important goals, like time with our children and the pursuit of a higher spiritual intimacy with the Goddess.

Material goals sometimes separate us from family, as our jobs require us to live in certain areas. Again, we must ask if this is indeed a necessity, or merely the fulfillment of a desire that might be better left waiting until young children need less direction from their kin. One of the most beautiful facets of the Norse Tradition is the emphasis on family, and the importance each member holds in relation to knowledge and understanding of the Goddess. Spirituality does not come from one person, one book, or one vision. It is an ongoing experience perpetuated through stories, walks, discussions, questions, and contemplation. Many heathens and pagans are solitary, and they suffer from the same lack of input as our children. While they are certainly more able to read a variety of texts and meditate on the wonder of the Goddess, human interaction within a spiritual setting is important as well. A new mode of communication has recently become available—the use of online computer resources. This development has bridged the gap for solitaries, and has helped them fulfill their desire and need to share their views and experiences of the feminine divine. It is also a wonderful tool to help heathens and pagans come together, which benefits both parents and children.

We really have to question our lack of desire or ability to teach morality and ethics to our young. We have to determine whether this stems from a lack of time, insufficient understanding, or incomplete spiritual guidance. In the heathen and pagan worldview, spiritual guidance is a constant. We are aware of our surroundings and pay close attention to subtle hints given to us by animal visitations, dreams, or intuitive visions. We normally make time to listen fully to these messages and, in many cases, meditate deeply on their meaning. This is in direct contrast to the monotheistic worldview where these same messengers are normally deemed unworthy and, by some sects, demonic. This difference in spiritual views puts a great deal of pressure on heathens and pagans concerning their children. The last thing any of us desires is to see our children suffer from negative peer pressure. We have all experienced this cruelty, and wish to protect our young. We cannot. We are obligated as parents to share these experiences with our children, and to help them develop their own spirituality and connection with the Goddess. This is what teaching morals and ethics is all about—sharing the good and bad, teaching the consequences for action and inaction, and learning to develop a secure, strong inner self.

THREE BASIC TENETS OF THE GODDESS OF THE NORTH

The Goddess of the North teaches us a basic creed to live our lives by. It is three-fold, in accordance with Her aspects of Mother, Daughter, and Grandmother.

Honor: In the Nordic worldview honor means that we honor the Goddess first and foremost; then ourselves, our children and spouse, our kin, our community, and our country. This means that we do all in our power to be the best we can be to each of these groups. We are active, participating elements in this membership. We are always prepared to love, protect, serve, listen, question, guide, and cherish each member within the whole. The word "honor" does not equate to "obey." We are individuals, with separate wants and needs. We do not partake, however, in any action that we know will have a negative impact on another member of our extended "family." This is honor (see figure 22, page 233). An example of honor can be seen in a myth of the Goddess in her Frigg aspect.

When Frigg's son, Balder, was murdered, she did everything in her power to bring him back from the underworld. She requested the tears of all beings to meet the demands of the giantess/goddess Hel. These tears, shed by every soul within the worlds, would have freed Balder from his imprisonment. Loki, however, would not comply, and Balder remained in Hel's domain. Eventually, in punishment, Loki was caught and bound in a cave to await Ragnarok.

Frigg exhibited honor in this myth, for she could have declared war upon Loki. She could have led the Aesir and the Vanir to a horribly bloody battle against Loki and his mortal followers. If she had done this, many mortals would have been slaughtered needlessly, and the Aesir and Vanir harmed in unknown ways. She would actually have caused a premature Ragnarok.

Instead, Frigg honored Hel's request, even though it failed to return Balder to her embrace. Frigg honored herself, her spouse, family, kin, friends, and worshippers by not requesting them to go to a battle destined to fail. Even though her love for her son was all-encompassing, Frigg continued to honor herself and all members of her world by biding her time. Eventually, Loki was destroyed and Balder returned to share the love of his mother.

To *be* honorable involves action, not inaction, as the circumstance requires. To *be* honorable emphasizes the need to strive constantly to *act* with honor. Frigg does this in her decision

Figure 22. Honor in the Norse Tradition.

to await Ragnarok. Fathers or mothers do this when they protect their children from harm. An employee exemplifies honorable action when she or he reports the wrongdoing of another employee or supervisor. A neighbor acts in an honorable fashion when she or he picks up a telephone to report signs of possible abuse. To have honor and to act honorably is one of the tenets of the Nordic Tradition.

Respect: From the Nordic viewpoint, respect is a key element on the path to spirituality (see figure 23, page 235). Respect is not merely a catchall term used to express how we view another individual. Respect is an *action*. We show respect to the Goddess through remembrance, study, conversation, meditation, and consideration of Her. Respect is shown through recycling, protesting the extermination of forests and species, protecting the precious water resources, and not littering. We show the Goddess our respect in the way we care for pets and even in the way we care for common household items. Respect for the Goddess encompasses all, but sometimes it can be twisted to encompass a more personal desire.

This can be seen in our attitude toward the ordinary lawn. In our country, property values and neighbors' good opinions are enhanced by the appearance of a well-kept green lawn. Many people also find it quite enjoyable to work in their yards as a hobby. With the exception of areas that receive a fairly high volume of rain, however, green yards are not only impractical, but disrespectful to the Goddess. A massive amount of precious water is wasted upon them every year. Not only is our limited water supply impacted, but the environment itself is altered to support these lawns. In some cases, this alteration actually prohibits native wildlife from flourishing. We need to remember that we are a *part* of the environment, which is the Goddess. We are not in control of it or of Her. For those of us not happy with the natural environment in which we live, it would be infinitely preferable to live in climates that conform to our desires, naturally, rather than changing the body of the Goddess to please ourselves.

We show respect for others by honoring the fact that each and every being has a life-force. We do not need to like or admire each individual or species. This has nothing to do with respect. We do, however, need to acknowledge their existence and respect their right to life. We also show respect by not forcing others, human or otherwise, to conform to our expectations of ourselves. Respecting another's choice of spirituality is a fundamental key to being a true heathen or pagan. None of us know the factual "truth" of the afterlife. Therefore, we must rely on our own personal experiences and insights, and share them if requested. For any of us to proclaim that we have found the one spiritual truth for all humankind is to act in distasteful arrogance, and to perpetrate an extreme act of disrespect. The wonders of the Goddess are many. She shows each of us a different painting, to be cherished and remembered forever.

As we discuss respect, we must consider our children, spouses, and immediate families. We hear the phrase "respect your elders" from a young age. This phrase appears to mean that we must *listen to and obey* our elders, simply because they are older than we are. This is not respect, but is actually closer to fear. Our elders do deserve our respect, as they have lived longer and experienced more. They should be our most cherished leaders, advisors, and educators. It is a shame that, in our society, people who have reached a certain age are considered expendable. In the past, these same people held high seats of respect and honor within their tribe.

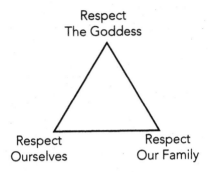

Figure 23. Respect in the Norse Tradition.

Our spouses, family members, and friends also deserve our undying respect. They are the ones who married us, birthed us, and have stood at our sides through countless sorrows and un-forgettable joys. Because of these people, we are who we are. We must not take these members of our "tribe" for granted, for there will come a day when we will sorely regret this in-action.

Children, too, deserve our respect. They are the true com-modities of the future of humankind. Too often, children are ex-pected to "be seen and not heard." We forget that they are a part of our "tribe," and have a voice, no matter how naive or young. We must progress to a stage where we are again ready to listen to, educate, cherish, and protect our children. They are the extension of ourselves. They are the most wondrous gift the Goddess has bestowed upon us.

In our hectic lifestyles, we forget that we deserve our own, personal respect. Most of us work hard, strive to achieve goals, do the very best we can, but always feel as if what we do is simply not good enough in comparison to our society's goals. We need to remind ourselves that we are of the Goddess, and we are good folk. We must again learn to respect ourselves.

Responsibility: This is probably the hardest tenet for most hea-thens and pagans to learn. Many of us are accustomed to the concept of redemption. In other words, most of us have been taught to request forgiveness for negative deeds and assume it will be granted. This is not the way of the Nordic Tradition.

We must again learn to be responsible for every action, or
inaction, we perform. If an action has negative consequences, we
are responsible for rectifying them. This is called making amends
or, in the Nordic Tradition, paying *weregild*. If we hit an animal
while driving, we do not drive off. We stop and assist the animal,
as it is our fault it is injured. If we see another driver hit an animal and drive off, we still stop. Whether we actually commit the
negative action or not, we are still responsible to react in some
fashion, even if we only watched one of our fellow species commit the wrongdoing (see figure 24, page 237).

This does not mean that we are responsible for every action
every human makes. It does mean that we are responsible for
making the choice of action or inaction if we perform, or see another perform, a negative deed. We are responsible for protecting
and nurturing the Goddess in Her Earthly form, just as She protects and nurtures us. By taking responsibility when we see a
negative action committed against Her or any of Her beloved
species, we actually become responsible for our own continuing
future.

We are responsible for our personal well-being and that of
our immediate and extended families. We are responsible for
providing shelter, clothing, food, education, spiritual guidance,
and models of moral and ethical conduct. We have this responsibility, not only to ourselves, our spouses, and our children, but
also to our kin, friends, and community.

One of the most depressing human tragedies facing us
today is that of homelessness. Our society views not only elders
as dispensable, but also those unable to fend for themselves and
meet societal standards. This includes those who have lost all of
their hard-earned belongings due to unemployment, those suffering from mental illness, those suffering from other personal
tragedies, and even children who have run away from home. It is
impossible to believe that these people have no family. It is also
impossible to believe that those families are not helping these
unfortunate individuals. Every person, in some fashion, needs a
helping hand at least once in their lives. None of us is perfect.
The homeless are, however, literally thrown away, destined to
drift endlessly through our city streets. This breakdown of the

Figure 24. Responsibility in the Norse Tradition.

family is an act of sheer irresponsibility—one that must be rectified by all members involved. If we do not again become responsible to our families, we cannot expect to be responsible either to ourselves or to the Goddess.

We are fortunate, however. We have the ability to become a closer family unit. We have the ability to learn change, and we certainly have the ability to expand our spiritual awareness. The Goddess has spoken to us in various ways, and with Her guidance, we can learn to be responsible again without depending on a fevered prayer begging for salvation. Many heathens and pagans have already learned this. They are the most fortunate of us all for having done so. As they can attest, learning responsibility to oneself and to others brings one ever closer to the realm of the Goddess, for She encompasses all life.

These three concepts of honor, respect, and responsibility are the basic tenets of the Goddess of the North (see figure 25, page 238). However, the Nordic Tradition is not set in stone. Other tenets can be found in Edred Thorsson's *A Book of Troth,* which contains good guidelines to consider and, if chosen, to include in one's personal observance.[1]

It should be noted that the heathen path is not a path of strict tenets and rules. The three tenets of honor, respect, and responsibility detailed above are merely suggestions from personal experience and research. While no one wishes to revert to living

---

[1]Edred Thorsson, *A Book of Troth* (St. Paul: Llewellyn, 1992).

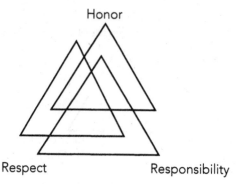

Honor

Respect   Responsibility

Figure 25. The three tenets of the Norse spiritual tradition.

in the times of early history, some of the ways of early people hold lessons that we, as humans, should consider bringing into the future. These early practices can be positive influences, leading us ever closer to the higher realm of spiritual enlightenment that is the entire purpose of our search.

The Goddess of the North has been misunderstood and hidden for centuries. Now, due to the development of complex communication systems and the overwhelming pull toward feminism and heathenism/paganism, the Goddess is coming to the fore again in our lives. This time, we will continue to look forward, while remembering the past, certain never to forget Her again.

GLOSSARY

Aesir: Originally used as a name for the race of gods fathered by Odhinn, Vili, and Ve. After the war between the Aesir and Vanir gods, the term Aesir came to be used for all gods. It is still common to use Aesir to describe battle and war gods in general.

Animism: Spiritual belief that all creatures and objects have life, are sacred, and have a soul.

Apples: Hallowed fruit of youth, health, and longevity. The apple tree is held just as sacred, since these same attributes resound throughout the tree's physical body.

Asatru: Term sometimes used as a name for the Norse Tradition. Due to negative connotations caused by a very small minority of Asatru members, some people prefer being called Norse polytheists, heathens, or pagans.

Asgard: World that stands at the highest level of the nine worlds and is normally thought to be the home of the Aesir gods.

Ask: Created by Odhinn, Vili, and Ve from a log, Ask became the first male of the human species.

Asynia: Singular term used for a Norse goddess.

Asyniur: Plural term used to refer to all Norse goddesses.

Audmula: In the creation myth, Audmula is the sacred aurochs who nursed the giant Ymir. Audmula is actually the Goddess of the North in metaphoric disguise.

Berserker: Warriors who are able to shape-change into bears or wolves during battle. These gifted people are almost unstoppable, and are valued members of any army.

Bifrost: Mythic rainbow bridge that connects the three levels of the nine worlds. Bifrost will be destroyed temporarily at the onset of Ragnarok.

Draupnir: Magical ring of gold belonging to Odhinn. When he gives it to his dead son, Balder, Draupnir begins to reproduce itself eight times every ninth night.

Drinking Horn: Sacred tool used throughout the centuries for Nordic rituals. Regardless of the material of which it is made, the drinking horn is symbolic of the aurochs, Audmula.

Embla: First female of the human race. She, along with her partner Ask, was created from a dead log by Odhinn and his two brothers.

Fatalism: Belief in no afterlife. Fatalism is totally contradictory to the Norse Tradition.

Fensalir: Frigg's hall, located presumably either on the world of Asgard or Vanaheim.

Fjorgyn: Mother of Frigg and grandmother of Freya. Fjorgyn is often called Mother Earth. Fjorgyn is the name humans gave the Grandmother Goddess.

Folkvang: Hall of Freya, positioned on the world of Vanaheim.

Freya: Daughter of Frigg. Freya is the goddess of love and youth, to name just two of her many attributes. Freya is the name humans gave to the Daughter Goddess.

Frigg: Queen of the Aesir and Asyniur. She is the human-given form of the Mother Goddess.

Ginnungagap: The void of space where Earth was created.

Gungnir: Odhinn's magical spear.

Heathenism: Spiritual practice of "nature" religions, polytheism, paganism, and animism. Many polytheists prefer to be named heathens.

Hel: Name for both the giantess/goddess of the underworld and one of the nine worlds lying at the lowest level in the Norse cosmos.

Hlidskialf: Magical chair in the hall of Valaskialf. This chair is used to view all of the nine worlds.

Hvergelmir: One of the springs of Yggdrasill.

Hyfjaberg: This is the sacred rock of the healer Mengloth and her attendants.

Idises: Another name for the feminine guardian spirits, Disir.

Jotunheim: World on the middle level of the cosmos, along with Midgard and Svartalfheim.

Keys: Revered symbol of Nordic femininity linked directly with the goddess Frigg. Keys are representative of the control a woman has over her chosen environment.

Laevateinn: Magical sword guarded by the giantess Sinmara that will supposedly be used in Ragnarok.

Lif: Mortal woman said to survive Ragnarok.

Lifthrasir: Mate of Lif, also thought to survive Ragnarok.

Ljossalfheim: World that sits on the same lofty level as Asgard.

Midgard: Earth.

Mimir: Name for both a god and a spring of Yggdrasill.

Mjollnir: Thorr's sacred and magical hammer.

Monotheism: Spiritual belief in only one supreme being, usually considered male.

Mothers: Groups of early Nordic women who traveled to assist other communities in the arts of healing, magic, and divination.

Muspellheim: World of the south, located on the same level as Hel. One of the worlds to help create Midgard. Muspellheim is the world of fire.

Nidhogg: Dragon who is constantly trying to destroy the Guardian Tree, Yggdrasill.

Niflheim: World of the north, filled with cold and ice, located on the same plane as Hel and Muspellheim. Niflheim was one of the worlds that helped in the creation of Midgard.

Orlog: Destiny of all known and unknown life throughout the universe and beyond.

Paganism: Term, like heathenism, for faiths based upon nature, polytheism, and animism. Some polytheists and heathens prefer the title of pagan.

Polytheism: Spiritual belief in more than one deity.

Ragnarok: Also called "The Twilight of the Gods." The Norse end-of-existence myth.

Ratatosk: Squirrel who dwells on the World Tree, Yggdrasill.

Ringhorn: Ship used to carry the god Balder's body out to sea.

Runemasters: People who are adept at runic workings.

Runes: Ancient sequence of spiritual symbols used for magic, divination, and, occasionally, communication.

Seidhr: Norse feminine practice of astral projection, magic, runic lore, herbal craft, and witchcraft.

Shamanism: Ability to commune spiritually on different levels of existence.

Shape-changing: Art of utilizing an animal skin or vision to physically and mentally become one with that specific animal.

Spae-wife: Norse term for a witch.

Spindle: Revered symbol of the goddess Frigg. The spindle characterizes the talents all women innately have.

Svartalfheim: World that lies on the same level as Midgard and Jotunheim.

Thorr's Hammer: Nordic spiritual symbol recognizing both the feminine and masculine powers of the divine. On a mythical level, Thorr's Hammer is named Mjollnir.

Urd: Name for a Norn and a spring of Yggdrasill.

Valas: Another term used for the goddesses of fate and destiny, the Norns.

Valaskialf: Hall of Odhinn that is roofed in silver. It is located in Asgard. Home of the magical chair, Hlidskialf.

Val-Halla: Odhinn's hall in Asgard, home of all slain warriors chosen by the Valkyries. These warriors are said to reside in Val-Halla until the coming of Ragnarok.

Valknut: Sacred symbol normally associated with Odhinn, but is also an ancient feminine symbol of the divine. The Valknut is a group of three intertwined triangles.

Vanaheim: World of the Vanir, located on the same level as Asgard and Ljossalfheim.

Vanir: Fertility gods. After the war of the gods, the Vanir became known as the Aesir.

Vedrfolnir: Hawk who sits in Yggdrasill.

Vigrid: Mythic battlefield where the destruction of Ragnarok will take place.

Vingolf: Hall of the Asyniur, overseen by the Queen of the Aesir and Asyniur, Frigg.

Volva: Woman who practices the sacred art of seidhr.

Weregild: Physical repayment given to rectify a wrong done toward another.

Wild Hunt: Divinely led search for lost souls in Midgard. This hunt is usually headed by Odhinn and/or the Valkyries.

Winternights: Norse polytheistic holy festival held yearly to honor the Disir of the family line.

Yggdrasill: Hallowed World Tree of the Norse.

PRONUNCIATION GUIDE

The following guide gives the pronunciations of the majority of names and places listed throughout this book. Names missing from this list should be pronounced using modern English techniques; such as the name "Bil," which is pronounced the same as the word "bill." This guide is based upon the pronunciations found in *Teutonic Myth and Legend,* by Donald A. Mackenzie, and *The Norsemen,* by H. A. Guerber.[1]

Aegir	ā′ jir
Aesir	ā′ sir
Angrboda	än – gur - bō′ dà
Asgard	as′ gärd
Ask	äsk
Asyniur	a – sin′ joor
Aud	owd
Audmula	ow – dum′ la
Aurboda	owr – bod′ a
Balder	bäl′ der
Bergelmir	ber – gel′ mir
Berserker	bēr′ serk - er
Bertha	bēr′ thà
Bestla	best′ la
Bifrost	bē frest
Bolthorn	bol′ thorn
Bor	bēr
Bragi	brä′ gē
Brechta	brek′ tà
Brisingamen	bri – sing′ à - men
Brisingr	bri – sing′ - ur
Brunnaker	brōōn′ na - ker
Buri	bur′ e

[1] H. A. Guerber, *The Norsemen* (London: Senate, 1994); and Donald A. Mackenzie, *Teutonic Myth and Legend: An Introduction to the Eddas and Sagas, Beowulf, the Nibelungenlied, etc.* (London: Gresham, n.d.)

Dain	dā′ in
Disis (Dis, Disir)	dis′ ez
Draupnir	droup′ nir
Duneyr	dōō′ nīr
Durathror	dōō′ ra thrôr
Dvalin	dvä′ lin
Eir	īr
Ellida	el – li′ - da
Elvidner	el – vid′ ner
Embla	em′ bla
Erce	er′ ka
Farbauti	far – bou′ tē
Fenia	fen′ yà
Fenris	fen′ ris
Fensalir	fen′ säl - ir
Fimbulvetr	fim′ bul - vet ur
Fjorgvin	fyôrg′ vin
Fjorgyn	fyôr′ gēn
Folkvang	fōlk′ vang
Forseti	fôr – set′ e
Frau Gode	frou gō′ dā
Frau Holle	frou hol - le
Freki	frek′ ē
Frey	frī
Freya	frī - ya
Frigg	frig
Friia	frī - a
Frithiof	frĭt′ yof
Frodi	frō′ dé
Fulla	ful′ à
Fylgie	fīl′ gye
Gefjon	gef′ yon
Gefn	gef′ n
Geirrod	gīr′ rod
Geri	gēr′ ē
Gersemi	gēr – se - mē
Gialp	gyälp

Gimle	gim' lē
Ginnungagap	gi – nōōn' gȧ - gap
Gna	gnä
Greip	grīp
Grid	greed
Groa	grō' ȧ
Gud	good
Gullveig	gul' vēg
Gungnir	gung' nir
Gunnlod	gōōn' lod
Hamingjes	ham' ing - yez
Hati	hä' tē
Heid	hīd
Heimdall	hī m' däl
Heith	hīth
Helge	hel' ge
Hermod	hēr' mod
Hild	heeld
Hjuki	hyuk' e
Hlidskialf	hlidz' kyȧlf
Hlodyn	hlo' dēn
Hraesvelg	hrā - svelg
Hugin	hōō' gin
Huldra	hul' drȧ
Hvergelmir	hver – gel' mēr
Hyrrokkin	hēr' ro - kin
Iarnaxa	yärn' sax - ȧ
Idavoll	eedä - vol
Idises	ē – dis' ez
Idun	ē' doon
Ilm	ēlm
Ingeborg	in' – ge - borg
Iord	yērd
Jormungand	yēr' mun - gand
Jotunheim	yē' tōōn - hīm
Kvasir	kvä' sir
Laevateinn	lā' va tīn

Lifthrasir	lĭf′ thrä - sir
Ljossalfheim	lyōs′ alf hīm
Lofn	lōfn
Loki	lō′ kē
Magni	mag′ nē
Mani	man′ ē
Mardel	mär′ del
Mengloth	men′ glôth
Menia	men ĭ′ - a
Midgard	mid′ gärd
Mimir	mē′ mir
Mjollnir	myēl′ nir
Modi	mō′ dē
Munin	mōō′ nin
Muspellheim	mus′ pels - hīm
Mysing	mee′ sing
Naglfar	nag′ el - får
Nanna	nan′ na
Nerthus	nēr′ thus
Nidhogg	nee′ dhoog
Niflheim	nĭfl′ - hīm
Njord	nyērd
Odhinn	ō′ din
Orion	o - rī′ on
Orlog	ôr′ log
Ostara	os′ tä - ra
Ottar	ot′ tar
Radgrid	rad′ greed
Ragnarok	råg′ nå - rok
Randgrid	rand′ greed
Ratatosk	ra′ ta - tosk
Reginleif	rā′ gen - lif
Rerir	rā′ rir
Ringhorn	reng′ - horn
Rugen	rē′ gen
Saga	sa′ ga
Schwartze See	shvärt′ se - sä
Sigyn	sē′ gēn

Sjofn	syōfn
Skadi	skä′ dē
Skialf	skyȧlf
Skiold	skōld
Skoll	skēl
Skuld	skoold
Sleipnir	slīp′ nir
Snotra	snō′ tra
Sokkvabekk	so − kvä′ bek
Surt	sōōrt
Suttung	sut - tōōng
Svafnir	svȧf′ nir
Svartalfheim	svärt − alf′ - hīm
Syn	sēn
Syr	sēr
Thorr	thôr′
Thrud	thrōōd
Thrymheim	thrim′ hīm
Tyr	tēr
Uller	oŏl′ er
Urd	oŏrd
Vafthrudnir	väf − thrōōd′ nir
Vala	vä′ lȧ
Valaskialf	vä′ la - skyȧlf
Valfreya	val − frī′ a
Val-Halla	väl − häl′ lȧ
Vali	vä′ lē
Valkyries	val′ keer - ez
Vanabride	väna − brē′ dȧ
Vanaheim	väna′ hīm
Vanadis	vȧn′ ȧ − dis
Vanir	vȧn′ ir
Vara	vä′ rȧ
Ve	vā
Vedrfolnir	ved ur fol′ ner
Verdandi	vēr − dän′ dē
Vidar	vē′ där

Vigrid	vig' rid
Vili	vi' lē
Vingolf	ving' golf
Volsung	vol' sung
Vor	vĕr
Vrou-Elde	vrōō – eld' e
Winnilers	win' i - lerz
Wode	wō' da
Wyrd	wērd
Ygg	ig
Yggdrasill	ig' drȧ - sil
Ymir	ē' mir

BIBLIOGRAPHY

To assist the reader, this bibliography has been separated into sections, although many of the texts actually encompass the majority of the listed categories. In these instances, I have selected the primary classification in relation to our specific study of the Goddess of the North. I have chosen not to annotate each entry for the simple reason that every book listed in the next few pages is highly recommended. Each work contains a truth pertaining to this Goddess study, although sometimes it may not always be easily discernible.

Comparative Spiritual and Mythological Studies

Andrews, Ted. *Animal Speak: The Spiritual and Magical Powers of Creatures Great and Small.* St. Paul: Llewellyn, 1995.

Biedermann, Hans. *Dictionary of Symbolism, Cultural Icons and the Meanings Behind Them.* James Hulbert, trans. New York: Meridan, 1992.

Buffalo Horn Man, Gary and Sherry Firedancer. *Animal Energies.* Lexington KY: Dancing Otter, 1992.

Bulfinch, Thomas. *Bulfinch's Mythology of Greece and Rome with Eastern and Norse Legends.* New York: Collier, 1962.

Carey, Ken. *Return of the Bird Tribes.* San Francisco: HarperSanFrancisco, 1988.

Conway, D. J. *The Ancient and Shining Ones: World Myth, Magic, and Religion.* St. Paul: Llewellyn, 1994.

Cunningham, Scott. *Wicca: A Guide for the Solitary Practitioner.* St. Paul: Llewellyn, 1994.

Dolfyn and Swimming Wolf. *Shamanic Wisdom II: The Way of the Animal Spirits.* Oakland: Earthspirit, d/b/a Sacred Earth in California, 1994.

Eagleman, Ed McGaa. *Native Wisdom: Perceptions of the Natural Way.* Minneapolis: Four Directions, 1995.

Graves, Robert. *The Greek Myths*, 2 vols. rev. ed. New York: Penguin, 1960.

Harner, Michael. *The Way of the Shaman.* 3rd ed. San Francisco: HarperSanFrancisco, 1990.

The Holy Bible, New Revised Standard Version. New York: American Bible Society, 1989.

Lake-Thom, Bobby. *Spirits of the Earth: A Guide to Native American Nature Symbols, Stories, and Ceremonies.* New York: Plume, 1997.

Matthews, John. *The Celtic Shaman: A Handbook.* Boston: Element, 1991.

McCoy, Edain. *Witta: An Irish Pagan Tradition.* St. Paul: Llewellyn, 1993.

Meadows, Kenneth. *Earth Medicine: A Shamanic Way to Self-Discovery.* Boston: Element, 1989.

Olson, Dennis L. *Shared Spirits: Wildlife and Native Americans.* Minocqua: NorthWord Press, 1995.

Pennick, Nigel. *The Pagan Book of Days: A Guide to the Festivals, Traditions, and Sacred Days of the Year.* Rochester, VT: Destiny, 1992.

Pickthall, Mohammad M. *The Glorious Qur'an.* Rev. ed. Des Plaines: Library of Islam, 1994.

Sams, Jamie and David Carson. *Medicine Cards, the Discovery of Power through the Ways of Animals.* Sante Fe: Bear & Company, 1988.

Sun Bear, Wabun Wind, and Crysalis Mulligan. *Dancing with the Wheel: The Medicine Wheel Workbook.* New York: Fireside, 1991.

Telesco, Patricia. *Folkways: Reclaiming the Magic and Wisdom.* St. Paul: Llewellyn, 1995.

Folk and Fairy Tales

Andersen, Hans Christian. *Hans Christian Andersen: The Complete Fairy Tales and Stories.* Erik Christian Haugaard, trans. New York: Anchor, 1974.

———. *Andersen's Fairy Tales.* Mrs. E. V. Lucas and Mrs. H. B. Paull, trans. New York: Grosset and Dunlap, 1945.

———. *Andersen's Fairy Tales.* Pat Shaw Iversen, trans. New York: Signet, 1987.

———. *Hans Andersen's Fairy Tales: A Selection.* L. W. Kingsland, trans. Oxford: Oxford University Press, 1984.

Booss, Claire, ed. *Scandinavian Folk and Fairy Tales: Tales from Norway, Sweden, Denmark, Finland, Iceland.* New York: Gramercy, 1984.

Grimm, Jakob and Wilhelm. *The Complete Grimm's Fairy Tales.* Margaret Hunt, trans. Revised, corrected, and completed by James Stern. New York: Pantheon, 1972.

———. *Grimm's Fairy Tales.* Mrs. E. V. Lucas, Lucy Crane, and Marian Edwardes, trans. New York: Grosset and Dunlap, 1945.

———. *Grimm's Tales for Young and Old.* Ralph Manheim, trans. New York: Anchor, 1977.

———. *The Complete Fairy Tales of the Brothers Grimm.* Expanded ed. Jack Zipes, trans. New York: Bantam, 1992.

Yolen, Jane, ed. *Favorite Folktales from around the World.* New York: Pantheon, 1986.

Goddess Studies

Adler, Margot. *Drawing Down the Moon.* Rev. ed. New York: Penguin, 1986.

Eller, Cynthia. *Living in the Lap of the Goddess.* New York: Crossroad, 1993.

Gimbutas, Marija. *The Civilization of the Goddess: The World of Old Europe.* San Francisco: HarperSanFrancisco, 1991.

———. *The Gods and Goddesses of Old Europe: Myths and Cult Images, 6500–3500 B.C.* New and updated ed. Berkeley: University of California Press, 1982.

———. *The Language of the Goddess.* San Francisco: HarperSanFrancisco, 1989.

Graves, Robert. *The White Goddess.* New York: Noonday Press, 1948.

Heath, Jennifer. *On the Edge of Dream: The Women of Celtic Myth and Legend.* New York: Plume/Penguin, 1998.

Johnson, Buffie. *Lady of the Beasts: The Goddess and Her Sacred Animals.* Rochester, VT: Inner Traditions, 1994.

Leeming, David and Jake Page. *Goddess: Myths of the Female Divine.* Oxford: Oxford University Press, 1994.

Matthews, Caitlin. *The Elements of the Goddess.* Boston: Element, 1997.

Monaghan, Patricia. *The New Book of the Goddesses and Heroines,* 3rd. ed. St. Paul: Llewellyn, 1997.

Neumann, Erich. *The Great Mother.* Ralph Manheim, trans., 2nd ed. Princeton: Princeton University Press, 1983.

Olson, Carl, ed. *The Book of the Goddess, Past and Present.* New York: Crossroad, 1983.

Pollack, Rachel. *The Body of the Goddess: Sacred Wisdom in Myth, Landscape and Culture.* Boston: Element, 1997.

Starhawk. *The Spiral Dance: A Rebirth of the Ancient Religion of the Great Goddess,* rev. ed. San Francisco: HarperSanFrancisco, 1989.

Stone, Merlin. *Ancient Mirrors of Womanhood,* 2nd ed. Boston: Beacon Press, 1990.

———. *When God Was a Woman.* San Diego: Harcourt Brace, 1976.

Nordic Spiritual and Runic Studies

Aswynn, Freya. *Northern Mysteries and Magick: Runes, Gods, and Feminine Powers,* 2nd ed. St. Paul: Llewellyn, 1998.

Conway, D. J. *Norse Magic.* St. Paul: Llewellyn, 1990.

Flowers, Stephen. *The Galdrabok: An Icelandic Grimoire.* York Beach, ME: Samuel Weiser, 1989.

Gundarsson, Kveldulf. *Teutonic Magic: The Magical and Spiritual Practices of the Germanic Peoples.* St. Paul: Llewellyn, 1994.

———. *Teutonic Religion, Folk Beliefs and Practices of the Northern Tradition.* St. Paul: Llewellyn, 1993.

King, Bernard. *The Elements of the Runes.* Boston: Element, 1993.

Metzner, Ralph. *The Well of Remembrance.* Boston: Shambhala, 1994.

Page, R. I. *Runes and Runic Inscriptions.* David Parsons, ed. Rochester, NY: Boydell Press, 1995.

Pennick, Nigel. *Rune Magic: The History and Practice of Ancient Runic Traditions.* London: Aquarian, 1992.

Thorsson, Edred. *A Book of Troth.* St. Paul: Llewellyn, 1992.

———. *At the Well of Wyrd: A Handbook of Runic Divination.* York Beach, ME: Samuel Weiser, 1988.

———. *Futhark: A Handbook of Rune Magic.* York Beach, ME: Samuel Weiser, 1984.

———. *Gildisbok: The Inner Workings of the Rune-Gild.* 1994. Privately issued by the Rune Gild.

———. *Green Runa: The Runemaster's Notebook: Shorter Works of Edred Thorsson, Volume 1 (1978–1985).* Second improved and expanded ed. Smithville, TX: Runa-Raven Press, 1996.

———. *Northern Magic.* St. Paul: Llewellyn, 1993.

———. *Runelore: A Handbook of Esoteric Runology.* York Beach, ME: Samuel Weiser, 1987.

———. *The Nine Doors to Midgard: A Complete Curriculum of Rune Magic.* St. Paul: Llewellyn, 1994.

Tyson, Donald. *Rune Magic.* St. Paul: Llewellyn, 1988.

Nordic Mythological Studies

Colum, Padraic. *The Children of Odin.* New York: Macmillan, 1920, 1948.

———. *Nordic Gods and Heroes.* New York: Dover, 1996.

Cotterell, Arthur. *Norse Mythology: The Myths and Legends of the Nordic Gods.* Oxford: Sebastian Kelly, 1997.

Crossley-Holland, Kevin. *The Norse Myths.* New York: Pantheon, 1980.

Davidson, H. R. Ellis. *The Gods and Myths of Northern Europe.* London: Penguin, 1964.

———. *Myths and Symbols in Pagan Europe: Early Scandinavian and Celtic Religions.* Syracuse: Syracuse University Press, 1988.

———. *Roles of the Northern Goddess.* New York: Routledge, 1998.

Eliot, Charles W., ed. *The Harvard Classics: Epic and Saga,* Vol. 49. New York: P. F. Collier, 1938.

Fell, Christine, trans. and ed. *Egils Saga.* Reissued London: Everyman's Library, 1993.

Gordon, R. K, trans. *Beowulf.* Shane Weller, ed. New York: Dover, 1992.

Grimm, Jacob (Jakob). *Teutonic Mythology.* 3 vols. James Steven Stallybrass, trans., 4th ed. New York: Dover, 1966.

Guerber, H. A. *The Norsemen.* London: Senate, 1994.

Hatto, A. T., trans. *The Nibelungenlied.* Rev. ed. New York: Penguin, 1969.

Hollander, Lee M., trans. *The Poetic Edda.* 2nd ed., rev. Austin: University of Texas Press, 1962.

———. *The Sage of the Jomsvikings.* Austin: University of Texas Press, 1955.

Jonasson, Bjorn, trans. *Havamal: The Sayings of the Vikings.* Reykjavik: Gudrun, 1992.

Jones, Gwyn. *A History of the Vikings,* 2nd ed. Oxford: Oxford University Press, 1984.

———, trans. *Eirik the Red and Other Icelandic Sagas.* Oxford: Oxford University Press, 1961.

Mabie, Hamilton Wright. *Norse Stories Retold from the Eddas.* New York: Dodd, Mead, 1882, 1900.

MacKenzie, Donald A. *Teutonic Myth and Legend: An Introduction to the Eddas and Sagas, Beowulf, the Nibelungenlied, etc.* London: Gresham, n.d.

Magnusson, Magnus and Hermann Palsson, trans. *The Vinland Sagas: The Norse Discovery of America.* Betty Radice, advisory ed. New York: Penguin, 1965.

———. *Njal's Saga.* Betty Radice, advisory ed. New York: Penguin, 1960.

Magoun, Francis Peabody, Jr. trans. *The Kalevala, or Poems of the Kaleva District.* Elias Lonnrot, comp. Cambridge: Harvard University Press, 1963.

Page, R. I. *Norse Myths.* Austin: University of Texas Press, 1990.

Palsson, Hermann, trans. *Hrafnkel's Saga, and Other Icelandic Stories.* Betty Radice, advisory ed. New York: Penguin, 1971.

Paul, Jim, trans. and ann. *The Rune Poem: Wisdom's Fulfillment, Prophecy's Reach.* San Francisco: Chronicle Books, 1996.

Rebsamen, Frederick, trans. *Beowulf: A Verse Translation.* New York: Icon Editions, 1991.

Roesdahl, Else. *The Vikings.* Susan M. Margeson and Kirsten Williams, trans. New York: Penguin, 1991.

Simek, Rudolf. *Dictionary of Northern Mythology.* Angela Hall, trans. Cambridge: D. S. Brewer, 1984, 1993.

Sturluson, Snorri. *Edda.* Anthony Faulkes, trans. London: Everyman's Library, 1992.

———. *Heimskringla: History of the Kings of Norway.* Lee M. Hollander, trans. Austin: University of Texas Press, 1964.

———. *The Prose Edda: Tales from Norse Mythology.* Jean I. Young, trans. Berkeley: University of California Press, 1954.

Terry, Patricia, trans. *Poems of the Elder Edda,* rev. ed. Philadelphia: University of Pennsylvania Press, 1990.

Titchenell, Elsa-Brita. *The Masks of Odin: Wisdom of the Ancient Norse.* Pasadena: Theosophical University Press, 1985.

Wagner, Dr. W. *Asgard and the Gods: The Tales and Traditions of Our Northern Ancestors, Forming a Complete Manual of Norse Mythology.* W. S. W. Anson, ed. New York: E. P. Dutton, 1917.

Philosophy and History

Daly, Mary. *Beyond God the Father: Toward a Philosophy of Women's Liberation.* Boston: Beacon, 1985.

Dennis, Andrew, Peter Foote, and Richard Perkins. *Laws of Early Iceland, Gragas.* Winnipeg: University of Manitoba Press, 1980.

Durant, Will and Ariel. *The Lessons of History.* New York: Simon & Schuster, 1968.

Eliade, Mircea. *Myth and Reality.* Willard R. Trask, trans. New York: Harper Torchbooks, 1963.

Kaufmann, Walter. *Critique of Religion and Philosophy.* Princeton: Princeton University Press, 1958.

Women's Studies

Anderson, Bonnie S., and Judith P. Zinsser. *A History of their Own: Women in Europe from Prehistory to the Present,* vol. 1. New York: Perennial Library, 1988.

Barstow, Anne Llewellyn. *Witchcraze: A New History of the European Witch Hunts.* San Francisco: Pandora, 1994.

Briggs, Robin. *Witches and Neighbors: The Social and Cultural Context of European Witchcraft.* New York: Penguin, 1996.

Carmody, Denise Lardner. *Women and World Religions,* 2nd ed. Englewood Cliffs: Prentice-Hall, 1989.

Eisler, Riane. *The Chalice and the Blade: Our History, Our Future.* San Francisco: HarperSanFrancisco, 1995.

Geis, Gilbert, and Ivan Bunn. *A Trial of Witches, a Seventeenth-century Witchcraft Prosecution.* New York: Routledge, 1997.

Girard, Rene. *Violence and the Sacred.* Patrick Gregory, trans. Baltimore: The Johns Hopkins University Press, 1977.

Haddad, Yvonne Yazbeck and Ellison Banks Findly, eds. *Women, Religion, and Social Change.* Albany: State University of New York Press, 1985.

Jochens, Jenny. *Women in Old Norse Society.* Ithaca: Cornell University Press, 1995.

———. *Old Norse Images of Women.* Philadelphia: University of Pennsylvania Press, 1996.

Karlsen, Carol F. *The Devil in the Shape of a Woman: Witchcraft in Colonial New England.* New York: W. W. Norton, 1998.

Kors, Alan C. and Edward Peters, eds. *Witchcraft in Europe, 1100–1700: A Documentary History.* Philadelphia: University of Pennsylvania Press, 1972.

Walker, Barbara G. *The Woman's Encyclopedia of Myths and Secrets.* San Francisco: HarperSanFrancisco, 1983.

Additional Works

Tolkien, J. R. R. *The Hobbit,* rev. ed. New York: Ballantine, 1966.

———. *The Fellowship of the Ring: The Lord of the Rings, Part One.* New York: Ballantine, 1965.

———. *The Two Towers: The Lord of the Rings, Part Two.* New York: Ballantine, 1965.

———. *The Return of the King: The Lord of the Rings, Part Three.* New York: Ballantine, 1965.

INDEX

ABOUT THE AUTHOR

Lynda C. Welch has been exploring Norse Goddesses, Mythology and Runes for a number of years. The birth of her son inspired her to write this book. Lynda has also run a small metaphysical bookstore, where she taught workshops on runes. She lives near Traverse City, Michigan where she and her husband raise Norwegian Fjord horses. Interested readers are welcome to correspond with her via e-mail at heithingi@aol.com, or in care of the publisher.